This symposium celebrates the 450th anniversary of the birth of William Byrd, one of the greatest English composers. Twelve scholars contribute essays which together cover all the genres of Byrd's prolific output. Topics discussed in this collection include authentication of the canon, applications of new technology to Byrd research, Byrd's relationship to earlier English traditions and his influence on his successors. There are studies concerned with manuscript sources and aspects of performance, and the final contribution is a comprehensive listing of Byrd recordings made between 1923 and 1988.

The essays in this volume show a variety of approaches to musical analysis and some of the conclusions are controversial, or offer revisions of earlier opinions. As a body of work, they consolidate Byrd research to date and indicate its future direction.

# Byrd Studies

A certificate in Byrd's hand requesting the payment of an annuity to Mrs Dorothy Tempest, dated 25 June 1581 (in the possession of O. W. Neighbour). A later version of this document (*GB-Lbl* Egerton 3722) is reproduced in MB 27, p. xxi

# *Byrd Studies*

EDITED BY
## ALAN BROWN
### AND
## RICHARD TURBET

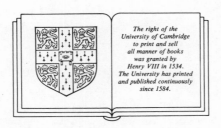

The right of the
University of Cambridge
to print and sell
all manner of books
was granted by
Henry VIII in 1534.
The University has printed
and published continuously
since 1584.

## Cambridge University Press

*Cambridge   New York   Port Chester*
*Melbourne   Sydney*

Published by the Press Syndicate of the University of Cambridge
The Pitt Building, Trumpington Street, Cambridge CB2 1RP
40 West 20th Street, New York, NY 10011–4211, USA
10 Stamford Road, Oakleigh, Victoria 3166, Australia

First published 1992

Printed in Great Britain at the University Press, Cambridge

*British Library cataloguing in publication data*
Byrd studies.
1. English music, Byrd, William. *1542 or 3–1623*
I. Brown, Alan *1941–* . II. Turbet, R. B. (Richard Beaumont)
780.92

*Library of Congress cataloguing in publication data*
Byrd studies/edited by Alan Brown & Richard Turbet.
p.    cm.
A symposium celebrating the 450th anniversary of the birth of William Byrd.
Discography: p.
Includes bibliographical references and index.
ISBN 0 521 40129 1
1. Byrd, William, 1542 or 3-1623 – criticism and interpretation.
I. Byrd, William, 1542 or 3-1623.   II. Brown, Alan, 1941–
III. Turbet, Richard.
ML410 B996B9 1992
780′.92–dc20   90–25640   CIP   MN

ISBN 0 521 40129 1 hardback

CE

# Contents

# *Plates*

# Preface

... my loving Maister (never without reverence to be named of the musicians) M. *Bird* ...[1]

Morley's tribute to the greatest of Elizabethan composers has been echoed by musicians of many later generations, not least in our own century. At the time of the tercentenary celebrations in 1923, a group of enthusiasts was responsible not only for performances of music which in many cases 'had lain in complete oblivion for nearly three centuries',[2] but also for a spate of persuasive articles and lectures. Thereafter Byrd research proceeded steadily, another landmark being the anniversary fifty years later which saw the inauguration of a second collected edition. *The Byrd Edition* is now nearing completion, and the music is being discussed in a series of monographs, *The Music of William Byrd*, whose scope goes well beyond that of the first full-length biographical and critical study.[3] In another recent publication, all known writings on Byrd have been listed and, where appropriate, annotated.[4] The present collection of *Byrd Studies*, not the first of its kind[5] but the most substantial to date, was planned as a way of bringing together some of the diverse strands of present-day Byrd scholarship, on the occasion of the 450th anniversary of the composer's birth in 1542 or 1543. Widely ranging in subject matter and approach, the contributions have in common that they will further encourage – directly or

[1] Thomas Morley, *A Plaine and Easie Introduction to Practicall Musicke* (London, 1597), p. 115.
[2] Edmund H. Fellowes, *William Byrd* (London, 1936; 2nd edn, 1948), p. v.
[3] Fellowes, *William Byrd*.
[4] Richard Turbet, *William Byrd: A Guide to Research* (New York and London, 1987), pp. 135–263. To be updated in Turbet, *Tudor Music: a Research and Information Guide* (New York, forthcoming).
[5] *The Chesterian* 5 (1923) included, on pp. 229–39, four short articles on aspects of Byrd's music, by W. Barclay Squire, J. A. Fuller Maitland, E. H. Fellowes and Gerald Cooper.

indirectly – the 'focussed admiration' implicitly called for by the authors of
*The Music of William Byrd*.

The ordering of the contributions reflects the categorisation of Byrd's
music established by Fellowes in his pioneering collected edition of
1937–50. In keeping with the historical trend in Byrd criticism, there are
more essays on the Latin music than on other categories. Peter le Huray
considers English cantus firmus composition in the sixteenth century, with
special reference to *Christus resurgens*, published in 1605. Querying
received wisdom, Owen Rees argues that the English psalm motet was not
so much a response to continental developments as a reflection of the
content of Primers in use in English religious institutions. John Morehen
describes a computer-assisted project to test the authenticity of eleven
Latin motets whose attributions to Byrd are dubious. Computer analysis
also plays a part in David Wulstan's account of Byrd's vocal scoring at
different stages during his career, supporting his view that the performing
pitch level of the Latin music was closely related to that of the English
church music. Continuing his involvement with Byrd's Anglican music,
Craig Monson considers the Services in respect of their debt to Tallis and
influence on Morley. Byrd's secular vocal output is celebrated by Joseph
Kerman in a close analysis of *Retire, my soul*. A subtheme of this symposium
is Byrd's influence upon his successors, a topic featuring in Monson's paper
already mentioned. From this point of view John Bennett looks at the
consort music of Byrd's young contemporary Richard Mico, and John
Irving investigates the instrumental music of his pupil Thomas Tomkins.
Two papers are concerned with My Ladye Nevells Booke: Hilary Gaskin
examines the 'Nevell' hand of the scribe, John Baldwin, and his copying
procedures, while Desmond Hunter reappraises keyboard gracing from
evidence in the manuscript. In another contribution dealing with questions of authenticity (but approached from a different standpoint), Oliver
Neighbour considers some anonymous pieces from two slightly later
sources, the Weelkes and Forster keyboard books. Finally, Michael Green-
halgh lists all recordings of Byrd's original music available commercially in
the United Kingdom between 1923 – the year of the tercentenary – and
1988.

Byrd's music contains within it a large potential for further research, and
indeed straightforward appreciation. Within a few years there will no
doubt be material available that could fill another volume of *Byrd Studies*;
and the contributions to the present book reveal that scope exists for the
performance of a much wider range of the music than is normally heard
even today. For example, the incomparable Mass Propers of the *Gradualia*

have rarely been recorded, and are seldom used, in anything approaching an appropriate liturgical or quasi-liturgical context. All musicological study must, in the end, be related to the sound of the music as re-created by the performer and perceived by the listener. If it is to have any worth beyond its own borders, our criticism must prepare the ground for those encountering Byrd's music for the first time, and take *cognoscenti* back to it with increased understanding, enjoyment and reverence.

We record with regret the death of John Bennett in July 1990. We should like to thank Judi Vernau and Clifford Bartlett for their encouragement when this book was being planned, John Milsom for his interest and assistance, and Penny Souster of Cambridge University Press for her valuable advice at all stages of the project.

Alan Brown
Richard Turbet

# *Abbreviations*

---

The following editions and books are referred to in abbreviated form:

BE  *The Byrd Edition*
1. *Cantiones Sacrae I (1575)*, ed. Craig Monson (London, 1977)
2. *Cantiones Sacrae (1589)*, ed. Alan Brown (London, 1988)
3. *Cantiones Sacrae II (1591)*, ed. Alan Brown (London, 1981)
4. *The Masses [1592–1595]*, ed. Philip Brett (London, 1981)
8. *Latin Motets I (from manuscript sources)*, ed. Warwick Edwards (London, 1984)
10a. *The English Services*, ed. Craig Monson (London, 1980)
10b. *The English Services II (The Great Service)*, ed. Craig Monson (London, 1982)
14. *Psalmes, Songs, and Sonnets (1611)*, ed. John Morehen (London, 1987)
15. *Consort Songs for voice and viols...from manuscript sources*, ed. Philip Brett (London, 1970; originally issued as a re-edition of vol. 15 of *The Collected Works of William Byrd*)
16. *Madrigals, Songs and Canons*, ed. Philip Brett (London, 1976)
17. *Consort Music*, ed. Kenneth Elliott (London, 1971; originally issued as a re-edition of vol. 17 of *The Collected Works of William Byrd*)

BK      *William Byrd: Keyboard Music I and II* (= MB 27 and 28),
        ed. Alan Brown (London, 1969 and 1971; 2nd edns, 1976;
        rev. reprint of vol. II, 1985)

BW      *The Collected Works of William Byrd*, ed. Edmund
        H. Fellowes
        5. *Gradualia (1605), parts ii and iii* (London, 1938)
        8. *Motets for three, four and five voices (recovered from
        manuscript)* (London, 1939)
        14. *Psalmes, Songs, and Sonnets (1611)* (London, 1949);
        rev. Thurston Dart (London, 1964)
        16. *Additional Madrigals, Canons and Rounds. Appendix:
        Fragments of Text* (London, 1948)

EECM    *Early English Church Music*
        8. *Fifteenth-century Liturgical Music: I Antiphons and Music
        for Holy Week and Easter*, ed. Andrew Hughes (London,
        1968)
        13. *Thomas Tallis: English Sacred Music: II Service Music*, ed.
        Leonard Ellinwood (London, 1971); rev. Paul Doe
        (London, 1974)
        22. *Fifteenth-century Liturgical Music: II Four Anonymous
        Masses*, ed. Margaret Bent (London, 1979)
        28. *Robert White: I Five-part Latin Psalms*, ed. David
        Mateer (London, 1983)
        34. *Fifteenth-century Liturgical Music: III The Brussels
        Masses*, ed. Gareth Curtis (London, 1989)
        38. *Thomas Morley: English Sacred Music*, ed. John Morehen
        (forthcoming)
        Supplementary Volume 2: *Latin Music in British Sources,
        c.1485–c.1610*, compiled by May Hofman and John
        Morehen (London, 1987)

EK      *Elizabethan Keyboard Music* (= MB 55), ed. Alan Brown
        (London, 1989)

MB      *Musica Britannica*
        5. See TK, below
        19. *John Bull: Keyboard Music II*, ed. Thurston Dart
        (London, 1963; 2nd edn, 1970)

24. *Giles & Richard Farnaby: Keyboard Music*, ed. Richard Marlow (London, 1965)

27, 28. See BK, above

48. *Orlando Gibbons: Consort Music*, ed. John Harper (London, 1982)

55. See EK, above

59. *Thomas Tomkins: Consort Music*, ed. John Irving (forthcoming)

MWB      *The Music of William Byrd*

1. Joseph Kerman, *The Masses and Motets of William Byrd* (London, 1981)

3. Oliver Neighbour, *The Consort and Keyboard Music of William Byrd* (London, 1978)

TCM      *Tudor Church Music*

2. *William Byrd, 1543–1623: English Church Music, part I* (London, 1922)

6. *Thomas Tallis, c.1505–1585* (London, 1928)

7. *William Byrd, 1543–1623: Gradualia, Books I and II* (London, 1927)

9. *William Byrd, 1543–1623: Masses, Cantiones* [1575], *and Motets* [recovered from manuscript] (London, 1928)

TK      *Thomas Tomkins: Keyboard Music* (= MB 5), ed. Stephen D. Tuttle (London, 1955); 2nd edn, rev. Thurston Dart (London, 1964)

Individual pieces within the above editions are designated as in *The Music of William Byrd*: thus, for example, 'BE 1/7' indicates 'Piece no. 7 in volume 1 of *The Byrd Edition*'; 'TK 61' indicates 'Piece no. 61 in *Musica Britannica*, volume 5'.

Libraries are referred to by the sigla used in the publications of RISM (Répertoire International des Sources Musicales, Kassel). The following libraries are cited in the course of *Byrd Studies*:

## D: Germany

Kl — Kassel, Murhardsche Bibliothek der Stadt und Landes-
bibliothek

## Eire: Ireland

Dtc — Dublin, Trinity College

## F: France

Pn — Paris, Bibliothèque Nationale

## GB: Great Britain

| | |
|---|---|
| Cfm | Cambridge, Fitzwilliam Museum |
| Ckc | Cambridge, King's College, Rowe Music Library |
| Cmc | Cambridge, Magdalene College |
| Cp | Cambridge, Peterhouse |
| En | Edinburgh, National Library of Scotland |
| Eu | Edinburgh, University Library |
| Lbl | London, British Library, Reference Division |
| Lcm | London, Royal College of Music |
| Ob | Oxford, Bodleian Library |
| Och | Oxford, Christ Church |

## US: United States of America

Cn — Chicago, Newberry Library

A date and number in the form '1556⁹' refers to a printed anthology listed
in RISM, volume BI (*Recueils Imprimés, XVIᵉ–XVIIᵉ Siècles*, 1960).

Pitch references are as follows (starting from bass C): C to B, c to b, $c^1$ (=
middle C) to $b^1$, $c^2$ to $b^2$.

# 1

## *Some thoughts about cantus firmus composition; and a plea for Byrd's Christus resurgens*

### PETER LE HURAY

No single work of Byrd's has been the subject of such conflicting opinions as *Christus resurgens*, that anachronistic cantus firmus motet which found its way into the first book of *Gradualia* motets in 1605.[1] For H. B. Collins the motet was 'caviare to the general', 'a wonderful meditation on the Plainchant, like nothing so much as some of Bach's Choral preludes, or the slow movements of his violin sonatas'.[2] For Joseph Kerman it was 'obviously ... the oldest piece in the collection by far – the oldest and crudest piece, in fact, ever published or anthologised by the composer'.[3] The conflict prompts a renewed search for the criteria that composers of Byrd's generation would have applied to cantus firmus composition, and indeed it prompts a reinvestigation of the relationship between the improvised art of descanting and the art of cantus firmus composition in England during the mid to late sixteenth century.

It may be helpful to begin with to see what Thomas Morley has to say about these matters in his unique *Plaine and Easie Introduction to Practicall Musicke* of 1597,[4] for Morley, after all, was a pupil of Byrd's. Moreover Morley dedicated the book to his beloved master, placing Byrd's name prominently at the head of the dedicatory page. Morley's preface is well worth reading, not least the section in which Morley acknowledges Byrd's presence in the book:

Accept (I pray you) of this booke, both that you may exercise your deepe skill in

---

[1] *Gradualia*, Book I (London, 1605), no. 10 of four-part fascicle. Ed. in TCM 7, p. 143 and BW 5, p. 64.

[2] 'Byrd's Latin Church Music for Practical Use in the Roman Liturgy', *Music & Letters* 4 (1923), p. 257.

[3] MWB 1, p. 62.

[4] Square-bracketed page references throughout are to the edition by R. A. Harman (London, 1952).

censuring of what shall be amisse, as also defend what is in it truely spoken, as that which somtime proceeded from your selfe. (Dedication [3])

Morley's book divides into three principal sections. The first deals with basic matters of pitch and rhythm; in it Morley draws upon a multiplicity of hallowed authorities, especially in the pretentiously overblown discussion of 'proportions', as if to establish his academic credentials as a 'learned' author. The other two sections are much more relevant to contemporary practice, and they are much more Morley's own. Indeed Morley goes as far as to declare concerning the second part – 'treating of Descant' – that 'there is nothing in it which I have seene set downe in writing by others . . . except the cords of descant, and that common rule of prohibited consequence of perfect cords [i.e. parallel fifths, unisons and octaves]'.[5] It is in this section especially that Morley is likely to have been reworking most closely the ideas which 'somtime proceeded' from that 'Father of music',[6] his master William Byrd.

In many respects the extensive second section is the nub of the entire book, for it describes the way in which the aspiring composer established for himself the ground rules of composition through the practical experience of improvising a melody against a *plainsong* (i.e. a cantus firmus; not necessarily a Gregorian chant). As Morley put it, 'singing extempore upon a plainsong is indeede a peece of cunning, and very necessarie to be perfectly practised of him who meaneth to be a composer . . .' (p. 121 [215]).[7] What then emerges from Morley's extensive discussion of descanting? Apart from such straightforwardly technical matters as the control of consonance and dissonance and the avoidance of 'consecutives', there are many fruitful insights into the ways that apprentice composers would have learned to create substantial pieces of imitative polyphony. The great importance that was attached to descanting suggests to begin with that the young composer was likely to have graduated first from cantus firmus *improvisation* to cantus firmus *composition*. Certainly the chronologies established by Kerman and Neighbour[8] suggest that the young Byrd may have progressed in that way. Indeed it is not too fanciful to suggest that the stages through which Morley takes the reader in the second and third parts of the book were broadly those that any experienced teacher would have

5 'Peroratio', p. 183 [307].
6 Entry in *The Old Cheque-Book . . . of the Chapel Royal*, ed. E. F. Rimbault (London, 1872; reprinted New York, 1966), recording Byrd's death in 1623, p. 10.
7 Morley's discussion here, however, suggests that practical descanting had by then gone out of fashion.
8 MWB 3, especially chapters 2, 3 and 6.

recommended to an aspiring pupil: first, the development of linear and vertical awareness through the simplest note-against-note improvisation on a slowly moving plainsong; then the creation of more elaborate lines against the cantus firmus (always in unvarying semibreves) in which the concepts of passing and suspended dissonance are explored, together with the nature and function of 'cadence' (p. 73 [145]). The reader is then introduced to the principle of 'formality' in which 'meaning' is given to the added line by shaping it imitatively, the imitation being internal – from point to point in the added line – as well as external, between the improvised line and the cantus firmus (p. 94 [174]). In this context Morley makes the particularly significant observation that important as imitation is in imparting 'meaning', on no account should the process involve simple repetition, 'without any alteration ... for it is odious to repeate one thing twise' (p. 84 [162]). In our discussion below of specific compositions there will be constant occasion to recall this crucial observation, for Byrd particularly excelled in the art of imitative *development*.[9]

Exactly *how* the necessary variety could be achieved was a problem that is largely left unsaid, perhaps because it is one that is best demonstrated in notes rather than words. Morley does nonetheless suggest (and the suggestion has very much the flavour of Byrd about it) that melodic activity is best seen as a cumulative process: in Morley's words, it is desirable that 'if your descant should be stirring in any place, it should bee in the note before the close' (p. 81 [158]); cadences, that is, at phrase ends may well be preceded by an increase in melodic activity.

It is a natural step from imitation to canon and to invertible counterpoint. These subjects lead conveniently from improvisation to the business of writing music, the subject of the third part of the book: 'treating of composing or setting of Songes'. There is comparatively little purely technical information here that has not been touched on in the second part. Although the section title implies that word-setting is to be the main topic, words are not discussed until the very end. Instead, Morley retraces a good deal of what has already been said about wordless descanting in two and three parts, observing that such additional rules of setting as are necessary for composition are 'fewe and easie to them that have descant' (p. 126 [222]). Further advice is given on how to write mellifluous polyphony, and examples of harmonic crudities are cited from pre-Reformation works

[9] In much mid-century English polyphony there is much almost mechanically repetitive imitation: even Byrd's master Tallis was not wholly immune from it, nor young Byrd himself; see for instance Tallis's *Absterge Domine*, TCM 6, p. 180, and Byrd's *Laudate pueri*, BE 1/7.

by English composers. More is said about texture and the need to avoid large gaps between one part and the next: as Morley put it, 'the best maner of composing three voices or how many soever is to cause the parts go close' (p. 126 [222]), a point that is restated later, thus: 'for the closer the partes goe the better . . . and when they stande farre asunder the harmonie vanisheth' (p. 146 [248]).

The important question of 'key' was left almost wholly unexplored in the descanting section, perhaps because the attendant plainsong supplied the basis of a tonal framework. Morley's comments here are very much in line with compositional procedures that are clearly evident in Byrd's music, if we only take the trouble to look for them. There is to begin with the question of 'key', and the emotive quality of 'key':

> you have in the closing [Philomathes's master declares] gone out of your key, which is one of the grosest faults which may be committed . . . for every key hath a peculiar ayre proper unto it selfe, so that if you goe into another then [than] that wherein you begun, you change the aire of the song, which is as much as to wrest a thing out of his nature, making the asse leape upon his maister and the Spaniell beare the loade.[10]

As Kerman and Neighbour have amply demonstrated, Byrd certainly thought in terms of 'key', using this as the basis for grouping together collections of pieces – notably those in the Latin publications. This is all obvious enough. What may be overlooked, though, is Morley's rider, to the effect that during the course of a composition the home 'key' may well be left temporarily for one (or more) adjacent keys. He writes:

> and though the ayre of everie key be different one from the other, yet some [keys] *love* [italics mine] (by a wonder of nature) to be joined to others so that if you begin your song in *Gam ut*, you may conclude [i.e. cadence] it either in *C fa ut* or *D sol re*, and from thence come againe to *Gam ut*: likewise if you begin your song in *D sol re*, you may end [again the implication is 'cadence'] in *A re* and come againe to *D sol re*, etc. (p. 147 [249])

The presence in so many of Byrd's compositions of significant areas of 'key' change, a quality that is not nearly so apparent in the music of his elders and immediate contemporaries, suggests that this idea too may have come from Byrd himself.

The lengthiest section in part three is the one devoted to cadence, a compositional element that is closely associated both with 'key' and with

---

[10] pp. 146–7 [249]. Here Morley refers particularly to Glareanus's *Dodecachordon* (Basle, 1547); tr. Clement Miller, Musicological Studies and Documents 6 (Rome, 1965): see especially book two.

word setting. It was a topic that Morley only touched on briefly in his instructions for descanting. Morley supplies well over a hundred examples of cadences.[11] 'Without a Cadence in some one of the parts, [Morley wrote] either with a discord or without it, it is unpossible formallie to close' (p. 127 [223]). The strongest form of cadence is the one in which the root-position triad on the tonic is preceded by the root-position dominant chord. In the discussion of word-setting, Morley observes that this kind of cadence has such a quality of finality that it should only be used when 'the full sence of the words be perfect' (p. 178 [292]). The cadence in other words was felt to articulate the music so strongly that it was the musical equivalent of the full stop; it had the nature of a highly conventional formula, offering only limited opportunity for variation. Indeed, Morley likened it to the 'Amen': 'I find no better word to saie after a good praier, then [than] *Amen*, nor no better close to set after a good peece of descant, then a *Cadence* . . .' (p. 82 [160]). Morley goes on to give examples of all forms of cadence, including 'passing closes', commonly called 'false closes', which 'shun a final end and go on with some other purpose' (p. 127 [223]). Whilst he does not define what these purposes might be, he would surely have been thinking of textual situations in which some perceptible, if not final, articulation was required – a comma or colon perhaps, rather than a full stop. Further on Morley recommended the use of 'passing closes' for the purely musical reason that the syncopations and dissonances help to 'drive' the music forward (p. 152 [256], and p. 160 [267]).

In one further respect Morley seems to be echoing what Byrd must have taught him (if with Zarlino's help), namely a sensitivity to word rhythms. 'We must also have a care [he pointed out] so to applie the notes to the wordes, as in singing there be no barbarisme committed: that is, that we cause no sillable which is by nature short be expressed by manie notes or one long note, nor no long sillable bee expressed with a shorte note . . .' He laments the fact that 'in this fault do the practitioners erre more grosselie, then [than] in any other, for you shall find few songes wherein the penult sillables of these words, *Dominus, Angelus, filius, miraculum, gloria*, and such like are not expressed with a long note, yea many times with a whole dossen of notes . . .' (p. 178 [291]).

Among the more important matters that Morley discusses, then, are the function of descanting in music instruction, the relationship between

---

11 Harman (*Introduction*, p. 241, fn. 1) examines the question of Morley's indebtedness here to Orazio Tigrini's *Il compendio della musica* (Venice, 1588), and draws attention to the fact that 53 of the 108 examples in Morley are identical to ones supplied by Tigrini.

descanting and the writing of polyphony upon a plainsong, the further extension of compositional techniques into freely imitative polyphony, and finally, techniques of word-setting. Important aspects of Morley's discussion cover key, key interrelationships, dissonance control, cadence, melodic structure, processes of imitation and principles of underlay. In what respects is all this relevant to Byrd's cantus firmus music?

The first full-scale cantus firmus composition that Byrd published was the Respond from the Office of the Dead, *Libera me, Domine, de morte* – no. 33 in the 1575 *Cantiones Sacrae*. Kerman has drawn attention to the existence of other settings of this text by Byrd's contemporaries, notably the one by Robert Parsons, who is best known today for his arresting setting of *Ave Maria*.[12] The opening and closing sections of Parsons's *Libera me, Domine, de morte* (transcription from *GB-Lbl* R.M. 24.d.2; words supplied from *GB-Och* 979–83) are shown in Example 1.1. Since, as Morley observed, 'imitation' gives meaning to the music, one of the principal characteristics of a satisfying cantus firmus composition would undoubtedly have been its imitative structure. How did the two composers set about organising this? The first task would surely have been to divide the text and its plainsong into suitable units. The two settings of *Libera me* follow a fairly similar plan, so similar indeed that it is difficult to believe that one composer was not working in the knowledge of what the other had done – and since Byrd succeeded Parsons, who was tragically drowned in the river Trent in 1570, the inference must be that the younger musician was emulating, and even commemorating, the elder.[13] Both composers set the same portions of the Sarum text, leaving out the verses 'Quid ergo' and 'Nunc Christe'. Both, oddly enough, cadence conclusively at 'tremenda' and 'terra', making it possible for the plainchant verses 'Tremens factus sum ego', 'Dies illa, dies irae' and 'Requiem aeternam' to be inserted, and thus suggesting that both composers had the possibility of liturgical performance in mind. On the other hand, the traditionally liturgical way of beginning the respond would have been for the choir to begin at 'de morte aeterna', the incipit being sung to its plainchant by a solo voice. Both settings, however, begin at the beginning. Despite these similarities, there are nonetheless two small but significant structural differences that already mark out Byrd as the more perceptive composer. Parsons divides the

---

[12] ed. John Milsom, Oxford, 1988 (no. 115 in Oxford University Press series Tudor Church Music).

[13] Morley describes (p. 115 [202]) in another context how Byrd 'contended with' Alfonso Ferrabosco [the elder] in canonic settings of the 'Miserere'; and Kerman has drawn attention to several compositions of Byrd's that seem to be based, however loosely, on pieces by his contemporaries.

Example 1.1 Parsons, *Libera me, Domine, de morte aeterna*

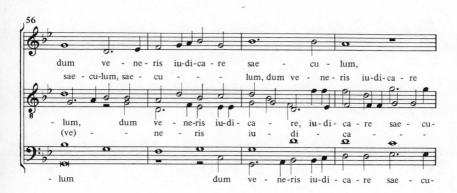

opening verbal phrase into two self-contained units: 'Libera me, Domine' and 'de morte aeterna'. He may perhaps have been aware of the difficulty of treating the thirteen-syllable phrase as a whole; such a lengthy phrase would have generated an overextended imitative point, and thus a diffuse imitative structure that would have blurred rather than enhanced the powerfully affective quality of the text. He may on the other hand have been doing what English composers had traditionally done, paralleling each imitative section with the progression of the words in the cantus firmus. Byrd, however, departs from the norm here. Long before the words 'Libera me, Domine' have come to an end in the slowly-moving chant, Byrd begins to develop a succinctly expressive imitative point to the words 'de morte aeterna'. The associated elements of suspended dissonance and syncopation which derive from this point add greatly to the impact of the section, and form a marked contrast to Parsons's ponderous successive treatment of the two phrases. By the time that the cantus firmus reaches the words 'de morte aeterna', Byrd has dropped the opening point entirely.

The technique here foreshadows the 'head and tail' procedure which Byrd used with such expressive effect to conclude his first two freely imitative motets in the 1575 *Cantiones Sacrae*, *Libera me, Domine, et pone* (no. 5), and *Peccantem me quotidie* (no. 6). In all three cases, it is very clearly the words that have given rise to the procedures.[14]

Byrd parts company with Parsons, too, in the final section of the motet. There is here, as at the beginning, the problem of text length: some fourteen syllables in all. Yet the words do not readily divide into sub-phrases. Parsons chooses to set the first eleven syllables as a unit: 'dum veneris iudicare saeculum', gradually introducing 'per ignem' as the music proceeds, cutting out at the same time the first two words, 'dum veneris'. Without a cantus firmus an eleven-syllable point would be difficult enough to manipulate: see for instance Byrd's very heavy handling of 'Attollite portas, principes vestras',[15] which is precisely the same length. What, after all, do the voices *do* when they are not singing the point itself? In the context of a cantus firmus, the problem is particularly acute, leaving Parsons no option but to fill in the free sections of each voice part with a good deal of non-motivic padding. Indeed only the first eight syllables of text recur in a recognisable melodic and rhythmic shape, and even here it is the ♩ ♩ ♩ 𝅗𝅥 rhythm that serves to identify 'iudicare', not a precisely defined melody. Byrd on the other hand adopts the normal procedure, keeping the imitative sections in line with the cantus firmus text: 'Dum veneris iudicare': 'saeculum per ignem'. A 'head and tail' structure would perhaps have been the ideal solution, the 'tail' 'saeculum per ignem' being introduced at an early stage to form an expressive counterpoint against the squarer 'head', 'dum veneris iudicare'. Byrd does not do this, but even so he achieves quite a lot with the final point, 'saeculum per ignem', recalling the opening point, now developed even more affectively in suspension and syncopation.

It is easy enough to list the simple linear ground rules that the Elizabethans followed in their compositions: predominantly conjunct movement, an absence of large and awkward leaps, the avoidance of unduly complex rhythms (mainly those expressible only in double-dotted values), natural verbal stress, and the 'imaging' of words in melodic shapes and

[14] In the preface to the 1605 *Gradualia* motets Byrd referred to the mysterious power of words, 'that as one meditates upon the sacred words and constantly and seriously considers them, the right notes, in some inexplicable manner, suggest themselves quite spontaneously' – the translation of E. H. Fellowes, in *William Byrd* (London, 1936; 2nd edn, 1948), p. 80.

[15] 1575 *Cantiones Sacrae*, no. 11 (BE 1/5).

rhythms. Such matters are all laid out by precept and example in Morley's *Plaine and Easie Introduction*. What is less obvious in this book, though, is the way in which an aspiring composer would have been trained to develop large melodic units – those, that is, covering not just a single imitative point, but the extension of that line to the end of the imitative section. A study of almost any Byrd motet nonetheless leaves a clear impression that the vocal line of each imitative unit was conceived as a whole, and in relation to every other line in the section; the process was not one of repetition but of development. This kind of thinking can be traced back to Taverner (and well beyond). Taverner's *Meane Mass* Sanctus, for instance, must surely have been the inspiration for Byrd's own four-part Sanctus.[16] The process here is cumulative, the greatest intensity in each case being reached towards the end of the section. Taverner's opening point well illustrates this. The first statement rises to $bb^1$; on its restatement it reaches $c^2$, the upward crotchet scale being extended by two notes. The line then reaches its most active moment just before the close, as Morley suggested (see above, p. 3). The cumulative shape of the Sanctus is the result not only of pitch rises and rhythmic acceleration but also of the changing time relationships between imitative entries; 'offbeat' entries break up the initial regularity as do the subsequently 'compressed' (and thus syncopated) entries. Byrd's masterly handling of all these techniques can be left to speak for itself.

The peculiar difficulty of doing all this against a cantus firmus has already been remarked. Morley leaves the reader in no doubt, though, that the development of such skills was a central part of the basic training.[17] How do Byrd and Parsons compare, in this respect? Parsons introduces his first point at regular (and lengthy) time intervals of five minims. The expansive point necessitates the use of much freely-moving polyphony in the surrounding voices. Within the section, the first tenor displays the most strikingly developed shape, whilst the highest and lowest voices are very largely repetitive. It is quite a different story in the brief section that follows – 'de morte aeterna' – where tension rises markedly as the music proceeds. Byrd's linear handling of the opening phrase has already been discussed. It should also be noted that the pitch level of the section has a

---

[16] The correspondence between the two settings has been commented on by Philip Brett; see his 'Homage to Taverner in Byrd's Masses', *Early Music* 9 (1981), p. 169.

[17] Indeed, the difficulties were even extended to the writing of canon against a plainsong. Byrd, as we have seen, vied with Ferrabosco in the writing of canons against 'Miserere'; canon also plays an unusually prominent role in several of his early compositions, notably *Similes illis fiant* (BE 8/2) and *Miserere mihi Domine* (BE 1/13).

much clearer shape. The *discantus* is the first voice to state the 'de morte aeterna' motive. Successive statements take on a kind of wave motion; there is an upward surge to bar 9, then downward (bar 12), upward again (bar 15), downward (though less so than bar 12) to 17, and finally upward (bar 19), ending strongly on a C minor cadence. This wave motion is also evident in the other non-cantus firmus voices, which together form a purposeful shape that gets the words across superbly well. The way in which Byrd handles the time intervals between entries here adds a good deal to the total effect. These are all much closer and less symmetrical than are those in the Parsons motet; moreover Byrd introduces a sixth ('redundant') entry in the lowest line, now out of 'key', a device that in itself creates a kind of tension. The increase of activity just before the section 'in die illa tremenda' is also worth recalling, as also are similar increases during the final 'tremenda' and at the very end of the piece. The Parsons setting, in this respect, moves at a more uniform pace and is less dramatically articulated.

One further aspect of the two settings deserves attention: that of harmonic structure. To some extent this is of course predetermined by the chant, although as neither composer places the chant in the lowest part there is quite a lot of room for manoeuvre. Perhaps the best way to compare the two is by means of a figured bass skeleton, in which non-harmonic notes are omitted (see Example 1.2). Read as a quickly-moving hymn tune, Byrd's setting gives a much clearer impression than Parsons's of a superimposed harmonic design, despite the fact that the recurring flattened seventh of the chant inevitably clouds cadences that might otherwise have been more clearly 'tonal'. The broad impression of the opening phrase (to 'aeterna') is G minor in both settings though Byrd sounds more tonal, if only because of the intermediate sharpward and flatward moves at bars 10, 13 and 19. The harmonic focus of Byrd's second phrase moves from G minor to F, which is prepared as far back as bar 28; from there to the cadence in bar 34 E♮ almost entirely displaces E♭. Parsons, apart from a fleeting E♮, remains centred on G minor, the important ending on F being quite unprepared. From there Byrd moves back to G minor (bars 35–9), then to B♭ (39–42) in anticipation of the B♭ key of bar 47. At this point, consciously or otherwise, Byrd changed the chant. Was it perhaps to avoid a return to G minor or was it simply carelessness? The fourth phrase (bar 48 onwards), as has been observed above, lacks a subphrase structure. It is for this reason, no doubt, that Byrd avoided any very obvious cadential articulation. Nonetheless, there are distinct areas of 'key' change sharpwards (bars 52–65) before the final (balancing) plagal cadence. Parsons,

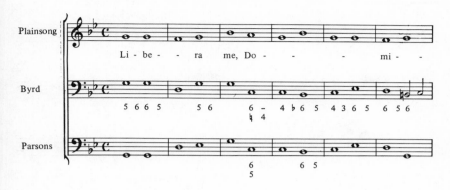

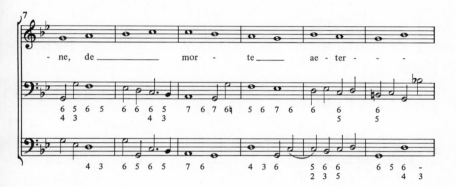

Example 1.2 *Libera me, Domine, de morte aeterna*: a harmonic analysis of settings by Parsons and Byrd

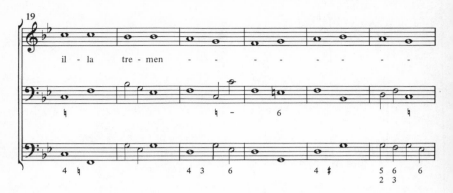

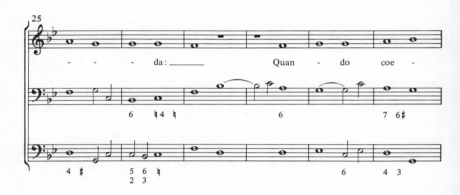

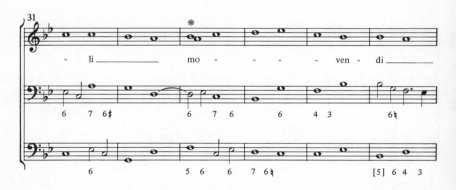

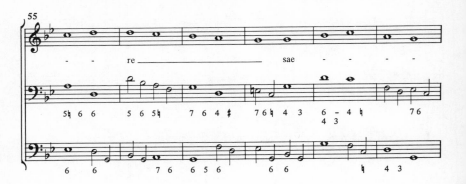

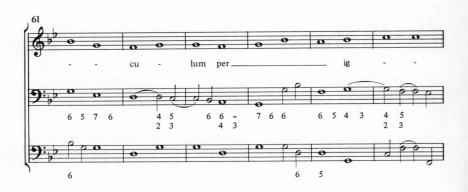

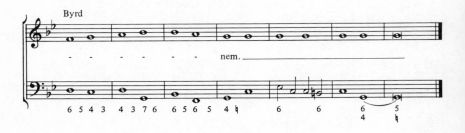

* Where two semibreves appear on the same beat, the first is set by Byrd, the second by Parsons.

on the other hand, harmonises the chant throughout in a rather 'modal' way, using in particular far more minor dominant chords than Byrd: compare for instance, bars 14, 17, 21, 23, 28–30, 34–5, 37, 47–8, 52, 54, 56–7, 66, 68, 70–1 and 74. Notes in the chant that belong to the tonic triad of G minor, moreover, tend to be more simply harmonised as tonic triads: compare for instance bars 15, 17–20, 22, 27–9, 31, 37, 39, 44, 47–8, 53, 62, 64–6 and 68–9.

Where then does Byrd's 'wonderful', 'crudest' cantus firmus motet *Christus resurgens* fit in? That the chant was set by so many of Byrd's elders and contemporaries is hardly surprising for it illuminates one of the most dramatic and joyous occasions in the Christian year.[18] The briefest comparison of the setting by Knight with Byrd's 'oldest' cantus firmus piece (as *Christus resurgens* has been described) will serve to illuminate the qualities of Byrd's own setting. The first 32 breves of Knight's setting (unedited transcription from *GB-Lbl* Add. 17802–5) are shown as Example 1.3. The Sarum chant itself runs from tonic (d) to dominant (a); only once is the sixth degree, b, touched, where unsurprisingly it is flattened.[19] Knight follows the open key signature of the chant, and he only sporadically flattens sixth degree notes in his polyphony during the course of the piece. Byrd uses a B♭ key signature, only sharpening the sixth degree very selectively. Knight's setting sounds very modal, being full of juxtapositions of chords containing B♭ and B♮.

The clearest indication of Byrd's comparatively 'tonal' idiom is to be found at those points in the chant where Morley would have used punctuating cadences of various kinds: taking the first verse and alleluia, the shape is as follows:

[18]  See May Hofman and John Morehen in EECM, Supplementary Volume 2: the composers named are Byrd, Dygon, Gerarde, Knight, W. Parsons, Redford, Tailer, and Tye. Settings by Lassus and Montanus are also in English sources.

[19]  Unsurprisingly, because the note is in the context of 'unum notum supra "la" semper est canendum "fa" '.

Example 1.3  Knight, *Christus resurgens*

Christus resurgens ex mortuis, iam non moritur;
mors illi ultra non dominabitur.
Quod enim vivit, vivit Deo.
Alleluia.

At each point of punctuation Byrd supplies clear cadences that involve
sharpened leading notes or emphatic plagal cadences. Only at the final
'vivit Deo' does Knight really articulate the music in this way, and he
cadences not on the tonic but on the fourth degree of the scale, using the
sharpened form of the triad.

The chant itself is not particularly accommodating to large-scale tonal
manipulation. Nevertheless, Byrd's carefully placed accidentals (C♯, F♯,
B♮, and towards the end G♯ – the 'dominant' of the 'dominant') do much
to modify the flattened-seventh modality of the chant. If *Christus resurgens*
is an early work, it is certainly a remarkably forward-looking one, at least in
respect of its tonality.

There are other reasons, though, that call into question the proposed
dating. The differences in horizontal design between the Knight and Byrd
settings are obvious enough. Knight rarely repeats text phrases. His
imitation is consequently spread out, and very impressionistic. It may well
be that the source of the setting is itself corrupt; even so the structure of the
lines is such that any attempt at 'rational' underlay is fraught with problems. Again, therefore, Byrd is light years ahead of Knight.

Perhaps then, more fruitful comparisons are to be drawn with Byrd's
own *Libera me, Domine, de morte*, since this cannot in any case be later than
1575. The fact that *Christus resurgens* is only in four parts is no indication
of age, for much of the 1605 *Gradualia* music is for four voices. It is in the
quality of the imitative writing that *Christus resurgens* emerges as a remarkably mature piece. Allowances must of course be made for differences in
text: *Libera me ... de morte* is after all a funeral piece, whilst *Christus
resurgens* is a joyous Easter 'Alleluia'. Even so, there is a markedly more
cohesive quality about the imitative structure of *Christus*. This is strikingly
evident, for instance, in the section 'Quod enim vivit, vivit Deo', and in the
succeeding 'Alleluia'.[20] Here the motives are particularly concise and
energetic, and there is a constant interplay between voices that recalls
nothing so much as the exuberant 'Alleluias' of the four-part Corpus
Christi mass.[21] There is moreover that feeling for cumulative design that so
distinguishes the best of Byrd's music: the acceleration towards the 'vivit

[20] Byrd, in any case, abandons the cantus firmus in the following section, 'Dicant nunc
Iudaei', a section that Kerman believed might have been a later addition (MWB 1, p. 64).
[21] See *Oculi omnium* and *Sacerdotes Domini*.

Deo' cadence, together with the masterly placing of the augmented-triad chord in that acceleration; the stretto-like relationship between the outer parts at the beginning of the 'vivit Deo' section; the antiphonal interplay of voices at the beginning of the 'Alleluia', high voices answering low; the intensification of melodic movement at the repetition of the 'Alleluias'; the rising bass line of the 'Alleluia', coupled four bars before the end with the tautest and most syncopated entries of the point in the two upper voices, both of which are also at the upper ends of their registers. To be sure, there are some odd spacings of texture in the freely imitative section, 'Dicant nunc Iudaei' (could this part perhaps have been a reworking of older material?). But such unusual spacings as occur in the first part of the piece, where the cantus firmus appears in unbroken semibreves, are easily explained. There is the gap between alto and tenor in bar 55 (the fourth bar from the end of the first Alleluia) through which Morley could certainly have driven a 'coach and horses'! But then, the spacing is in large measure imposed on the music, given Byrd's evident concern to create a final climax by keeping the tessitura of each free part high. There are some remarkable dissonances too. But these are also a feature of the *Gradualia* style, especially at full cadences where the very formality of the harmonic process challenged him to invent elegant variations on the basic formula. Morley was certainly aware of the danger of stereotyped cadences, for as he put it, 'In *Cadence* there is little shift or varietie, and therefore it shoulde seeme not so often to be used, for avoiding of tediousnesse' (p. 82 [160]). In this very typical passage from *Pascha nostrum*, for instance, Byrd doubtless considered that the cadential procedure would help the ear to grasp the logic of some unconventional dissonances:

Example 1.4  Byrd, *Pascha nostrum* (*Gradualia*, 1607)

Might *Christus resurgens* then be a comparatively late work – Byrd's last great tribute, perhaps, to the ancient English disciplines of descanting and cantus firmus composition? No early manuscript copies, after all, have yet come to light.

# 2

# The English background to Byrd's motets: textual and stylistic models for Infelix ego

## OWEN REES

Many questions remain to be addressed before we reach a full understanding of Byrd's attitude to the *cantio sacra*: why did he (or a patron) choose particular texts? What associations (religious or musical) did those texts have for Byrd and for those who copied or heard his music? Did these associations influence his use of particular styles and techniques? What were the specific models, English and continental, from which he acquired such techniques? Compared with his English predecessors, Byrd could exercise great freedom of choice as a composer of Latin polyphony, since such music was for the first time largely independent of the demands of a liturgy and of liturgical propriety. Furthermore, the London in which he worked presented an increasingly cosmopolitan environment in which a growing class of musically literate amateurs were acquiring and performing sacred and secular music of the international repertory. In seeking answers to the above questions our enquiries will need to be correspondingly wide-ranging.

One major task must be the investigation of the motet as it existed in England and on the Continent during Byrd's formative years. With regard to the position in England between about 1540 and 1570 there has emerged a general consensus of musicological opinion. The surviving repertory of what are now called 'motets' by English composers from this period is dominated by settings of complete psalms (or complete sections of Psalm 118) without doxology.[1] Joseph Kerman has claimed that the origins of this 'special category of non-liturgical motet . . . can be traced . . . to the Continent via Scotland'.[2] Kerman and Frank Harrison use the term

---

[1] The only such motet to include a setting of the doxology is Tallis's *Laudate Dominum*.

[2] MWB 1, p. 29. A similar view is expressed by Frank Ll. Harrison, 'Church Music in England', in Gerald Abraham, ed., *New Oxford History of Music*, vol. 4 (Oxford, 1968), p. 479, where it is suggested that most 'psalm motets' 'were probably composed in Queen

'psalm motet' to describe such pieces, and this designation has become widely accepted. Kerman has supported his thesis that English composers were following a continental fashion in writing extended psalm settings with the observation that 'The psalm-motet had been a favorite continental genre since the time of Josquin'.[3] The established view of the 'psalm motet' sees it as in some sense the successor of the 'votive antiphon'[4] in terms of function and style; however, it is claimed that since the texts of 'psalm motets' were apparently taken straight from the Bible, such motets (which do not set the doxology) cannot be regarded as fitting any specific liturgical context, and that they should therefore be seen as a symptom of the process of reformation and in particular of the freeing of Latin polyphony from the liturgy.[5]

To what extent was the 'psalm motet' indeed a 'favorite continental genre'? Thirteen of the ninety-nine motets which evidence suggests can safely be ascribed to Josquin fit the definition of the 'psalm motet' given above.[6] This proportion of psalm settings is, however, much higher than that found in the surviving works of Josquin's contemporaries and successors. In a 'comprehensive survey of Latin psalm motets in European sources from 1500 to 1535' Edward Nowacki is able to list only fifty-five

---

Mary's reign, perhaps under the impulse of their cultivation on the Continent'. The claim that the impetus for composing psalm settings came to England from Scotland seems to depend solely on the fact that Thomas Wode's copy of *Deus misereatur* by Robert Johnson (*GB-Eu* La.III.483) includes the observation that the piece was composed 'in Ingland ten or xii yeiris before reformation'; it should be pointed out that this reference could be either to the English reformation or to the Scottish (of 1560). If the latter is the intended meaning, then this motet need not be any earlier than a number of psalm settings by English composers.

[3] Joseph Kerman, 'The Elizabethan Motet: a Study of Texts for Music', *Studies in the Renaissance* 9 (1962), p. 282.

[4] It should be remembered that the terms 'motet' and 'votive antiphon' were not apparently in use in England during the period when psalm settings were being composed. It may be that this nomenclatural division of the repertory into these two supposedly distinct 'genres' has itself strengthened the view that the 'psalm motet' was simply a *replacement* for the 'votive antiphon'.

[5] Kerman, 'Elizabethan Motet', p. 282, states that 'the psalm-motet ... represents a link or a middle stage between the composer's impersonal handling of a liturgical unit and his personal choice of words from the Bible or elsewhere'.

[6] Eighteen motets by Josquin are settings of complete psalms or complete sections of Psalm 118. However, five of these include the doxology or shorter doxology, and do not therefore conform to this definition of the 'psalm motet'. It should also be noted that no fewer than seven of Josquin's psalm settings employ patterns of text-repetition (usually the recurrence of the opening phrase at the end) which are untypical of works by English composers (although Sheppard's *Beati omnes*, exceptionally, employs just this type of repetition).

works which conform to the above definition.[7] Very few surviving works
by such composers as Gombert, Clemens, and Willaert could be given the
label 'psalm motet'.[8] The music of these men, and of Clemens in particular,
features prominently in many of the continental motet anthologies
published during the middle decades of the century, several of which were

[7] Edward Nowacki, 'The Latin Psalm Motet 1500–1535', in Ludwig Finscher, ed.,
*Renaissance-Studien: Helmuth Osthoff zum 80. Geburtstag* (Tutzing, 1979), pp. 159–84.
The above total excludes those works listed by Nowacki which include a setting of the
doxology or shorter doxology, or which incorporate an antiphon, alleluias, or other types
of refrain.

[8] In the modern complete edition of Gombert's motets (Corpus Musicae Mensurabilis 6, ed.
Joseph Schmidt-Görg, Rome, 1951–75) only 10 out of 145 works are settings of complete
psalms. The same applies to only 4 out of 231 motets by Clemens (Corpus Musicae
Mensurabilis 4, ed. K. Ph. Bernet Kempers (Rome, 1951–76)). Approximately one in
twenty of the motets by Willaert which were published during the composer's lifetime
could be labelled 'psalm motets'.

It is true that 'psalm motets' were written in some numbers by German composers such
as Ludwig Senfl (who, though of Swiss origin, worked in Germany) and Thomas Stoltzer.
Fourteen settings of Latin psalms by Stoltzer survive. However, over a third of these
include the doxology and/or a repetition of the opening text verse at the end. For a modern
edition, see Denkmäler deutscher Tonkunst, Series 1, vol. 65: *Thomas Stoltzer, Sämtliche
lateinische Hymnen und Psalmen*, ed. Hans Albrecht and Otto Gombosi, revised by Hans
Joaquim Moser (Wiesbaden, 1959). Eleven Latin psalms by Senfl are edited in *Ludwig
Senfl Sämtliche Werke*, vol. 3: *Motetten. I. Teil: Gelegenheitsmotetten und Psalmvertonungen*,
ed. Walter Gerstenberg (Basle, 1939). More than a quarter of these works set the doxology
and/or conclude with a repeat of the opening text. Both Stoltzer and Senfl seem to have had
Lutheran sympathies, and this may explain their unusual preoccupation with the composition of Latin psalms.

Some manuscripts of German provenance are devoted almost entirely to settings of Latin
psalms. See Willem Elders, 'Ein handschriftlicher "Liber Psalmorum" aus deutscher Überlieferung', in Ludwig Finscher, ed., *Formen und Probleme der Überlieferung mehrstimmiger
Musik im Zeitalter Josquins Desprez*, Quellenstudien zur Musik der Renaissance I (Munich,
1981), pp. 47–69, and Wilibald Nagel, 'Johann Heugel (ca. 1500–1584/5)', *Sammelbände
der Internationalen Musikgesellschaft* 7 (1905–6), pp. 102–5. Elders describes a part-book
now in Utrecht which contains fifty-two works conforming to the definition of 'psalm
motet', of which thirty-one can be ascribed to a particular composer. However, twenty-five
of these were written by Germans, while only six belong to the more 'international' musical
repertory (three by Josquin, and one each by Isaac, Claudin de Sermisy, and La Rue). The
inventory of *D-KL* MSS 4° Mus. 24/1–4 provided by Nagel shows that, while many of the
106 psalms which it contains are ascribed to German composers, and no fewer than 19 to
Josquin, there are very few by non-German composers of the generations after Josquin
(and some of these are not 'psalm motets': for example, the text of Gombert's *Vias tuas*
includes material from two psalms).

There is no evidence that the repertories of psalm settings by Josquin or by German
composers influenced by him reached England. The list of Latin works by foreign
composers preserved in British manuscripts which has been compiled by May Hofman and
John Morehen and published in EECM, Supplementary Volume 2, includes no works by
Senfl or Stoltzer, and only one 'psalm motet' by Josquin.

acquired by the Earl of Arundel as additions to his library at Nonesuch. If the musicians of the Chapel Royal had had access to this collection, perhaps during Elizabeth's progresses to Nonesuch, they would have found there nothing which could act as a model for their own cultivation of the 'psalm motet'.[9] As for the surviving manuscripts of continental provenance which came to England in the first half of the sixteenth century, these too contain very few settings of complete Latin psalms.[10] Similarly, it seems that no impetus towards the composition of such motets could have come from foreign musicians working in this country: only six of the eighty-nine surviving Latin works which have been ascribed to Dericke Gerarde (who was 'composer in residence' to the Earl of Arundel) are settings of complete psalms,[11] while out of forty-nine extant

[9] See Charles W. Warren, 'Music at Nonesuch', *Musical Quarterly* 54 (1968), pp. 47–57. Warren concludes (p. 57) that under the Earl of Arundel and Lord Lumley this house and its library 'probably served as a showcase of continental taste and a source of instruction to English musicians in that critical period of stylistic evolution between the death of Taverner in 1545 and the publication of the Byrd–Tallis *Cantiones* in 1575'. For a modern edition of the library catalogue of 1609 see Sears Jayne and Francis R. Johnson, *The Lumley Library: The Catalogue of 1609* (London, 1956). This catalogue gives little idea of the true extent of the collection, as has been pointed out by John Milsom in 'English Polyphonic Style in Transition: a Study of the Sacred Music of Thomas Tallis' (Diss., U. of Oxford, 1983), p. 79: 'Many of the partbook sets contained not a single publication but several – in a few cases, as many as fourteen – bound together in tracts; and of these, only the top tract is described in the 1609 catalogue.' Milsom goes on to list those volumes that were held in the library. Even among these very extensive motet anthologies there are extremely few 'psalm motets': only three are included in the first seven surviving volumes of *Cantiones Sacrae* published by Phalèse (Louvain, 1553–5), while Gombert's *Motectorum . . . Liber Secundus* (Venice, 1541) contains none at all.

[10] John Milsom lists nine manuscripts containing continental music which came to England (or were copied in England) between about 1500 and 1540 ('English Polyphonic Style', Appendix 3.2). A textual analysis of the motets included in these sources reveals very few 'psalm motets'. For example, of the thirty-six motets included in *GB-Lbl* Royal 8.g.vii (sent as a gift to Henry VIII and Catherine of Aragon and later in the Arundel/Lumley Library) not one is a setting of a complete psalm. Music of a later generation (that of Verdelot) is found in the 'Newbury/Oscott' part-books (*US-Cn* 1578. M91, and Sutton Coldfield, Oscott College, Old Library. MS Case B no. 4), which Colin Slim had argued were presented to Henry VIII by a Florentine embassy in, probably, 1527–8 (H. Colin Slim, *A Gift of Madrigals and Motets* (Chicago, 1972), vol. 1, pp. 105–16). In this case only four out of thirty motets set a psalm text complete, and one of these (Lhéritier's *Qui confidunt*) includes the doxology. Of the other four manuscripts listed by Milsom which contain motets, *GB-Lbl* Add. 35087 and *GB-Cmc* 1760 contain no 'psalm motets', *GB-Lbl* Royal 11.e.xi has one, and *GB-Lcm* 1070 has three (out of thirty-nine sacred motets). Thus, only 8 out of the 148 sacred motets which these manuscripts contain could be described as 'psalm motets'.

[11] Charles W. Warren, 'The Music of Derick Gerarde' (Diss., U. of Ohio, 1966).

motets by Alfonso Ferrabosco the Elder only three set a psalm text complete.[12]

In the light of such information, it seems highly unlikely that the impetus for the composition of 'psalm motets' in England came from the Continent. We are therefore left anew with the task of explaining the appearance and cultivation of such works by Byrd's English predecessors between about 1540 and 1570.[13] In particular, the exact nature and extent of the relationship between the 'votive antiphon' and the 'psalm motet' remains to be clarified. One resource which could shed light on this matter has remained largely untapped by musicologists: the *Horae* or Primers which were published in great numbers between the end of the fifteenth century and the 1570s, and which played a central role in the devotional and educational life of the literate classes.[14]

Although Primers were essentially books of private devotion, it is clear that in many respects they closely reflect institutional devotional practices. In the first place, the Hours of the Blessed Virgin (*Horae beatae Virginis Mariae*) which forms the heart of pre-reformation Primers was an Office very widely observed in England, both in monasteries and in secular communities. However, it is the collection of *Orationes* (the terms *Suffragia* and *Precationes* are also found) which follows the Office in Sarum Primers which is of special relevance to the present enquiry. A number of these

---

[12] One of these psalm settings by Ferrabosco, *Benedic anima mea*, is a multi-sectional 'cyclic' work and thus hardly comparable with the 'psalm motets' by English composers. See David Humphreys, 'Aspects of the Elizabethan and Jacobean Polyphonic Motet, with Particular Reference to the Influence of Alfonso Ferrabosco the Elder on William Byrd' (Diss., U. of Cambridge, 1976), p. 7. Such sectional construction is akin to that of Lassus's settings of the Seven Penitential Psalms, which with few exceptions treat each verse as a separate musical unit (and which also include settings of the doxology). Transcriptions and a discussion of Ferrabosco's surviving motets can be found in J. V. Cockshoot, 'The Sacred Music of Alfonso Ferrabosco, Father (1543–88) with Critical Commentary' (Diss., U. of Oxford, 1963).

[13] As with all such discussions of repertories of Tudor music, the lack of contemporary sources and paucity of biographical data make the dating of this repertory largely a matter of speculation.

[14] The basic bibliography and summary of the contents of Primers published in England or for the English market is to be found in Edgar Hoskins, *Horae Beatae Mariae Virginis or Sarum and York Primers* (London, 1901). See also Charles C. Butterworth, *The English Primers (1529–1545): Their Publication and Connection with the English Bible and the Reformation in England* (Philadelphia, 1953), and Helen C. White, *The Tudor Books of Private Devotion* (Madison, 1951).

Hoskins describes the variations between the contents of the Primers which claimed to follow Sarum Use. However, the 'core' of material included in all such editions until the reformation is sufficiently stable to justify the use of the term 'Sarum Primers' in the discussion which follows.

*Orationes* correspond exactly in form (and sometimes in content) with the types of sung evening devotion cultivated in all kinds of religious institutions. In those institutions which had a polyphonic choir, this devotion included as its central feature the performance of an elaborate piece of composed music, the 'votive antiphon' as it is now called. Such devotions conformed to a basic pattern: the antiphon(s) followed by versicle(s) and response(s), and a concluding collect.[15] The majority of these *Orationes* included in Sarum Primers are based on an antiphon addressed to the Virgin. The relationship between the antiphon texts found here and those set by English composers is very close: Hugh Benham has found that in cases where the texts of polyphonic votive antiphons can be traced to non-musical sources, those sources are, almost without exception, Primers.[16] However, there also exist some devotions, both within the Primers and as specified in ordinals and statutes of institutions, in which a psalm or psalms take the place of the Marian antiphon. Thus many Sarum Primers include the following devotion among the *Orationes de beata Maria*:

Psalmus .cxxix. in quo monet ad penitentiam. De profundis ... Kyrieleyson ... Pater noster ... [$\breve{V}$] Requiem eternam ... [$\mathbb{R}$] Et lux perpetua ... [$\breve{V}$] A porta inferi. [$\mathbb{R}$] Erue domine animas eorum. [$\breve{V}$] Credo videre bona domini. [$\mathbb{R}$] In terra

---

15  For example, in his statutes for Cardinal College, Oxford, Wolsey requires that every evening the choristers shall come into the church and there 'intortu cantu canant antiphonam de Sancta Maria, cum versiculo "Ave Maria", et oratione "Meritis et precibus", per unum chorustarum cantata. [Ac deinde, genuflexis omnibus, "Ave Maria" trina vice campanae sonitu intervallo distinguente, solemniter cantetur]' (reproduced in *Statutes of the Colleges of Oxford* (Oxford and London, 1853), vol. 2, Statutes of Cardinal College, p. 57). Hugh Benham, *Latin Church Music in England c. 1460–1575* (London, 1977), p. 153, notes that the form of Taverner's *Ave Maria* indicates that it was probably composed for this very devotion. Some devotions were included in ordinals: such *memoriae* are described by Frank Ll. Harrison, *Music in Medieval Britain* (London, 1958), pp. 76–7, as 'miniature services added at the end of Lauds and Vespers'. These followed exactly the same pattern, namely 'an antiphon without psalm followed by versicle, response, and collect'. Harrison goes on to explain that 'some memorials, for example those of the Virgin, of All Saints and of the patron saint of the church, were observed throughout the year, and were called *memoriae consuetae*. Others, which might be described as "short-term" memorials, were sung during their appropriate season or week, for example those of Advent, of the Resurrection, of the Trinity, of the Cross, or of a particular saint or day.' It is interesting in this connection to note that certain psalms are associated in Sarum Primers with devotions 'of the Trinity' and 'of the Cross', as is discussed below. Since, for example, *Deus misereatur* (Psalm 66) retains this Trinitarian significance in the *Preces Privatae* of 1564, one wonders whether the appearance in the same book of Psalm 50 (*Miserere mei Deus*) among the *Psalmi ... De resurrectione Domini* indicates a similarly long-lived association with devotions 'of the Resurrection'.

16  Benham, *Latin Church Music*, p. 20, and note 25 (p. 225). Another text which survives both in a polyphonic setting (in the 'Gyffard' part-books, *GB-Lbl* Add. 17802–5) and in a

viuentium. [℣] Domine exaudi orationem meam. [℞] Et clamor meus ad te veniat. Oremus. Absolue quesumus domine ... Et anime omnium fidelium defunctorum ... Pater noster. Ave Maria. Credo. God have mercy on all cristen sowles amen. God save the kynge and brynge us to the blysse that neuer shall have endynge. Amen.[17]

At Wolsey's Cardinal College, a devotion following exactly this pattern (except that the concluding prayers are for Wolsey and his family, as well as for Henry VIII) was to be said twice daily in choir, as well as privately. Of particular interest is the fact that after Vespers the *De profundis* devotion was to follow immediately the performance of three polyphonic votive antiphons.[18]

To judge by their appearance within Sarum Primers, other psalms were considered 'proper' to specific types of devotion. Thus Psalm 85, *Inclina Domine*, is associated with veneration of the Holy Cross:

Oratio S. Crucis. A blessing by the virtue of the holy cross with the psalm, Inclina Domine aurem tuam, and an orison. Signum sancte crucis defendat me ... Amen. Psalmus. Inclina Domine aurem tuam. Kyrie eleyson. Pater noster. Ave. ℣. Adoremus crucis signaculum. ℞ Per quod salutis sumpsimus sacramentum. Oremus. Sanctifica quesumus Domine famulum tuum ... Amen.[19]

There is evidence (for example from Salisbury Cathedral) for the performance of sung devotions S. *Crucis* before the great cross in the nave, devotions which seem often to have preceded or followed the singing of the

---

devotion of the standard pattern in Sarum Primers is the prayer ascribed to St Bernard, *O bone Jesu*. See Hoskins, *Horae*, p. 112.

[17] *This prymer of Salysbury use* ..., published by François Regnault, Paris, 1527 (no. 15995 in A. W. Pollard and G. R. Redgrave, *A Short-Title Catalogue of Books Printed in England, Scotland, and Ireland, and of English Books Printed Abroad, 1475–1640* (2nd edn begun by W. A. Jackson and F. S. Ferguson, completed by Katharine F. Pantzer, London, 1986), hereafter *STC*), f. li.

[18] *Statutes of the Colleges of Oxford*, Statutes of Cardinal College, p. 57: 'tres canant intortu cantu antiphonas; videlicet, unam de Trinitate, alteram de Sancta Maria, tertiam de divo Willielmo deinde exeuntes stallos dicant ut supra post nonam "De Profundis", cum versiculis et orationibus supradictis'. These 'versiculis et orationibus' are set out on p. 54. A similar devotion was specified in an Exeter Ordinal, which directed that 'the psalm *De profundis*, the *Kyrie eleison*, and some versicles, responses and prayers were to be said by all, standing at the choirstep and around the presbytery, at the end of Compline' (Harrison, *Music in Medieval Britain*, p. 82). The devotions established at Lincoln by Bishop Bokingham in 1380 also included the recitation of the psalm *De profundis*: see Harrison, p. 83. An almost identical combination of the psalm *De profundis, Kyrie, Pater noster*, versicles and responses, and collect to that found in Sarum Primers was used during the Bidding Prayers before Mass according to the Sarum Rite: see Nick Sandon, ed., *The Use of Salisbury: the Ordinary of the Mass* (Newton Abbot, 1984), p. 8.

[19] Hoskins, *Horae*, p. 117.

Marian antiphon. Other psalms apparently had Trinitarian associations, to judge from the context within which they are found in the Primer:

Ad S. Trinitatem. To the holy Trinity a prayer in Latin with certain psalms. Domine deus omnipotens, Pater et Filius et Spiritus Sanctus ... Amen. In nomine. Pater noster. Ave. Psalmi. Deus in nomine. Deus misereatur. De profundis. Voce mea ad Dominum. Ad te levavi oculos meos. Levavi oculos. Beati omnes. Jesus autem transiens per mediam illarum ibat.[20]

It is interesting to note that one of these psalms, *Deus misereatur*, was still considered 'proper' to the Trinity in the early part of Elizabeth's reign, since it appears among the *Psalmi, Lectiones, et Preces ... de sancta Trinitate* from the *Preces Privatae* of 1564.[21]

The fact that the *Orationes* included in Sarum Primers seem to reflect institutional practice rather closely, and that the correlation between the votive antiphon texts set by English composers and those which appear in such Primers is so close, suggests that we may be justified in drawing conclusions about the original function of some 'psalm motets' from the context within which their texts appear in Primers. Since, as has been shown, certain psalms occupy exactly analogous positions within Primers to votive antiphons, it may be that polyphonic settings of these texts were written for sung devotions of this type. It might in this connection be significant that there survive two settings by Sheppard of *Inclina Domine*, a psalm which, as was noted above, appeared in devotions S. *Crucis*; Sheppard also wrote settings of three of the seven psalms included in the devotion *Ad S. Trinitatem*.[22] Indeed settings of all but one of these psalms survive in English manuscripts. Other works may also have been written for Trinitarian devotions: there survives a single voice part from a *Te Deum laudamus* by Tye in which the text is set complete rather than in *alternatim* fashion. Benham concludes that this work must have been written as 'an antiphon of the Trinity or a motet'.[23] A piece by Aston is given the text *Te matrem Dei laudamus* in one source, but *Te Deum laudamus* in another; Benham here notes that 'the words of this latter are not those of the normal

---

[20] *Ibid.*, pp. 116–17.

[21] *Ibid.*, p. 259. With regard to Trinitarian devotions, it is interesting to note that at Cardinal College one of the three antiphons sung in polyphony after Vespers each day was to be 'de Trinitate': see above, fn. 18.

[22] This total presumes that the piece preserved in *GB-Ckc* 316 with English text but with the title *Voce mea ad dominum clamavi* might have had a Latin original. The hypothesis is somewhat strengthened by the fact that the section of the manuscript in which this piece is found includes other works with English texts for which Latin-texted versions also survive, such as Taverner's *Mater Christi*.

[23] Benham, *Latin Church Music*, p. 209.

Te Deum from Matins of which *Te Matrem Dei laudamus* is a Marian adaptation, but were quite clearly derived (possibly for use as an antiphon of the Trinity . . .) from the "Te matrem Dei" text'.[24] Another piece by Tye suggests that psalmody could indeed serve a votive function. The text of *Peccavimus cum patribus* begins with the penitential sixth verse of Psalm 105 ('Peccavimus cum patribus nostris / injuste egimus / iniquitatem fecimus'), but continues with words which in their direct appeal for intercession are typical of the votive antiphon ('tuae tamen clementiae spe animati ad te supplices confugimus benignissime Jesu').

Thus it may be that, at least in their origins, settings of complete psalms were as closely related to the pre-reformation devotional practices of English religious institutions as the votive antiphons they are usually claimed to have 'replaced'. However, Sarum Primers include a great deal of psalmody besides that which occurs in the type of devotions described above. In addition to those psalms incorporated in the Hours of the Virgin, there were several fixed groups of psalms: the Seven Penitential Psalms, Fifteen Gradual Psalms, Placebo and Dirge, Commendations, and the Psalms of the Passion, as well as the Psalter of St Jerome, which included an abridged version of Psalm 50.[25] A comparison between the psalms included in these groups and those set by English composers seems to reveal some correlation. For example, no fewer than fourteen 'psalm motets' – or about a quarter of the total of such works – are settings of one of the Fifteen Gradual Psalms. In addition, those psalms which appear most frequently in the fixed groups of psalms or in the Hours of the Virgin are to a surprising degree those for which more than one musical setting has survived.[26]

---

[24] *Ibid.*, p. 158.

[25] For details of the appearance of particular psalms within Sarum and reformed Primers see the table in Butterworth, *The English Primers*, pp. 288–9.

[26] Psalm 50, *Miserere mei Deus*, appears four times within Sarum Primers; certain editions (for example, that published by Thomas Petyt in 1542, *STC* 16028) also direct that it should be recited after the general confession. In addition, it was to be used as a replacement for the *Te Deum* during Lent. Settings of this psalm by Whyte and Mundy survive (although the latter used a translation of the text by François Vatable rather than the Vulgate version). Johnson, Sheppard, Whyte, and Ferrabosco all set Psalm 66, *Deus misereatur nostri*, which makes three appearances within the Sarum Primers. Psalm 119, *Ad Dominum cum tribularer*, appears twice within the fixed groups of psalms, and also in settings by More and Byrd. Psalm 122, *Ad te levavi oculos*, is included in Sarum Primers at no fewer than five points: there is an anonymous setting as well as those by Whyte and Ferrabosco. Four settings survive of Psalm 130, *Domine non est exaltatum*, which appears three times in the Primer. In addition, the following psalms each make two appearances in the Primer, and survive in two settings in English manuscripts: Psalm 116, *Laudate Dominum omnes gentes*, Psalm 132, *Ecce quam bonum*, and Psalm 133, *Ecce nunc benedicite*.

In contrast to the psalms which appear within formal devotions, Sarum Primers provide no specific ritual context for many of these texts. Could it be that, through their inclusion in devotions of so many antiphons, psalms, and prayers which had traditionally formed part of sung devotions and which had therefore received polyphonic treatment, Primers had come to be regarded as a natural source of texts for music? Whereas Primers had at first merely reflected ritual and musical practice, they may, especially as the institutions and devotional practices of pre-reformation England disappeared, have encouraged the growth of a particular musical repertory. There is other evidence that Primers may have provided a fund of texts to be set to music: Peter le Huray has pointed out that 'during the years immediately before the publication of the first English Prayer Book, the Primers furnished the most readily available and most acceptable translation of the daily offices, and it is hardly surprising therefore to find that many of the Wanley texts come from these books'.[27]

Other factors may have encouraged English composers to turn to Primers for Latin texts. These books must have been very widely available in comparison with the succession of new liturgical books issued by the Government. Primers were published in huge numbers between 1530 and 1560: Hoskins lists 253 printed and manuscript Primers which appeared in England between 1478 and 1580. Furthermore, these numerous editions of the Primer represented relative stability in a period of constant – and often, no doubt, confusing – liturgical change. As Butterworth explains, the Primer was a great survivor: 'All three of [Henry VIII's] children were to sponsor fresh editions of the Primer. In Edward's reign, the Primer of 1547 re-embodied virtually the whole of Henry's Primer. In Mary's reign, though much was brushed aside with the return of Roman Catholic influence, yet the "uniforme and Catholyke Prymer" of 1555 retained a great many of the same psalms and prayers that were in her father's edition. Even as late as the beginning of Elizabeth's reign, an authorised Primer was set forth to carry on the long tradition.'[28]

While it is true that the Primer survived and that its textual content remained relatively constant, it underwent a transformation in one most important respect: the Marian element which had formed the core of the original Sarum Primers was reduced in scope and finally removed entirely.

[27] Peter le Huray, *Music and the Reformation in England, 1549–1660* (London, 1967; Cambridge, 1978), p. 177. The appearance of Primer texts in the Wanley source is discussed in James Wrightson, *The 'Wanley' Manuscripts: a Critical Commentary* (New York, 1989), pp. 91–4. On p. 93 Wrightson concludes that 'the *King's Primer* was of paramount importance as a source of *Wanley*'s texts'.

[28] Butterworth, *The English Primers*, p. 274.

However, the role of psalmody in Primers suffered no comparable attack. As the requirement for the composition of votive antiphons addressed to the Virgin declined, the obvious alternatives would seem to have been, in addition to Jesus antiphons, those psalms which had become closely associated with sung devotions or with the Primer in general.

The emergence of the 'psalm motet' as such an important feature of the English music of this period may thus reflect a natural desire for continuity in textual and musical practice, a continuity also apparent in the stylistic similarities between many votive antiphons and psalm settings. Even after the types of devotions at which certain 'psalm motets' as well as votive antiphons may have been sung had disappeared together with the institutions which maintained such devotions, the association of psalm texts with Primers perhaps encouraged their continued use as 'texts for music'. It is interesting to note that the production of Primers declined very markedly during the first decade of Elizabeth's reign, and thereafter ceased almost entirely:[29]

| Year | Number of new Primers issued |
|------|------------------------------|
| 1555 | 13 |
| 1556 | 11 |
| 1557 | 3 |
| 1558 | 5 |
| 1559 | 3 |
| 1560 | 4 |
| 1566 | 2 |
| 1568 | 1 |
| 1575 | 1 |
| 1580 | 1 |

(Then none until 1627)

As far as can now be told from biographical and other evidence, the period of the greatest production of Primers (c.1535–56) was also that

[29] The figures in the following table are based on the 'Concise List of Horae or Primers' compiled by Hoskins (*Horae*, pp. xli–xlviii).

when most 'psalm motets' were composed;[30] furthermore, the 'psalm motet' and the Primer seem to have died out at the same time.[31]

If there did exist a tradition of taking 'texts for music' from Primers in England during the middle decades of the sixteenth century, the young William Byrd would certainly have been aware of it, just as he would have been intimately acquainted with the styles and forms employed by such composers of psalm settings as Whyte, Mundy, Sheppard, and Parsons. However, although it has long been recognised that certain Byrd motets are 'archaic' in that they are indebted to Latin polyphony by older English composers, the exact nature of that debt, in textual as well as stylistic terms, has rarely been examined. Thus Joseph Kerman describes certain works by Byrd as 'motets in votive antiphon form',[32] and characterises one of these, the setting of *Infelix ego*, with the phrase 'new matter poured into [an] old mould'; he goes on to remark that in this piece 'the Tudor votive antiphon – archaic, monumental, decorative, impersonal – accommodates a Continental text' which Byrd 'most likely took . . . from Lassus's *Sacrae Cantiones* of 1566'.[33] It is obvious that our appreciation of Byrd's achievement in this piece depends on an accurate identification of the 'old mould' so that the 'new matter' can be distinguished.

Besides the setting of *Infelix ego* by Lassus, others survive by Willaert, Rore and Vicentino (as well as a setting of part of the text by Clemens). The text consists of the opening section of the *Expositio* upon Psalm 50, *Miserere*

---

30 As already noted, the application of dates to the 'psalm motet' repertory involves a great deal of speculation, and depends almost entirely on the little we know about composers' lives and on observations regarding the development of musical style, rather than on the dates of sources contemporary with the music, which in large part have not survived from the period c. 1545–60. Joseph Kerman's view that there was 'a sensible increase' in the production of 'psalm motets' in the first part of Elizabeth's reign is apparently based on the fact, first, that 'not a single psalm-motet is preserved in any source prior to the 1560s', secondly, that 'stylistic progress within the corpus' of Whyte's psalm settings 'points clearly to composition over a span of time', and that 'so large a proportion of his output cannot be reasonably placed in his earliest years as a composer', and, thirdly, that Parsley's *Conserva me Domine* and Tye's *In quo corriget* are given the date 1568 in two manuscripts (Kerman, 'The Elizabethan Motet', pp. 279–80). The first of these arguments is, owing to the lack of sources of *all* types of music in the period before 1560, inconclusive. With regard to Whyte's motets, if the composer was born around 1528, as seems likely, then the 1550s were hardly his 'earliest years as a composer'. Finally, if stylistic criteria are to be used in dating this repertory, it seems most unlikely that Tye wrote the highly archaic *In quo corriget* in 1568: more probably this indicates the date of copying.

31 Although some of the psalm settings by Byrd, as well as those by Morley and John Mundy, are likely to postdate 1580, these isolated works no longer dominate the Latin polyphony of their period as do 'psalm motets' in the middle decades of the century.

32 MWB 1, p. 177.      33 *Ibid.*, p. 179.

*mei Deus*, written by Girolamo Savonarola in prison shortly before his death in 1498. This work appeared in print almost immediately, and during the sixteenth century it circulated throughout Europe in numerous editions.[34]

The editions of Savonarola's *Expositio* which appeared in England differed from those published in the rest of Europe in one important respect. Whereas on the Continent the meditation was typically printed either on its own or together with one or more of the other psalm meditations by the same author (on Psalms 30 and 79), it has been shown that the great majority of English editions were associated with a particular edition of the Primer, and often survive bound with their 'concomitant' Primers.[35] Moreover, in certain Primers the *Expositio* is incorporated into the body of the book (for example, in *The Prymer in Englyshe, and Latyn* published by Toye in 1542; *STC* 16027). If there existed an association between the Primer and musical practice, and if the Primer had come to be regarded as a source of 'texts for music', it would have seemed quite natural to Byrd to set a text which, in England, had become closely connected with the Primer. Even if it was Lassus's motet which first suggested to Byrd the idea of writing a motet on this text, the style which he adopted may well have been determined by the association between the Primer and a body of 'motets' and 'antiphons' by older English composers.

The text set by Byrd differs from that found in the works of Willaert, Vicentino and Rore to an extent that makes it very unlikely that the Englishman used these works as his source. Most notably, both Vicentino and Rore set the phrase '*ubi* confugiam' rather than '*ad quem* confugiam' found in printed sources of the *Expositio* and in the motets of Lassus and Byrd. Willaert uses a different version again: 'ad quem fugiam'. Since, in addition, Vicentino's work was apparently never published, and Rore's only in 1595, it seems improbable that Byrd could have known them.[36]

---

34 See Mario Ferrara, ed., *Operette Spirituali*, vol. 2 of *Edizione Nazionale delle opere di Girolamo Savonarola* (Rome, 1976), pp. 361–8, where no fewer than seventy-eight editions of the *Expositio* dating from 1498 to 1600 are listed.

35 See Charles C. Butterworth, 'Savonarola's Expositions on the Fifty-First and Thirty-First Psalms', *The Library*, Fifth Series, vol. 6 (1951–2), pp. 162–70.

36 All these settings of *Infelix ego*, and the possible relationships between some of them, are discussed in Patrick Macey, 'Savonarola and the Sixteenth-Century Motet', *Journal of the American Musicological Society* 36 (1983), pp. 422–52. Macey does not, however, refer to the textual variants between the motets.

Willaert's setting of *Infelix ego* was published in Montanus and Neuber's *Sextus tomus Evangeliorum* (1556⁹), and in addition seems to have reached Britain around the middle of the sixteenth century, since four of the six parts were copied into *GB-Eu* 64 among a group of continental motets. Kenneth Elliott ('Church Musick at Dunkell', *Music & Letters* 45

Byrd's text also fails to agree at several points with that used by Lassus. Firstly, while Lassus – and apparently all other printed sources of the text – has the phrase 'ad coelum oculos levare non audeo', in the version set by Byrd the words 'oculos' and 'levare' are transposed.[37] The rhythms employed by Byrd at this point indicate that he intended this word-order when composing the piece,[38] and that the variant is not the result of an error in the edition of 1591. Of course, Byrd may simply have made a mistake in copying Lassus's text, if that is what he was indeed doing. However, a study of other texts set by Byrd for which a likely continental model exists reveals no 'mistakes' of this kind, even though Byrd's versions occasionally depart from their 'models' in ways which suggest a deliberate alteration.[39] Perhaps, then, in the case of *Infelix ego* Byrd was not copying a text from a written source, but rather recalling (not entirely accurately) one that he had learned by heart as a boy. It should be remembered that one of the principal functions of the Primer was educational: it was through the Primer that the young acquired not only good doctrine but also their letters. If Byrd's family had possessed one of the several editions of the Primer which were intended to be bound with, or which incorporated, Savonarola's *Expositio*, it seems not at all unlikely that the boy would have learned this famous text by heart.

There exists one other variant between the texts used by Lassus and Byrd: while Lassus's motet includes the phrase 'cum oculos levare non aude*am*', Byrd sets the word 'audeo'. This use of the indicative form rather than the subjunctive is grammatically correct, and indeed is rather more vivid than the version set by Lassus. Nevertheless, printed editions of the

(1964), pp. 228–32) suggests that the likely owner of this manuscript, Robert Douglas (provost of Lincluden), gathered this collection of foreign music during a sojourn in Paris in the early 1550s. The existence of three variants between Byrd's and Willaert's texts makes it improbable once again that the latter acted as a source for the former. However, see fn. 51 below with regard to a possible connection between Willaert's setting and another motet by Byrd.

37 Every version of the *Expositio*, whether musical or otherwise, which I have examined agrees with Lassus's reading rather than with Byrd's at this point. The critical commentary in Ferrara, *Operette Spirituali*, p. 371, does not mention any printed edition of the *Expositio* which has 'levare oculos', as set by Byrd.

38 See BE 3, pp. 184–5, bars 36–48.

39 There are, for example, no textual variants between Byrd's and Clemens's settings of *Vide Domine afflictionem nostram*; the same applies to the two composers' settings of *Tristitia et anxietas*, except that in place of 'sit igitur nomen tuum benedictum nunc et semper et in secula seculorum amen' (Clemens) Byrd has 'et miserere mei'. The fact that neither of these texts has been traced to a liturgical or scriptural source (except for a reference to Lamentations in the latter) makes it more likely that Byrd copied them from a musical source such as Clemens's settings.

*Expositio* seem all to have the form 'audeam'.[40] Once again, it would not apparently have been characteristic of Byrd to make an alteration of this kind – one that merely attempted to improve the grammar – if he were copying a text. Perhaps this variant too was the result of Byrd's less than perfect recall of a meditation memorised in childhood. In this case the mistake would have been an easy one to make, since a very similar phrase, but employing the form 'aude*o*', occurs earlier in the text: 'ad coelum levare oculos non audeo'. The original cause of this confusion may have been a printer's error: the English/Latin Primers published by William Bonham or Robert Toye in 1542 (*STC* 16025–7) and by Thomas Petyt in 1543 (*STC* 16029) both contain the phrase 'cum oculos levare non aud*i*am'. Anyone with a basic knowledge of Latin would have noticed the confusion here between the verbs audere (to dare) and audire (to hear), and might well have corrected the word to 'audeo' (since they might have had no reason to know that the original reading was 'audeam'). Perhaps it was one of these editions that Byrd's family owned, and from which the young man learned the text.[41]

The sound worlds and formal ideals of the motets by Lassus and Byrd are far apart, and the stylistic debt which Byrd owes here to older English practice is clear. While this debt has generally been acknowledged in discussions of the piece, such discussions have tended to reflect an undue concentration on a restricted part of the English motet repertory of the mid sixteenth century, a concentration which has obscured the nature of the relationship between Byrd's technique and that of his predecessors.

Discussions of the so-called 'psalm motet' have dealt principally with works – mostly by Whyte and Mundy – which fall into two categories. First, there are those which retain the formal conventions characteristic of large-scale pieces, and particularly votive antiphons, written by English composers from the late fifteenth century until the middle of the sixteenth: a division into two 'major sections', each built up from a succession of 'scoring sections' (usually of some length) for a reduced number of voices, followed by passages for the full choir. Secondly, there are works which employ full textures throughout, and are indeed characterised by thick scoring. Such accounts ignore a group of pieces (mostly psalm settings) in which the traditional form based on contrasts of texture evolved as follows:

---

40 See Ferrara, *Operette Spirituali*, p. 371.

41 Considering Byrd's own religious inclinations, it would seem likely that those of his parents were traditional rather than Protestant. This being so, the family would have been more likely to possess a Primer 'after the Use of Sarum' such as these versions by Toye and Petyt, rather than a book such as those published by William Marshall which reflected a more Protestant outlook.

the length of 'scoring sections' was reduced to the extent that such sections no longer act as major elements of the large form but are rather contrasted with other vocal groupings to create small-scale antiphonal effects; these passages based on antiphony are combined with full textures in a flexible pattern, so as to produce pieces whose principal characteristics are discontinuity and textural and 'tonal' variety, and which are far removed from the stereotyped schemes of the 'votive antiphon' style and of those motets by Mundy and Whyte which retain a simplified version of such schemes.

Works which are based on what might be called the 'antiphonal' technique include Sheppard's *Inclina Domine* and *Confitebor tibi Domine*, Tye's *Omnes gentes* and *Quaesumus omnipotens* (as well as the *Missa Euge bone*, based on the last-named), Parsons's *Domine quis habitabit*, and Tallis's *Blessed are those*, as well as Taverner's setting of the votive antiphon *Mater Christi*. Particularly common in such pieces are passages in which a single text phrase is first presented by a duo or (more usually) trio of high voices and then by a group of low voices; this pattern was developed – for example by Sheppard in *Confitebor tibi Domine* and Parsons in *Domine quis habitabit* – by overlapping high and low trios to create textures which approach fully-scored imitation, so that the vestigial distinction between semichoir and 'full' sections disappeared. Certain motets, such as Tallis's *Suscipe quaeso Domine*, show how the highly articulated structures of the 'antiphonal' style and its ideals of variety and contrast were retained within works which are now more generally imitative. Indeed, a continuous line can be traced from such works into the music of Byrd, whose *Aspice Domine quia facta est* owes much to Tallis's *Suscipe quaeso Domine*. The first parts of both motets follow the same textural pattern: lengthy double points[42] employing similar motives and ending with flurries of crotchets are followed successively by free homophony (in which the 'harmony' follows what would now be termed a 'cycle of fifths'), stretto imitation, and antiphonal passages employing what Kerman has termed 'cell' technique. In addition, the animated and syncopated rhythms of the homophony at 'non est qui consoletur eam' in Byrd's motet are reminiscent of the treatment of the words 'qui se dicere audeat' in Tallis's.

I believe that an examination of those works by English composers which employ an 'antiphonal' technique contrasting in many respects with the style of the 'votive antiphon' must lead to a fundamental alteration in our view of Byrd's *Infelix ego*. Kerman delineates the old and the new in this work by stating that it 'takes over the actual style of the votive antiphon

---

[42] 'Double imitation' is defined by Kerman (MWB 1, p. 98) as 'imitation in which the two parts of a single composite subject are developed flexibly together throughout a point'.

only in the semichoir sections; the "full" sections . . . sample the entire range of styles, techniques and textures that Byrd was developing at that time. *Infelix ego* offers a regular compendium of block-chord homophony, half-homophony, single and double points, and "cell" constructions of various kinds. But while the contrapuntal technique is up to date, the harmonic idiom . . . remains close to that of the earlier period.'[43] The problem with this view of the piece is that English composers had already written motets that are themselves 'regular compendia' of all the textures and structures described here.

One of the principal ways in which *Infelix ego* differs from the Tudor votive antiphon or those motets by Whyte and Mundy which preserve its formal plan is in the use of antiphonal effects on the small scale (bars 22–6, 102–8), and more particularly in the blurring and overlapping of the passages for high and low voices, so removing the distinction between semichoir and 'full' sections (bars 48–52). A typical method of achieving such blurring is to re-introduce the high voices during the course of what had seemed to be a semichoir passage (bars 57–61, 190–200); when this technique is used to produce the pattern high semichoir – low semichoir – full, it corresponds with what Kerman calls 'cell' technique. This pattern occurs regularly in the 'antiphonal' works mentioned above, as for example in the passage from Sheppard's *Confitebor tibi Domine* shown in Example 2.1.[44]

Other striking features of *Infelix ego* turn out to be commonplaces of the 'antiphonal' style. The sudden entry of all the voices in homophony after a passage of reduced scoring at 'solus igitur' (bars 122–6) and 'miseri-cordiam' (bars 257–60) might be compared, for example, with the very similar effects at 'elegit nobis' in Tye's *Omnes gentes* (bars 34–6), or with the passage from Sheppard's *Confitebor tibi Domine* shown in Example 2.2. In the 'antiphonal' motets it is particularly common for such passages of homophony to break down after just a few semibreves into stretto imitation, which itself leads rapidly to a florid cadence, as in the Examples 2.2 and 2.3.[45] Byrd chose to use exactly this structure (reduced texture – homophony – stretto – sudden florid cadence) at the end of *Infelix ego*

---

[43] MWB 1, p. 178.

[44] A transcription of this and other psalm settings by Sheppard is included in the author's M. Phil. thesis, 'Settings of Latin Psalms in England c. 1545–1570' (Diss., U. of Cambridge, 1987). The sole source for Examples 2.1 and 2.2 (*GB-Och* 979–83) has a key signature in voice V only; voice IV is lacking.

[45] Examples 2.3a and 5a are transcribed from *GB-Cp* 471–4, except for voice IV, which is transcribed from *GB-Ob* Mus.e.4. Example 2.3b is transcribed from *GB-Ob* Mus. Sch.e.376–81.

Example 2.1

(Example 2.4). Thus, what at first seems the most striking and original compositional device in the whole piece, the newest of the 'new matter' with which Byrd fills the 'old mould', turns out once again to be itself part of that 'mould'.

Still other characteristics of the 'antiphonal' motets are to be found in *Infelix ego*. For example, homophonic passages tend to be harmonically fluid or unstable (Example 2.5).[46] Furthermore, it is generally true of the 'antiphonal' motets that cadences are not only frequent but also highly varied with regard to the notes on which they are formed. Tye's *Quaesumus omnipotens*, *Omnes gentes*, and the *Gloria* of the *Missa Euge bone*, Sheppard's *Confitebor tibi Domine*, and Tallis's *Blessed are those* all cadence on four different notes within overall spans of less than 150 breves; similarly, the *prima pars* of *Infelix ego*, which is 97 breves long, includes cadences on Bb, G, C, and F.

[46] For sources used for Example 2.5a see fn. 45. Example 2.5b is transcribed from *GB-Och* 984–8.

Example 2.2

Example 2.3a  Taverner, *Mater Christi*

Example 2.3b  Tye, *Missa Euge bone*

Example 2.4  Byrd, *Infelix ego*

Example 2.5a Taverner, *Mater Christi*

Example 2.5b Tye, *Omnes gentes*

Example 2.5c Byrd, *Infelix ego*, bars 113–18

Byrd's achievement in writing *Infelix ego* did not consist in the fragment-ation of the basic reduced/full plan employed by Whyte and Mundy. Such fragmentation had already occurred in works that Byrd would surely have heard in his youth. Byrd's contribution lay rather in seeing that this way of setting an extended Latin text – using a form built from often tiny units articulated by clear and highly varied cadences, and emphasising contrast of texture, scoring, and 'tonality' – could serve an expressive purpose and result in colourful musical rhetoric: in particular it lent itself to the reflection of sudden changes of textual mood, to the matching of textual punctuation to musical articulation, and to the achieving of emphasis through varied repetition. Thus, in setting the threefold question 'Quo ibo? Quo me vertam? Ad quem confugiam?' Byrd employed three phrases, scored for low voices, high voices, and the full choir respectively, a structure which matches in a clearly audible and rhetorically effective way the inner articulation, overall unity, and cumulative effect of the text. It is true that the 'antiphonal' motets by Tye, Sheppard, Tallis, and Parsons contain many striking examples of musical rhetoric, but there is nothing in these works that can equal in power the setting of the words 'miserere mei Deus secundum magnam misericordiam tuam' with which *Infelix ego* ends. This power is due partly to the fact that Byrd carefully reserves the structure used here (homophony – stretto – florid cadence) for the conclusion of his motet, and also because he has limited the number of 'general pauses' (with which many 'antiphonal' motets written by his predecessors are liberally sprinkled) which might make that before 'miserere mei' (bar 233) less striking. This discrimination in his employment of the various textural devices of the 'antiphonal' style ensures that Byrd's motet achieves a continuity and rhetorical effectiveness lacking in, for example, Sheppard's *Confitebor tibi Domine*, where these effects occur with such regularity that they lose much of their impact.

David Humphreys has suggested that in lavishing special attention through the use of homophony on the final passage of text Byrd was following the example of Lassus.[47] However, as we have seen, there are passages in works by English composers which match Byrd's treatment here much more closely. Besides, Byrd would have needed no prompting from Lassus in deciding to highlight these words: in every edition of Savonarola's exposition which I have examined there is either a change in the size of type or a new decorative initial (or both) at the opening words of the psalm, 'Miserere mei Deus'. If Byrd was alluding to the work of another composer at this point, it was probably to an English predecessor of his, for

[47] Humphreys, 'Aspects of the Elizabethan and Jacobean Polyphonic Motet', p. 90.

it would be quite natural for Byrd to think of Robert Whyte's setting of this very psalm.[48] Probably the most striking feature of Whyte's motet is the recurrent appearance of homophony. In such passages one of the five voices typically anticipates the others by a semibreve; also characteristic is the use at the opening of these phrases of a chord whose root is a major third away from that of the preceding cadence.[49] Whyte usually allows his homophony to dissolve quickly into stretto imitation. Byrd's setting of the words 'miserere mei Deus' (bars 233–41) reveals all of these features.

As it happens, there existed a continental precedent for the allusion to a setting of Psalm 50 in musical treatments of *Infelix ego*: Patrick Macey has remarked on the fact that the motets of Willaert, Rore, and Vicentino based on the latter text all pay homage to Josquin's *Miserere mei Deus* by incorporating the *soggetto ostinato* (or a variant of it) employed in that work.[50] Indeed, it may be that Byrd too intended a motivic reference to Josquin's *soggetto ostinato*, with its rise and fall of a semitone: in Byrd's *Infelix ego* the topmost voice twice outlines this same shape, at the homophonic setting of 'miserere mei Deus' (Example 2.6).[51] However, there exists another good reason for an *English* composer to regard *Infelix ego* and *Miserere mei Deus* as closely related texts, beyond the obvious connection. Psalm 50 occurs at no fewer than five points within the Sarum Primer,[52] with which, as has been shown, Savonarola's meditation was also associated.

To a considerable extent, the style and techniques which Byrd chose to employ in *Infelix ego* were a natural consequence of the associations which the text probably held for him. In order to be able to recognise such associations with regard to other motets by Byrd, and in general to uncover the likely sources of the texts set by him and by other composers, a broader appreciation of the devotional literature of the period is required. It seems

[48] Modern edition in EECM 28, p. 23.

[49] See bars 58–65, 86–91, 186–98, 208–13, and 220–5.

[50] Macey, 'Savonarola', pp. 440–1.

[51] If Byrd *was* referring to a continental work at this point, that work is more likely to have been Josquin's *Miserere mei Deus* than Willaert's or Rore's settings of *Infelix ego*, since in the latter two motets the *soggetto ostinato* assumes a different shape, employing three pitch-classes rather than two. See Macey, 'Savonarola', p. 441, Example 5. However, it seems more than coincidental that Byrd's motet *Miserere mei Deus* employs for the opening words the shape of the *soggetto ostinato* used by Willaert and Rore. This apparent reference appears first in the *superius* of Byrd's motet, at the same pitch as at the opening of Willaert's piece; in Byrd's next phrase the *medius* repeats the *soggetto ostinato* shape a fourth lower (see BE 3, p. 157). It is not impossible that Byrd had access to a copy of Montanus and Neuber's print (1556[9]) containing Willaert's motet.

[52] See fn. 25.

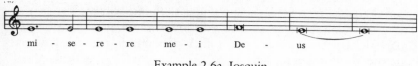

Example 2.6a  Josquin

Example 2.6b  Byrd

not unlikely that within the numerous editions of the Primer there remains a great deal of information that would be relevant to such enquiries.

It also seems important that in attempting to understand Byrd's compositional technique, the net should be cast as widely as possible when searching for possible influences. As I have attempted to show, a broader and yet more detailed approach can transform our view of what is 'traditional' and what 'original' in Byrd's style, and can help in identifying which elements might have come to Byrd's notice in music by his English predecessors and foreign contemporaries. For example, it may be that the 'cell' technique[53] which contributes much to the forcefulness of Byrd's musical rhetoric in the mature motets was derived as much from the 'antiphonal' works of Tye, Sheppard, Tallis, and Parsons as from Ferrabosco. In this and other ways, *Infelix ego* should perhaps be seen not simply as an isolated experiment in creating modern musical rhetoric using traditional English materials, but as the clearest example of a set of formal and textural ideals which might have wider importance for Byrd's technique. After all, within a year of the publication of this motet in which a long text is set using a highly articulated style which emphasises cadential and textural variety, Byrd had issued another work in the central movements of which a similar compositional challenge is faced by employing the same formal ideals: the Mass for Four Voices. These ideals are also fundamental to the construction of many *Gradualia* motets, in which, as Kerman has observed, 'the music is ... organised largely by the careful balancing of phrases that are both shorter and more clearly articulated than before'.[54] Since this description could be applied very well to the 'antiphonal' motets of Taverner, Tye, Sheppard, and Parsons, perhaps we should recognise that the influence of Byrd's English musical heritage can be seen not only in

[53] This term was coined by Joseph Kerman. See MWB 1, p. 117 and *passim*.
[54] *Ibid.*, p. 347

those *Gradualia* trios which adapt 'the half-canonic semichoir style of the Tudor votive antiphon',[55] or in Byrd's fondness for rich sonorities, 6–5 progressions and false relations, but also in his formal thinking as a composer of liturgical music.

[55] *Ibid.*, p. 348.

# 3

## Byrd's manuscript motets: a new perspective

### JOHN MOREHEN

Computer-aided musicology is a well-established discipline with a proven track record extending back over more than three decades.[1] The majority of analytical projects undertaken during that period have concerned statistical or 'quantitative' analysis, much of which has concentrated on pre-Classical music, where the music text as transmitted by contemporary sources is notationally economical. This economy has the dual merits of simplifying the encoding of the music and of ensuring the exclusion from the analysis of extraneous and irrelevant data. Most computer-aided statistical analyses have concerned what is sometimes described as 'stylistics', and have sought to discriminate between composers' styles, to identify geographical provenance, or to establish chronology. Although such projects inevitably pose formidable problems of methodology,[2] the application of computer techniques to Byrd's music would appear to offer many possibilities.

Byrd was the most prolific and versatile musician of his generation, exploiting virtually every genre favoured by Elizabethan and Jacobean composers. It is hardly surprising, then, that his legacy includes a large corpus of liturgical music, covering both the Latin and Anglican rites. Virtually all of Byrd's Latin church music was published during his lifetime

---

[1] Stefan M. Kostka, *A Bibliography of Computer Applications in Music*, Music Indexes and Bibliographies, 7 (Hackensack, 1974); Marc Battier, *Documents, Musique et Informatique: Une Bibliographie Indexée* (Ivry-sur-Seine, 1978); Deta S. Davis, *Computer Applications in Music: A Bibliography* (Madison, 1988)

[2] See John Morehen, 'The Tallis/Byrd "Cantiones Sacrae" (1575): An Appraisal of Current Methodology in Computer-Assisted Analysis', in *Informatique et musique: session musicologique de l'International Computer Music Conference*, Paris, 1984, textes réunis et présentés par Hélène Charnassé (Ivry-sur-Seine, 1984), pp. 59–76, and John Morehen, 'Computer-Assisted Musical Analysis: A Question of Validity', *Proceedings of the International Computer Music Conference* (San Francisco, 1986), pp. 337–9.

in editions of unquestionable authority. However, several additional Latin motets have survived in sixteenth- and seventeenth-century manuscript sources with attributions to Byrd. While many of these pieces display features which broadly conform to Byrd's style, their omission from his printed collections must inevitably place a question mark over the manuscripts' attributions. The case study described here involved an analysis of nine such works. Although all nine have been published under Byrd's name in modern scholarly editions, the authenticity of all nine has at some time provoked scholarly debate. It was decided to include within the study two further motets which survive with manuscript ascriptions to Byrd, although they can now be shown to be the work of other composers: their inclusion was considered useful for their value as a control, or reference group. The complete group of eleven motets is as follows:[3]

> *Alleluya. Confitemini Domino* (a 3)[4]
> *Ave regina coelorum* (a 5)[5]
> *Decantabat populus* (a 5)[6]
> *Dies illa* (a 5) (by ROBERT PARSONS; section of *Libera me Domine*)[7]
> *Domine Deus omnipotens*/part 2: *Ideo misericors* (a 5)[8]
> *Noctis recolitur* (a 5); verses 2, 4 and 6 of the hymn *Sacris solemniis iuncta*[9]
> *Quia illic* (a 4) (by VICTORIA; section of *Super flumina Babylonis*)[10]
> *Reges Tharsis et insulae munera* (a 5)[11]
> *Sanctus* (a 3)[12]
> *Similes illis fiant* (a 4); second part of *In exitu Israel* by JOHN SHEPPARD[13]
> *Vide, Domine, quoniam tribulor*/part 2: *Quoniam amaritudine* (a 5)[14]

---

3   Other works whose authenticity has been questioned, but for which various reasons have been excluded from this study, are: *Christe qui lux es* (a 5) (BE 8/4); *De Lamentatione Ieremiae* (a 5) (BE 8/5); *Salve regina* (a 4) (ed. Dart, Stainer & Bell Church Choir Library, No. 577, 1955; see MWB 1, p. 162); *Sponsus amat sponsam* (a 5) (BW 16, pp. 128–9; see MWB 1, p. 57); *Incola ego sum* (by Robert Parsons, TCM 9, p. 241; second part of *Retribue servo tuo*, unpublished and misattributed to Byrd in same source, *GB-Ob* Tenbury 354–8).

4   BE 8/1. See MWB 1, p. 62 *et passim*.      5   BE 8/10. See MWB 1, pp. 161–2.

6   BW 8/10. See MWB 1, p. 82.

7   TCM 9, p. 303. See MWB 1, p. 67.

8   TCM 9, p. 213 and BW 8/11. See MWB 1, pp. 176–7.

9   TCM 9, p. 248 and BW 8/13. See MWB 1, pp. 57–8.

10   TCM 9, p. 312. This is a four-part section from the eight-part Psalm setting *Super flumina Babylonis*. See F. Pedrell, ed., *T. L. de Victoria: Opera omnia*, 8 (Leipzig, 1911), pp. 55–6.

11   TCM 9, p. 295 and BW 8/17. See MWB 1, pp. 57–8.

12   BW 8/3. See MWB 1, p. 209.

13   BE 8/2. See MWB 1, p. 59 *et passim*. The third part of this motet, *Benedixit omnibus*, is attributed to 'Mundye'.

14   BW 8/18. See MWB 1, p. 161.

The project involved the application of quantitative analytical methods to the eleven motets, and entailed a comparison of each motet against a stylistic model of Byrd's Latin music in order to determine the likelihood of each individual piece being by Byrd. The model itself represented a profile of Byrd's compositional grammar, and was constructed from an exhaustive analysis of virtually all the Latin church music which Byrd composed during the twenty-year period 1575–95 – a total of some sixty-four individual 'movements'.[15] These sixty-four movements were taken from the three collections of *Cantiones Sacrae* (1575, 1589 and 1591), and from the Masses for Three, Four and Five Voices, which, although published without title-pages, have been shown on typographical evidence to have been printed between 1592 and 1595.[16] Not every piece in these collections contributed towards the model, however: for reasons which will be explained later, motets in *note nere* notation or involving passages in triple metre were omitted. Each of the seventy-five motets was tested for 11,328 musical features, covering melodic contour (152 observations), temporal features (1,454 observations), text setting (9,719 observations), phrase structure, and rest patterns. Two points should be made at this stage: first, the Byrd 'model' does not necessarily represent Byrd's style at any period of his life, but rather represents a crystallisation of his styles over a period of more than twenty years; secondly, some (at least) of the dubious motets may be amongst Byrd's *juvenilia*, and would thus predate the earliest music represented by the model.

The methodology required the initial identification of a homogeneous repertory of Byrd's Latin music – here termed the 'database' – against which the questionable works would be compared. A fundamental requirement of this database was that its readings be authoritative. This effectively required the musical text to have been transmitted through holograph copies or through prints assembled under Byrd's supervision. However, even sources of such primacy do not necessarily reflect the composer's true intentions or expectations. There is, for instance, the vexed problem of *musica ficta*: on what basis does an analytical project discriminate between the pitches that composers/scribes committed to paper and those melodic inflections which contemporary performers may have substituted? Whereas erratic or 'accidental' readings within a musical text may be of little

---

[15] The figure of sixty-four assumes that motets in more than one section are counted as a single work and that each Mass comprises five items. Where possible the music texts were encoded from BE 1–4 and 8.

[16] Peter Clulow, 'Publication Dates for Byrd's Latin Masses', *Music & Letters* 47 (1966), pp. 1–9.

consequence in the context of a reductive (e.g. Schenkerian) or motivic (e.g. Rétian) analysis, such matters as the interpretation of *musica ficta* might well be significant in the context of a quantitative analysis.

Since most of Byrd's Latin music was published during his lifetime the establishment of an authoritative database was not of itself problematic. It might be argued that the database should exclude any motet which might be externally influenced (examples of external influence include Gregorian chant, word painting, or the derivation of a vocal work from an instrumental original). In the present database there were relatively few obvious instances of word painting, although there were examples of a *bassus* part being demonstrably influenced by identifiable Gregorian chant (e.g. *Miserere mihi Domine*, 1575). There was one instance of a vocal work derived from an instrumental fantasia (*Laudate pueri*, 1575) and one motet which may derive from a consort song (*Emendemus in melius*, 1575).[17]

Musical polyphony presents a *prima facie* analytical predicament, since by definition it comprises complementary (but sometimes contrasting) textural strands. Since these various strands serve different functions and possess different musical characteristics and identities, it would clearly be unacceptable to aggregate the statistical information for each voice part and to regard the results as representing the piece as a whole. However, since it is not always possible to determine the actual voice type for which a given polyphonic strand was conceived, it would be invalid to embrace all the voice parts meaningfully in a linear analysis. For most purposes it is probably preferable to analyse only a single strand of the texture, even although this would preclude consideration of issues of harmonicity. Once this decision had been taken the choice of an outside voice part seemed preferable. The decision to concentrate the analysis on the *bassus* voice was prompted largely by the assumption that this part, by virtue of its position within the textural hierarchy, is more functional and therefore more musically 'informative' than its counterparts.

The most intractable problem was that of determining those features of the motets which were to be analysed. An initial decision was taken that it was inappropriate to include within the analysis any musical information which is exclusively notational, since such information might merely reflect scribal or compositorial idiosyncrasy. Consequently, the analysis took no account of features such as ligatures, key signatures, clef formations, etc., even though early copyists and printers may have adhered closely to

---

[17] See Joseph Kerman, 'On William Byrd's *Emendemus in melius*', *Musical Quarterly* 44 (1963), p. 435.

composers' copy in such matters, and despite the possible value of such features as musicological evidence for other purposes.

It seemed important to pay proper regard to intervallic structures, since valuable insight into a composer's style is presumably available from a study of the way in which melodic intervals are juxtaposed. Since ascending and descending intervals differ fundamentally from each other all intervals needed to be broken down into two categories – ascending and descending. As an indication of the importance of discriminating between ascending and descending intervals we need only cite Byrd's eight-part cancrizans canon *Diliges Dominum* (1575); were we not to discriminate between ascending and descending intervals the two *bassus* parts would be statistically identical as to interval, since they are mirror images of each other.[18]

But how is an 'interval' to be defined? Is it the difference between two consecutive pitches? If so, why must the notes be consecutive (i.e. 'first-order' intervals) to merit consideration? Surely the relationship between alternate notes is as stylistically informative as that between consecutive notes? This is certainly true if one accepts the proposition put forward by students of natural language that it is the most subliminal features of a work – i.e. those which the composer least consciously controls – that hold the greatest clue to stylistic identity. But how far can this principle be extended? Should fifth- or tenth-order intervals also be measured? Were one to decide to include up to $n$th-order intervals – and any cut-off point is quite arbitrary – how are those phrases to be treated which consist of fewer than $n+1$ notes? Are they simply to be excluded from the analysis? As a compromise the present project embraced first-, second- and third-order intervals, both ascending and descending.

However tempting it initially seemed to analyse absolute (i.e. sounding) pitches in addition to intervals, to have done so would have been very provocative in this precarious and controversial area of performance prac-tice. Pitch analysis is often measured through such tests as highest/lowest notes, tonal density, modal/median pitch, etc. Yet it has been clearly established that in Renaissance music certain clef combinations implied transposition, and that the notated pitch thus comprised a notational code. This transposition theory has been cited by theorists from Rocco Rodio

---

[18] We may at this point interject two relevant but provocative questions: first, is an ascending fifth closer to a descending fourth than it is to a descending fifth? Secondly, is the harmonic affinity between a unison and an octave sufficiently strong for these two intervals to be deemed identical, and, by analogy, may all compound intervals legitimately be reduced to their 'simple' form?

(c.1600) onwards, and has been revived in recent years by a succession of scholars.[19] So far as the clef combinations involving downward transposition – conventionally described as *chiavette* – are concerned, there is considerable disagreement amongst early writers as to precisely which clef combinations the *chiavette* formations embrace, and as to the degree of transposition which they were intended to imply. It would clearly have been dangerous to have taken the original notation of pieces in *chiavette* clefs at face value; on the other hand, to make *a priori* editorial adjustments would have been tantamount to the falsification of data, and might well have resulted in the destruction of valuable information.

Similar problems concerned note values, especially in the case of pieces notated in *note nere* – the notational practice whereby a composer notated his music in a lower scale of note values than would normally have been the case, usually involving the use of the 'full' crotchet, rather than the 'void' minim, as the basic unit of movement. Although the motives which underpinned the use of *note nere* notation are not fully understood, it would appear that composers intended to influence the visual, rather than the aural, effect of the music. In order, therefore, to bring *note nere* pieces into the same frame of reference as other compositions their note values ought logically to be increased, and usually doubled. Yet such data transformation presents a serious procedural dilemma, since it is arguably tantamount to falsification, and may be counter-productive through concealing a potentially significant compositional feature. For this project, therefore, pieces in *note nere* notation were excluded from the database. Another potential problem associated with note durations concerns the unacceptability of regarding the temporal values of pieces in perfect and imperfect mensurations as equivalent. Early mensural practice still holds certain secrets, and it is well known that some composers, scribes, and printers' compositors used certain mensuration signs to convey something other than their literal meaning. The mensural problem is perhaps most acute in works such as *Laudibus in sanctis* (1591), which involve changes of

---

[19] Arthur Mendel, 'Pitch in the 16th and Early 17th Centuries', *Musical Quarterly* 34 (1948), pp. 28–45, 199–221, 336–57, & 575–93; H. K. Andrews, 'The Transposition of Byrd's Vocal Polyphony', *Music & Letters* 43 (1962), pp. 25–37; David Wulstan, 'The Problem of Pitch in Sixteenth-Century English Vocal Music', *Proceedings of the Royal Musical Association* 93 (1966/7), pp. 97–112; Andrew Parrott, 'Transposition in Monteverdi's Vespers of 1610', *Early Music* 12 (1984), pp. 490–516. See also Kenneth Kreitner, 'Very low Ranges in the Sacred Music of Ockeghem and Tinctoris', *Early Music* 14 (1986), pp. 467–79.

mensuration. All motets containing passages in triple metre were therefore excluded from the database.[20]

In many motets, and in all Mass settings, the music is structured into motet *partes* or liturgical movements. In such works all sections needed to be taken into account. Yet simply to have aggregated the statistics for the individual sections and average them across the piece would have obvious disadvantages: it would have destroyed the integrity of the individual sections, and it would have distorted the work's organisation, since the sequence of the component sections or movements would have become irrelevant. Indeed, 'synchronic' analysis of this type is open to serious criticism in that it takes no cognisance of the development process. Yet it is arguably the only possible procedure in the case of a statistical analysis.

An additional problem associated with formal structure concerned the treatment of repeats. A liturgical performance is incomplete if non-formal repeats – as, for instance, in *Attollite portas* (1575) – are omitted. Although such repeats were often indicated at this period by *ut supra* indications, they were sometimes fully notated, perhaps in order to accommodate an alternative text.[21] It might be argued that to include repeats would be to accord undue weight to one segment of a composition. There are further difficulties in defining a repeat. Must it be exact? How extensive must the repeated passage be, bearing in mind that any pair of notes used more than once in any transposition constitutes a repeat? And how is a passage to be treated where only certain voices have a repeat? The problem is compounded by the fact that in the case of some motets scholars are in dispute as to whether or not a repeat was intended.[22] Consequently, repeats were excluded from the encoded music.

It seemed reasonable to assume that composers working within a *lingua franca* conceived musical ideas in terms of different phrase lengths, and that the determination of the 'average phrase length' of a composition might prove fruitful. But what constitutes a musical 'phrase'? While it might be proposed that no phrase may extend beyond a rest, and that a phrase may therefore be defined as the musical statement delimited within consecutive rests, a knowledge of the medieval 'hocket' principle rapidly informs us that such a definition is anything but watertight.

Perhaps the most fundamental problem concerned weighting and

---

[20] The excluded works are *O lux beata Trinitas* (1575), *Siderum rector* (1575), *Laudibus in sanctis* (1591), *Cantate Domino* (1591), and *Haec dies* (1591).

[21] Tallis's *O nata lux* (1575) may be cited as an example.

[22] *Emendemus in melius* (1575) and *Aspice Domine de sede* (1589) may be cited as contentious cases.

sample size. Clearly, for reliable results many features of each composition needed to be taken into account, covering intervals, durations, *tessiture*, text-setting, and other features. But should these features be weighted, and, if so, how? Are intervals as important as note values? Are first-order intervals of equal importance to second-order intervals? Is a composer's word setting more or less important than his exploitation of vocal *tessiture*? Any decision concerning weighting must be subjective, and therefore dangerous. Yet even a decision *not* to weight the various features of itself reflects a subjective decision that all features of a composition are of equal importance. The least objectionable procedure seemed to be to deem all features to be equal.

So far as sample size is concerned, it is questionable whether a typical sixteenth-century motet is of adequate length, in view of the large number of tests to which works may be subjected. Clearly, there is no problem so far as the database is concerned, since this is treated as a single corpus, and is of substantial size. But sample size was undoubtedly problematic in the case of some of the dubious motets: whereas the average length of pieces in the database was over 200 notes, only three of the nine dubious pieces are of this length, most of the remainder being significantly shorter. The shortest of the dubious pieces, the setting of *Sanctus*, has a mere fifty-six notes. This concern over sample size is especially persuasive in motets such as *Miserere mihi Domine*, which consists of a total of only about seventy musical 'events'.

The opening phrase of the *superius* voice of *Emendemus in melius* (1575), although it did not form part of the study (since it is not the lowest voice part), illustrates the type of statistical information which the computer programs extract from the database. (The figures are shown in raw form, prior to 'scaling'):

E - men-de - mus  in   me - li - us

## Intervals

Unisons:
  First order    3
  Second order   1
  Third order    2

|               | Minor 2nd | Major 2nd | Minor 3rd | Major 3rd |
|---------------|-----------|-----------|-----------|-----------|
| **Ascending:** |          |           |           |           |
| First order   | 1         | –         | –         | –         |
| Second order  | 1         | –         | –         | –         |
| Third order   | –         | –         | –         | –         |
| **Descending:** |         |           |           |           |
| First order   | 2         | 1         | –         | –         |
| Second order  | 2         | 2         | –         | –         |
| Third order   | –         | 1         | 2         | –         |

Although this short phrase provides only eleven basic intervallic observations, this number may legitimately be increased to twenty-seven by expressing all ascending intervals both as a percentage of the total *ascending* intervals and as a percentage of the *total* intervals, and by treating descending intervals similarly.

## Durations

Durations were treated by examining all one-, two- and three-event patterns. For the phrase in question this yielded the following fifteen observations:

| one-event: | two-event: | three-event: |
|------------|------------|--------------|
| 𝅝.   2 (=25%) | 𝅝. 𝅗𝅥   2 (=25.00%) | 𝅝. 𝅗𝅥 𝅝   2 (=28.57%) |
| 𝅝   4 (=50%) | 𝅝 𝅝.   1 (=12.50%) | 𝅝 𝅝. 𝅗𝅥   1 (=14.29%) |
|  | 𝅝 𝅝   2 (=25.00%) | 𝅝 𝅝 𝅝.   1 (=14.29%) |
|  |  | 𝅝 𝅝 𝅝   1 (=14.29%) |
|  | 𝅝 (rest) 1 (=12.50%) |  |
| 𝅗𝅥   2 (=25%) | 𝅗𝅥 𝅝   2 (=25.00%) | 𝅗𝅥 𝅝 𝅝   1 (=14.29%) |
|  |  | 𝅗𝅥 𝅝 (rest) 1 (=14.29%) |

## Text-setting

The combination of durations and syllables potentially offers a much larger number of observations than can be extracted from temporal features alone, since any note may or may not take a syllable. However, since this particular example is completely syllabic the number of observations yielded is identical, i.e. fifteen.

## Other observations

Certain features of the analysis yield only a single observation for each piece. In the above example these are:

| | |
|---|---|
| note-per-syllable ratio | 1.00 |
| percentage of piece occupied by rests | 5.88% |
| Average phrase length in crotchets | 32.00 |
| melodic range (in semitones) | 4 |

It must be conceded that there are grounds for questioning the validity of much computer-assisted statistical analysis, since there have been few conspicuously successful projects to date. The researches of Frederick Crane and Judith Fiehler into a corpus of fifteenth-century French chansons by Pierre Fontaine, Nicolas Grenon and Jacques Vide has enabled these scholars to establish tentative groupings of the twenty works by composer. Yet their conclusions can be regarded as sound only if one accepts that several of the twenty pieces which they examined are incorrectly attributed in the surviving manuscripts (which, of course, is possible but not demonstrable).[23] Alastair Pearce's work on Troubadour songs has similarly postulated clear differences between the songs of Giraut Riquier and those of Bernart de Ventadour. But his work did not identify those differences to the extent that it would be possible to place a given song within the canon of one composer rather than another.[24] Hofsetter's work on 'nationalistic' fingerprints in nineteenth-century instrumental ensemble music falls short in the same way.[25]

Although some doubt may thus be cast on certain aspects of current

---

[23] See Frederick Crane and Judith Fiehler, 'Numerical Methods of Comparing Musical Styles', in Harry B. Lincoln, ed., *The Computer and Music* (Ithaca, 1970), pp. 209–22.

[24] Alastair Pearce, 'Troubadours and Transposition: a Computer-aided Study', *Computers and the Humanities* 16 (1982), pp. 11–18.

[25] Fred T. Hofsetter, 'The Nationalistic Fingerprint in Nineteenth-Century Romantic Chamber Music', *Computers and the Humanities* 13 (1979), pp. 105–19.

methodologies, musical stylometry remains nonetheless a widely practised discipline. Some recent studies certainly suggest that the practice holds out some promise, as in the recent study of the joint Tallis/Byrd *Cantiones* (1575). Since the collection was assembled by the composers themselves, the musical texts and attributions are above reproach. And since each composer contributed seventeen pieces to this collection it was clearly an excellent corpus on which to test the extent to which quantitative methods are a reliable indicator of authorship. Even by examining only about 120 features of each composition it proved possible to account confidently and accurately for the authorship of about two thirds of the thirty-four pieces in that collection.[26]

The findings concerning the nine Latin motets of questionable authorship may now be summarised. As has already been explained, each piece was tested for over 11,000 features.[27] Of these, only 1026, or about 9%, were found to be present either in the dubious pieces or in the model. Each of the dubious pieces was then tested against the model for these 1026 'active' observations. By recourse to standard statistical routines it was possible to show which of the dubious works were most likely to have emanated from Byrd's pen. The present study used the Pearsonian (i.e. 'third moment') coefficient of correlation. This coefficient takes a value within the range $+1$ to $-1$, depending on the strength and direction of the (linear) relationship, with $+1$ indicating a perfect positive relationship. The results of this correlation exercise were as follows:

| | |
|---|---|
| *Domine Deus omnipotens* | 0.946 |
| *Alleluya. Confitemini Domino* | 0.944 |
| *Reges Tharsis et insulae munera* | 0.923 |
| *Ave regina coelorum* | 0.874 |
| *Noctis recolitur* | 0.873 |
| *Vide, Domine, quoniam tribulor* | 0.870 |
| *Decantabat populus* | 0.764 |
| *Dies illa* (by Robert Parsons) | 0.747 |
| *Similes illis fiant* | 0.732 |
| *Sanctus* | 0.718 |
| *Quia illic* (by Tomás Luis de Victoria) | 0.700 |

Such coefficients are normally capable of statistical interpretation to indicate the absolute (as opposed to the relative) likelihood of each work

---

[26] See fn. 2 above.

[27] Crane and Fiehler, in their computer-aided study of fifteenth-century French chansons (see fn. 23), covered 145 parameters of each work.

being by a given composer. In the present instance, however, no such test of significance is possible. This is because there is inevitably a stylistic affinity between all composers working within a given period or *lingua franca*, as a result of which the coefficients are almost invariably positive, and are usually artificially high. The *relative* importance of the coefficients, however, remains.

The relegation of *Quia illic* to the foot of the table is hardly surprising, since, despite manuscript attribution to Byrd, it is now known to be by Victoria. The presence of the other 'control' piece – Robert Parsons's *Dies illa* – three places higher suggests that the two works which lie between them in the above hierarchical ordering are not by Byrd. In the case of the setting of *Sanctus*, some scholars consider this piece most unlikely to be by William Byrd; it is also exceptionally short, with perhaps too few analysable features for it to be capable of high correlation with the Byrd model. Only one place above *Sanctus* is *Similes illis fiant*; its position here would appear to justify Joseph Kerman's opinion that 'it seems hard at first to rationalize into the composer's musical development'.[28] Kerman was no less worried by the ascription of *Alleluia. Confitemini Domino*;[29] however, its high correlation with the model perhaps vindicates Warwick Edwards's decision to include this motet in BE 8. The presence of *Domine Deus omnipotens* at the head of the list should dispel any reservations about its authenticity, and perhaps endorses its virtues as espoused by Kerman.[30] This is especially so since it is of reasonable length and is therefore unaffected by concern over sample size. As for the remaining five pieces – *Reges Tharsis, Ave regina coelorum, Noctis recolitur, Vide, Domine, quoniam tribulor* and *Decantabat populus* – one can say only that this ordering represents the decreasing likelihood of their being the work of William Byrd.

The tests to which these seventy-five pieces were subjected by no means exhausted all the possibilities, and the above results could almost certainly be further refined by additional tests. Even on the basis of the results so far, however, the computer-aided analysis convincingly endorses, and arguably supplements, the conclusions reached by scholars on musicological and other criteria.

---

[28] MWB 1, p. 59. *Similes illis fiant* is clearly influenced by Gregorian chant, a fact which may contribute to its position in this list.

[29] 'if *Similes illis fiant* and *Alleluia. Confitemini Domino* can indeed be considered authentic ...' MWB 1, p. 59.

[30] 'there is something appealing about the many unassertive upward scale motives and their attendant trains of gently striving ascending sixth chords; and the last of the phrases in question ... attains a certain distinction'. MWB 1, p. 177.

# 4

## *Birdus tantum natus decorare magistrum*

### DAVID WULSTAN

The death of Tallis in 1585 obviously affected Byrd to a profound degree. The elegy which Byrd wrote on this occasion, *Ye sacred muses*, overflows with a loss which is manifestly personal and unfeigned. Many medieval *planctus* are as eloquent, but their finely chiselled marble often feels cold to the senses. Byrd, like Blow in his *Ode on the death of Mr Henry Purcell*, displays real grief: the tears, we feel, are almost tangible. The relationship between Blow and Purcell was unusual, of course, in that the older composer selflessly stepped aside from his post as Organist of the Chapel Royal in favour of his admired junior. Although the circumstances were different, it seems obvious that the considerably senior Tallis must likewise have thought very highly of the younger man, to judge from his collaboration with the youthful Byrd in the 1575 *Cantiones*. Yet despite this, their musical relationship is far from obvious when the evidence is examined in some detail.

The general impression left by many writers is that Byrd was Tallis's pupil, and Heybourne's phrase, quoted as the title of this article, does nothing to belie the idea: indeed, later in the same prefatory poem to the 1575 *Cantiones*, Heybourne (alias Richardson) speaks of 'our common master'. Are these sentiments merely eulogistic? An examination of several facets of Byrd's technique (as for example in the solo songs such as *Ye sacred muses*) does not readily reveal the expected evidence for this musical lineage. Most conspicuously, Byrd's voice ranges differ markedly from those of Tallis; indeed, they differ similarly as between Byrd's English and Latin works. His English church music is found in 'eponymous' sources, whose ranges can more easily be established, for these sources include organ scores. Organ pitch of the time is known to have been roughly a minor third higher than today's pitch.[1] Can this pitch be assumed also for

[1] See David Wulstan, *Tudor Music* (London, 1985), pp. 194ff.

63

Byrd's Latin church music? If so, the transpositions already indicated by the clefs[2] must be read in conjunction with an additional pitch correction, a minor third higher.

In order to test this question as scientifically as possible, recourse has been made to a computer analysis of the music, kindly undertaken by John Duffill, whose expertise as a mathematician and computer scientist is matched by an interest in music. I suggested that he might analyse the voice ranges of the Byrd English church music found in TCM 2 and of the Tallis and Byrd *Cantiones* of 1575, printed in TCM 9. In these editions, the music is printed at the original written pitch, and there is no indication of the clefs of the sources. In any case, Duffill did not know of the possible significance of the latter, nor of the possibility of transposition, nor yet of my own or others' work on the subject. The experiment was therefore in the nature of a 'blind tasting', for in my asking as to whether the works in volume 9 relate to the same, or different, pitch base(s) in respect of those in volume 2, Duffill had no idea of what I should expect, nor indeed how to go about the task.

The works by Tallis and Byrd in the 1575 *Cantiones*, and the three masses and other works by Byrd found in TCM 9, showed remarkable correlations between their probable pitch level and the clef configurations of the sources. The level was the same as that found in Byrd's English church music, which because of the associated organ parts can be established as being a minor third higher than modern pitch, and was the level eventually taken by Duffill as his computer bank base pitch.

The most pointed consistency in the calculations, however, concerns *O nata lux, In manus tuas, Dum transisset* and *Candidi facti sunt*, since (unknown to the computer) these works are all scored for upper voices quite unlike those displayed by Byrd's English church music. The 'mean' is the highest voice used by Byrd in his English church music, ascending to $eb^2$ (taking the minor third pitch difference into account) or sometimes $f^2$; the four Tallis works mentioned, on the other hand, employ the 'treble' voice a fourth or fifth higher. The top $bb^2$s of *Candidi* or the rather high mean range of *In ieiunio* caused no problems to the computer once it had developed a 'soprano' range combining mean and treble voices. The ranges i–v given below in Example 4.1 are those employed by Tallis and others in earlier music involving the 'treble' voice;[3] those of ii–v correspond with those of Byrd's church music and earlier music without 'trebles'. The highest notes of the treble and mean ranges are particularly significant: the mean can be seen rising in compass (see *In ieiunio*) as the century pro-

[2] *Ibid.*, pp. 203ff.    [3] *Ibid.*, chapter 9.

gresses, but the treble, before dropping more or less entirely out of use (apart from a brief revival in the 1610s or so), tended to descend slightly from the $bb^2$ favoured by Sheppard and the earlier Tallis (see *Candidi*) to $ab^2$ (see *O nata lux, In manus tuas* and *Dum transisset*). The alto range is remarkably stable. This typical range, together with that of the tenor, often contrasts sharply with that employed by Byrd in his Latin music, as can be seen in Example 4.1.

Note that the alto voice (iii) was frequently, whereas the tenor (iv) was infrequently, doubled. Other voices were doubled from time to time, though not as often as the alto; and a baritone voice (midway between the tenor and bass ranges) is occasionally found.

Example 4.1

Turning to Byrd's contribution to the 1575 *Cantiones*, the peculiarities of his voice ranges are surprisingly well negotiated by the mathematics. The computer assigned nearly all of them to offset 0, i.e. the same pitch base as for Byrd's English church music and for Tallis's 1575 pieces. The exceptions are extremely interesting. *Tribue*, and its following section *Te deprecor*, were assigned to offset 0, but there remained some difficulty with the third section, *Gloria Patri*. This three-section votive antiphon is the only Byrd piece of 1575 to have an old-style scoring for treble, mean, two altos (though the second is low and tenor-like), tenor and bass. The uncharacteristic high $c^2$ of many alto parts did not give the computer pause, nor did the occasional presence of two tenor parts, sometimes with wide-ranging compasses (see *Da mihi* or *Domine, secundum actum meum*, displaying both of these characteristics). But it did find difficulties with *Emendemus, Peccantem, Libera me ... de morte, Libera me ... et pone* and *Siderum rector*: all were assigned at first to an offset of −3 semitones, but later wavered, to −5, 0, 0, −3 and −3 respectively.

Of these five pieces, the first two have F3 and C5 clefs, respectively, implying an offset of −5 semitones; the computer offset is therefore aberrant for *Peccantem* by 5 semitones, which is quite a serious margin of error. Both of these pieces exhibit the 'terraced' scoring in which the ranges of the voices descend gradually through the texture, as is seen in many Ferrabosco pieces such as *Qui fundasti* (the model for *Emendemus*), rather than employing the scoring involving the characteristic doubling, especially of the alto voice, found in English music. The terraced scoring doubtless accounts for this computer mismatch. The C5 clef, however (together perhaps with the F3 on occasion, when it may have been wrongly assumed to have the same function), sometimes implies a different transposition, *down a tone* (which gives, with the addition of the minor third pitch difference, total *upward* transposition of a semitone in modern terms, offset −2). This transposition is demonstrated in a service by Farrant[4] and other instances. If the two works in question are transposed by this factor, they both approximate to the 'treble' scoring of *Tribue*, owing to their 'terraced scoring', and they are certainly more singable, and sound more characteristically English, at this pitch. Nonetheless, Byrd must have meant the pitch of *Emendemus* to correspond with that of his model, which has the same clefs: the voice ranges are moreover characteristic of Ferrabosco, rather than of Tallis.

The voice ranges of *Siderum rector* and the two *Libera me* pieces are also untypical of those which were fed into the computer bank: this, too, has resulted in a tentative computer offset of −3 which contradicts the normal clefs (implying offset 0). At normal pitch the high $gb^2$s and $ab^2$s of these pieces are considerably higher than the extreme notes of Byrd's English church music, as are the $db^2$s for altos (the computer seems to take the high $c^2$s of other Latin pieces in its stride): the computer mismatch is therefore unsurprising. On the contrary, bearing in mind that virtually all of the ranges of Byrd's 1575 pieces are more or less untypical, the offsets are remarkably accurate reflections of the clef configurations: despite this lack of correct information, the computer analysis matches the clefs in all but three out of seventeen pieces (counting the three sections of *Tribue* as separate items).

4 *Ibid.*, p. 209.

John Duffill's computer calculations have therefore revealed that the 1575 *Cantiones* of Tallis and Byrd are to be performed at the same pitch base (a minor third higher than that of today) as Byrd's English church music; that the clef configurations known from theorists and from sources in conflicting pitches require additional transpositions; and that although Tallis's voice ranges are broadly consistent with the mainstream of church music, English and Latin, Byrd's compasses, particularly those for alto, are idiosyncratic.

These conclusions are important, since this additional proof for systematic transposition removes many possible uncertainties for the performer which are engendered by the singularity of Byrd's ranges (on the handful of problems which still remain, see Appendix 1). This further corroboration is evidential not only in regard to Byrd, but in relation to the generality of English, and indeed continental, music of the sixteenth and early seventeenth centuries: it adds a Keplerian dimension to the Galilean purview (for a recent geocentric view, however, see Appendix 2).

The peculiarities of Byrd's voice ranges cannot be ignored in a study of the chronology of his works. These ranges are often so unlike Tallis's, so like Ferrabosco's, that they must be accounted as an integral part of the influence of the Italian, and give credence to the references by Morley and East concerning the friendly rivalry between the two composers. Other important aspects of style, such as the question of underlay, should also be taken into account, but this topic must be left severely alone for the present. Instead, therefore, let us look back to Byrd's early years, to find features of his vocal scoring as clues to his formative influences. (In the following, all stated pitches assume a minor third pitch correction and transposition, according to the clefs.)

The high alto parts, reaching as high as $c^2$ or $db^2$, are typical of Byrd in all of his printed Latin music; so, too, is the duplication (and often high extreme of its range) of the tenor voice, not an English characteristic, common throughout Byrd's music. The use of two equal mean voices is also considerably more common than in English music as a whole. None of these features, nor yet the terraced scoring discussed earlier, are characteristic of Tallis, but (apart, perhaps, from terraced scoring) it is not wise to lay these traits entirely at the door of Ferrabosco. High alto parts, for example, are found in Van Wilder's music. His impressive wedding anthem *Blessed art thou that fearest God*[5] has one of the few high $c^2$s to be seen in the early anthem repertory, and there are two mean parts and a high tenor part. His *Aspice Domine, quia facta est*, found in many English

[5] Edited by David Wulstan in *An Anthology of English Church Music* (London, 1971), p. 141.

sources,[6] has a pair of alto parts, both reaching up to $c^2$. This is the piece upon which Byrd modelled his own setting, seen in the 1575 print. To judge from the musical quality, this is one of Byrd's fairly early efforts, so this work may be ascribed to the pre-Ferrabosco influence, attributable to Byrd scoring and studying manuscripts in his own account.

The presumably earlier *Reges Tharsis* displays the ranges characteristic of the Sheppard model, as one would expect – top $bb^2$ for trebles and typical English ranges for the lower voices. *Christe qui lux* imitates White's clefs (C5 in the bass) which also imply top $bb^2$s for treble if transposed up a semitone: Byrd's ranges are similar, but with a more modest $ab^2$. The English compasses continue with some later works such as the three-section *Tribue* (1575): this is for Tr M A A T B, though, as already observed, the second alto is slightly lower, veering towards the continental style of scoring. *Laudate pueri* and *Memento homo*, deriving (the second possibly) from instrumental pieces, may not be significant in regard to ranges; nonetheless, for all their continental influence, the alto parts ascend only to $bb^1$; on the other hand, *Laudate* has two bass parts, and *Memento* two tenors. *Da mihi* also requires two tenors, but here the high alto $c^2$ appears. The same features appear in the 1575 *Domine, secundum actum meum*, where the certain musical dependence upon Ferrabosco is seen. Byrd follows Ferrabosco in having two tenors of high range (to $ab^1$) and an alto compass to high $c^2$, but he has a high treble (to $ab^2$) rather than Ferrabosco's two equal sopranos (to $g^2$), the latter having only one alto whereas Byrd has two, not quite committing himself.

Meanwhile, in his *Credo quod redemptor*, Parsons follows Ferrabosco in much the same way. *Ave Maria* (*GB-Och* 984–8 etc.) and *Domine quis habitabit* (*Och* 979–83) exhibit the same high $c^2$ in the alto part, in contrast to his Magnificat (*GB-Ob* Tenbury 807–11), *Iam Christus ad astra* (*Och* 979–83) and other earlier works. Nonetheless, the high alto $c^2$ is found earlier in English sources: Mundy's contribution to *In exitu* has a solitary $c^2$, whereas his later *Adolescentulus sum ego* has several high $c^2$s in both alto parts. The same piece has two bass parts, which is a feature found in sections of pieces such as votive antiphons (e.g. Sheppard's *Gaude virgo Christiphera*) or even for a whole piece (e.g. Tye's *Peccavimus*). The same is true for doubled mean parts: incidental gimells for trebles and/or means are common enough, and the use of pairs of voices throughout a piece was widespread, if not entirely characteristic of earlier music. Thus Byrd's use of two means in *Exalt thyself* (whose missing parts were discovered and

---

[6] See Jeremy Noble, 'Le répertoire instrumental anglais: 1550–1585', in Jean Jacquot, ed., *La musique instrumentale de la Renaissance* (Paris, 1954), pp. 91–114.

restored by Peter James[7] and on which Gibbons modelled his *Hosanna to the Son of David*) may be considered as normal English scoring, as is the occasional use of two basses in English church music generally. Tallis's *Suscipe*, with doubled means and basses, was clearly influenced by continental practice; but such features cannot always be dissociated from the indigenous vocal scoring, and even when they can, Byrd's use of them cannot necessarily be ascribed to the influence of Ferrabosco, for other continental influences had been at work.

This having been said, Byrd's 1575 *Emendemus, Siderum rector* and *O lux beata* are certainly modelled on Ferrabosco, and the scoring reflects this dependence; the $db^2$s of the alto parts of *Siderum rector* derive from *Ecce quam noctis* (though only one of Ferrabosco's altos has this extreme note, the other has $c^2$); the same high $db^2$s are found in the two *Libera me* settings of 1575. *Libera me ... de morte*, however, has much to do with Parsons and his setting of the words.

By now, Byrd was at the Chapel Royal (1570 or so), perhaps meeting or just missing Ferrabosco on his second visit (1564–9).[8] The years in London up to the publication of the *Cantiones* of 1575 must have been fruitful. Some of the works already discussed (e.g. *Memento homo*, and one or two dependent upon Ferrabosco) may date from this period rather than earlier; *Attollite portas*, despite its un-Englishness, especially in its vocal angularities, may date from this time; and it is possible that Tallis may have exerted a light guiding hand in some of these pieces. He may also have persuaded Byrd to go back to the more traditional English textures, as reflected in some of the earlier works printed in the *Cantiones Sacrae* of 1589 and 1591. That they were not printed in the 1575 collection is explained by the avowed intention of Tallis and Byrd to produce a manifesto of English music displaying up-to-date techniques. To this end, Tallis may in turn have learnt a trick or two from Byrd, possibly even from Ferrabosco, who was now (1571–7) on his final visit.

In the light of what has been said about the doubling of the tenor voice in his Latin music, it is remarkable that Byrd also demonstrates this propensity in his English music for the church. The anthems *Help us, O God, O Lord make thy servant Elizabeth* and *Christ rising* (printed in 1589) all have two tenor parts: the apparently early works *Arise, O Lord* or *How long shall mine enemies* (nor yet the dubious *Out of the deep* and *Save me, O God*) do not however; this characteristic would accord with their

---

[7] Oxford, 1981.

[8] See Richard Charteris, 'New Information about the Life of Alfonso Ferrabosco the Elder (1543–1588)', *Royal Musical Association Research Chronicle* 17 (1981), pp. 97–114.

being works for Lincoln, where the size of the choir might not easily support irregular divisions of the voices. The double-tenor works therefore might arguably date from when Byrd joined the Chapel Royal. It may also be significant that Ferrabosco's only known English anthem, *O remember not our old sins*,[9] is scored for conventional English forces (M M A A T B) and ranges. As to Byrd's service music, the psalm *Save me, O God* has two tenor parts, as do the First and Second Services. Using the same argument, these works would also date from Chapel Royal years (in the case of the First Service it is possible that the two tenor parts might arise from a Chapel Royal revision of an earlier Lincoln work). It is notable that the Third Service has no doubled tenor, which reinforces Monson's view that this service is earlier than the other two.[10] Similarly, *Help us, O God* is unlikely to have been composed as an integral part of *Arise, O Lord*: it was surely composed later, whether or not it was Byrd who attached it as the second part of *Arise, O Lord*.

It is difficult to know how much of Byrd's English music was composed after the publication of the *Gradualia*: it may be true, as is nowadays generally assumed, that he wrote very little of any kind after this, his avowed swansong. *Pace* Turbet[11] however, it is caution, rather than 'ignorance of some recent research' which makes me await reasonably strong evidence, perhaps proof, before concurring with what is after all opinion rather than fact. Again, *pace* Turbet,[12] that Byrd's Second Service predated the verse service attributed to 'Mr. Farrant' is a possibility rather than a probability, in my view. When Byrd came to the Chapel Royal, we know that he picked up ideas from Hunnis for one of his earliest verse anthems (*Alack, when I look back*).[13] Byrd, equally, may have borrowed ideas from Richard Farrant's *When as we sat in Babylon* and Mr. Farrant's verse service, as he doubtless learned some of his solo song technique from the choirboy songs of Hunnis, Farrant and others. If Richard Farrant, a not wholly incompetent composer, had modelled a verse service (or indeed *When as we sat*) on Byrd, it would surely have been considerably more accomplished. Whether Richard or another Farrant composed this service

---

[9] Edited by Richard Charteris in *Alfonso Ferrabosco the Elder (1543–1588) Opera Omnia*, Corpus Mensurabilis Musicae 96/2 (Stuggart, 1984), p. 181.

[10] BE 10a, p.x.

[11] Richard Turbet, *William Byrd: A Guide to Research* (New York and London, 1987), p. 197.

[12] Turbet, *ibid.*, and 'Homage to Byrd in Tudor Verse Services', *The Musical Times* 129 (1988), p. 487.

[13] Craig Monson, 'Authenticity and Chronology in Byrd's Church Anthems', *Journal of the American Musicological Society* 35 (1982), pp. 280–305.

(Turbet's evidence against Richard Farrant's authorship is by no means persuasive), it does not rank as 'a fine expansive work': it is difficult to see this middle-order composition owing as much as it should to a supposed Byrd model.

The 'Great Service' is exceptional. It does not have a doubled tenor pure and simple, as in works instanced previously, for all the voices are divided at various points (the habitual pair of altos therefore becoming doubled in turn), a richness of forces which can hardly have been commanded by many choirs, if any, outside the Chapel Royal. This work may date from a third period when Byrd returned to a more conventional disposition of vocal forces, and it may be that the epithet in one of the MSS, 'Mr Byrd's new sute'[14], is to be interpreted more literally than Byrd's declaration in the preface that the *Gradualia* were to be his 'swansong'. There is some evidence, if somewhat circumstantial, to suggest a reversion to earlier scoring in his English music. The pieces published by Leighton in his *Teares or Lamentacions* of 1614 show conventional scoring (though there are high $c^2$s, not found in 'liturgical' church music) and cannot have been composed earlier, for Leighton's words date from only a year or so prior to the 1614 publication. Similarly, apart from *Have mercy* (which appears to be very similar in date to *Christ rising* of 1589) the 1611 *Psalmes, Songs, and Sonnets* contains several anthem-like pieces which again make use of more traditional forces (indeed, *O God that guides* is for Tr M A T B if performed at church pitch, which is consistent with a known revival of treble music at the Chapel Royal in these years). This evidence cannot be pressed very far, of course, since the domestic nature of these anthems does not allow a true comparison. Nonetheless, their testimony does suggest that Byrd returned to more conventional textures toward the end of his life; furthermore, in the *Gradualia* he moves away from the idiosyncratic choral forces found in his earlier publications of Latin music.

In the *Cantiones Sacrae* publications, as already noted, several earlier works were printed some time after their composition. The vocal forces involved are an important piece of evidence in connection with the chronology. Three particular works must be singled out which have archaic scoring: *Cunctis diebus*, *Infelix ego* and *Exsurge Domine*, all published in 1591. The first two are for Tr M A A T B, the third for Tr M A T B. In all cases the top treble note is conservative, at $ab^2$: this follows the Tallis of *Videte miraculum* and *O nata lux*, not the Tallis of *Gaude gloriosa*. These three 1591 treble pieces clearly follow on from the 1575 *Tribue*, though

---

[14] Peter le Huray, *Music and the Reformation in England, 1549–1660* (London, 1967; Cambridge, 1978), p. 237.

their scoring is actually more archaic, in that the divided alto parts have more similar ranges. *Infelix*, in particular, has many resemblances to *Tribue*, as Kerman has pointed out.[15] Both works have three long sections, and both are in the same written key of Bb. Morley was much exercised by the sight of these flats, complaining 'what can they possiblie do with such a number of flat *bb*, which I coulde not as well bring to passe by pricking the song a note higher?'[16] *Cunctis diebus* also shares the same signature (by no means unusual in Byrd): all three are found 'pricked a note higher' in other sources (see Appendix 1, where the question of keys, and the mistaken use of 'mode', is also referred to).

Although the key of *Infelix* is remarkable, the 5-3 chord on the flat seventh of the scale towards the end is a telling moment. Despite the work being for an old-style disposition of voices, this harmonic touch is distinctly continental, as is the text, which as Kerman has pointed out was also set by Lassus and other continental composers.[17] Its scoring, however, owes nothing to Lassus; this fine work is manifestly English, and (*pace* Kerman's reservations) is a landmark in Byrd's corpus.

It is noteworthy that these archaising treble-style works were not published until 1591. Both the *Cantiones Sacrae* collections of 1589 and 1591 contain, however, works whose ranges approximate to the scoring and ranges found in the majority of English music (and indeed in Byrd's church music in English). Examples from 1589 are *O Domine adiuva me, Tristitia et anxietas* and *Memento Domine congregationis tuae*, and there are many others from this and the 1591 collection. Then there are 'intermediate' pieces such as the first item of the 1589 set, *Defecit in dolore*: this is for men's voices of conventional English compasses (the alto parts do not stray above bb[1]), but the scoring for A A T T B evinces Byrd's predilection for a doubled tenor. So too *Descendit de coelis* (1591) has conventional alto ranges but two tenor parts (M A A T T B): *Afflicti pro peccatis* also has the same forces. *Deus venerunt gentes* and *Domine tu iurasti* (1589), on the other hand, are conventionally scored (M A A T B) but have high alto c[2]s: *Domine exaudi* and *Circumdederunt* in the 1591 collection share the same features.

Although the 1589 and 1591 collections contain several old-style pieces, some of which are more conventionally scored than many of Byrd's contributions to the 1575 *Cantiones*, the proportion of new-style pieces

---

[15] MWB 1, pp. 72, 177f, 341.

[16] Thomas Morley, *A Plaine and Easie Introduction to Practicall Musicke* (London, 1597), p. 156 [p. 262 in edition by R. A. Harman (London 1952)].

[17] MWB 1, p. 179.

becomes larger in the later collections. The doubling of the alto parts is no longer typical (true, the 1591 *Levemus corda* and *Recordare Domine* have M A A T B scoring, but both altos have db²s): instead the two means are doubled, as with *O quam gloriosum* (1589) or *Quis est homo, Domine non sum dignus, Domine salva nos, Haec dies* and *Laudibus in sanctis* (1591), the latter showing much use of the high g²s which were to become Byrd's norm (see also *Cantate Domino*, where both mean and bass parts are doubled). The most significant doubling however is that of the tenor, found thrice in 1589 (*Defecit in dolore, Aspice Domine de sede, Domine secundum*) and five times in 1591 (*Fac cum servo tuo, Apparebit in finem, Domine non sum dignus, Domine salva nos* and *Haec dies*). The most telling trait of all is the increase of 'terraced' scoring: *Vide Domine, Vigilate, In resurrectione tua, Ne irascaris, Tribulationes civitatum* and *Laetentur coeli* (1589) and *Salve regina, Tribulatio proxima est, Haec dicit Dominus, Exsurge Domine, Miserere mei Deus, Afflicti pro peccatis* and *Cunctis diebus* (1591).

The pieces listed above as exhibiting terraced scoring include several (e.g. *Vide Domine, Civitas sancti tui*) having a specifically 'recusant' message, as pointed out by Kerman. They also show an often pronounced influence of Ferrabosco. Byrd's more entrenched recusant position seems therefore to be associated with the time in which he became especially influenced by Ferrabosco, surely when he can be presumed to have met him in the period 1571–7. But Ferrabosco can hardly have been an evangelist in this regard: as Charteris has shown, he was in fear of the Roman Church.[18] At best he was an intermediary, bringing over continental Catholicism through music of the counter-reformation, which may have inspired Byrd to adopt a more assertively recusant stand: this seems to have happened well before the time Byrd moved to London in 1571 or so. The question is not helped by two herrings of a dubious colour: the supposed correspondence with Monte, and the setting of *Ad Dominum cum tribularer* (discussion of this interesting problem must be left for another occasion).

In the matter of Byrd's recusancy, all that can be said is that its influence on his texts can be seen clearly in the publications of 1589 and 1591, where it is often associated with the terraced scoring which he appears to have learnt from Ferrabosco. Terraced scoring is not a prominent feature, however, of the *Gradualia*, although there are some instances where the disposition of voices verges towards this format. What is remarkable in this collection is the Bach-like propensity for using extremely wide vocal ranges, which frequently cover over an octave and a fifth. In the first book

18  Charteris, 'New Information', pp. 97–114.

of the *Gradualia*, the tenor of *Speciosus forma* spans nearly two octaves (Bb to ab$^1$), as does the second mean of *Unam petii*, ranging from g to f$^2$; altos regularly have the compass eb to db$^2$, as in *Plorans plorabit*. The bass often has an octave and a sixth (Ab–f$^1$) to contend with, as in *O rex gloriae* or *Reges Tharsis* (*Gradualia* II). These extremes blur the identification of voices, and sometimes give an impression of terraced scoring. The difficulty is more apparent than real, however, for the scoring of the *Gradualia* is remarkably consistent in regard to two characteristics of the collection as a whole.

First, with the exception of reduced-voice sections and the like, the Propers assembled in the *Gradualia* are scored for the same disposition of the choir throughout each individual mass. Secondly, the doubling of the tenor voice is conspicuously absent: the more traditional division of the mean or alto voices is evident instead (though with extreme compasses). The Mass for Five Voices, therefore, stands apart from the *Gradualia* despite being generally reckoned to be closely connected: on the contrary, because of its two tenor parts (incidentally labelled eponymously, as *primus* and *secundus tenor*) it has more in common with the *Cantiones* collections. Both of these observations concerning the scoring of the *Gradualia* force the obvious conclusion that the choirs available to the recusant chapels for which Byrd wrote his Propers were unable to support the luxury of his favoured double tenor. Because of these traditional choral dispositions, the music of the *Gradualia* often seems surprisingly conventional in respect of vocal scoring; this impression is quickly dispelled, however, in the face of the many extremes of ranges.

The idiosyncratic ranges might be taken to argue for idiosyncratic pitches; but ranges as extensive as two octaves leave even less room for manoeuvre in the matter of transposition. Furthermore, any deviation from normal pitch, or the possibility that pieces were habitually transposed eccentrically, is precluded by evidence of the kind adduced earlier, in connection with the 1575 *Cantiones*. *Timete Dominum* (*Gradualia* I), for example, is printed with high (F3) clefs, but the regular transposition is confirmed by *Ob* Tenbury 374–8, which have the piece written in normal (F4) clefs a fourth below the printed pitch. The opposite is the case with *Viri Galilei* (*Gradualia* II), which in the same MSS is written (F3) a fourth above the printed pitch.

It is hoped that the foregoing remarks have suggested that several facets of vocal scoring are technical features quite as important as other characteristics of a composer's style. The discussion of dating is demonstrably affected by the same features, particularly in the case of Byrd, who in his use of voices differed markedly from his contemporaries. This article has not sought principally to answer questions, but perhaps by pointing to their existence it may encourage profitable discussion.

One problem, raised by way of an exordium, must form the subject of the peroration. What influences did Byrd absorb from Tallis; and were they enough to justify the assumption of pupillage? It has been seen that Byrd's propensities in regard to the use of vocal forces show very little evidence of his being Tallis's student. The early *Lamentations* are the nearest to Tallis in style. Later works, though they may betray one or other stylistic aspect attributable to Tallis, often have contrary features: such a work is *Plorans ploravit* (*Gradualia* I). This non-liturgical piece opens with a Ferrabosco-like 'reverted' point (to use Morley's useful word for the stupidly ambiguous modern term 'inversion'); similarly, the second section opens with a 'paired entry' (Morley's less felicitous phrase was 'two severall points in two severall parts at once').[19] In the bouquet of influences which make up Byrd's heady style, these and other continental perfumes are at least as strong as the old musk of the *Lamentations*. Taverner may provide the headstone of the Mass for Four Voices, but the traditional voice ranges are at the same time rejected. Similarly in *Gaude Maria*: despite one or two passing resemblances to works of the older English tradition, the scoring does not belong to that tradition, quite apart from the remarkable freedom of the opening points. Byrd's setting of the *Gaude Maria* tract has absolutely nothing to do with Sheppard's respond *Gaude, gaude, gaude, virgo Maria*. Examples of non-insular characteristics could be multiplied well beyond the point of tedium. Paired and reverted entries abound, both separately and in combination. Another interesting feature is worth mentioning: the *dux* is often a 'tonal answer' in respect of the *comes*. This feature (the 'tonal answer' being answered by a 'subject') is occasionally found in the Baroque fugue, causing consequent disarray on the part of analysts; but the device has its roots in the late Renaissance contrapuntal techniques which were espoused by Byrd, but rarely by his English confreres.

Continental influence is manifest in Byrd's music: the mark of Clemens, Lassus, Van Wilder and many others can be traced in many works; but the most pervasive influence was that of Ferrabosco, one which is demonstrable in the melodic outlines displayed in a remarkable number of pieces, to be found everywhere in Byrd's printed collections. For example, Ferrabosco's *Surge propera*[20] opens with a compound point, also taken up, modified, in the second section of the piece. It may be compared with a

---

[19] Morley, *Introduction*, p. 167 [276].

[20] Ed. Charteris in Corpus Mensurabilis Musicae 96/2 (see fn. 9 above), p. 89.

host of Byrd's opening points, from *In resurrectione tua* (1589), *Circum-
spice* (MS) to *Alleluia . . . Vespere autem*, *Ave maris stella*, *Salve regina*, *Felix
es* and *Felix namque* of the *Gradualia*. In the two last-named pieces there is
a striking similarity of the phrases to which the word 'Felix' is set. In *Salve
regina*, 1591, *Salve Sancta parens* and *Salve sola Dei* from the *Gradualia*, the
word 'salve' seems to conjure up a motive similar to that of *Felix namque*.
Many words – e.g. 'Domine' – seem to conjure up a particular idea in
Byrd's mind (illustrating his concept of the *aptissimi numeri* mentioned in
the *Gradualia* preface), witness also the word 'senex' in the two *Gradualia*
settings. Similar kinds of points are abundant in both Ferrabosco and
Byrd: the use of these and other particular scalar figures in central or
concluding melismas are also a distinctive mark of Byrd's style which can
be traced to Ferrabosco.

Although a legion of examples shows the debt which Byrd owed to
Ferrabosco, he repaid it by writing some of the most sublime music in the
history of polyphony, usually leaving the Italian's often fine, but rarely
outstanding, efforts far behind. What brought Byrd's music to a higher
level was something which is less obvious than the technical features
instanced so far. It is more a 'profound and hidden power' (*abstrusa atque
recondita vis*) to which Byrd alludes in the oft-quoted preface to the
*Gradualia*. This expressiveness, which seems to transcend mere technique,
though assuredly it is the mark of a more exalted technique, seems to be
inly felt throughout Byrd's music. It is partly explained by the English use
of voices, whereby the shape of the musical outline is suited to vocal
proclivities, rather than the voice having to follow the stonier path indicated by more abstract musical ideas. This is the notable quality of the
Tallis of *Videte miraculum* and *O nata lux*, of *Absterge Domine* and *In
ieiunio*; in these works, too, there is that profundity of expressive power
whose artifice is concealed by art. Perhaps here, after all, *Birdus tantum
natus decorare magistrum*.


## Appendix 1

It is important to point out that May Hofman[21] tabulated Byrd's voice
ranges for each of his works (along with those of all English composers of
Latin church music between 1485 and 1610): it is singularly unfortunate
that these important data were excluded from her catalogue published in

---

[21] 'The Survival of Latin Music by English Composers, 1485–1610' (Diss. U. of Oxford,
    1973).

the series *Early English Church Music*.[22] As she showed in 1973, the transpositions demanded by the clef configurations result in remarkably few exceptions or anomalies (which she discussed at some length, particularly in her Appendix VII). She makes clear that, various kinds of arrangements having been discounted, the exceptions to the proper working of the clef convention are few (indeed, there are even fewer, for she assumed that the C4 clef in the bass implies only one transposition, whereas the evidence of the Byrd sources confirms the Praetorius formula, whereby when there is no flat in the signature, the same transposition as for F3 in the bass is implied).

Among the more interesting exceptions are the 'Bb' pieces. *Cunctis diebus* and *Tribue*, which Byrd printed with a two-flat signature, are both transposed up a tone, but with incorrect clefs, in the Paston MSS *Ob* Tenbury 379–84. *Infelix ego* is treated similarly in the Paston MSS Tenbury 369–73, as is *Tribulationes civitatum* (this and *Cunctis diebus* occur thus in several other MSS). In all these instances it is clear that unlike Baldwin (who had no such qualms) the scribes involved, or their exemplars, were clearly in agreement with Morley that a two-flat key signature was beyond the pale. In transposing the work, however, they did not use (or did not know of) the correct clefs which would have normalised this transposition.

The concept of 'mode' appears to have an undue fascination for the twentieth century. The white purity of these modes, untouched by accidentals, is nevertheless a modern misconception, as is our view of medieval sculpture: garish colours and sharps and flats were the reality. Whatever 'mode' originally meant, it applied to melodic music: transferred to polyphonic music, the concept could only apply to a tenor, such as a *cantus firmus*. The only time the Renaissance musician would be exercised by the mode (or more usually the *tone*) of the polyphonic piece, was when chanted intonations, verses, antiphons and the like were conjoined.

Tallis's *Videte miraculum* has a cantus firmus on the third tone, but this hardly forces it to be called 'Phrygian': on the contrary, the setting abounds with F♯s and D♯s, so if anything, it is in E minor; and, in any case, the sounding key is G minor in regard to modern pitch. Similarly, *Infelix ego* is written as though in Bb. It is Pickwickian to attempt to call this key the 'transposed Ionian', particularly when the 'Ionian' was a last-ditch stand by theorists to make sure that no music should be modeless, however secular in its tonal proclivities, and should be able to enjoy the final comfort of the church modes. As Morley remarks, this ersatz system was promulgated in

22 Supplementary Volume 2.

Glareanus's *Dodecachordon* of 1547, 'which he tooke in hand onely for the explanation of those modes'.[23]

The terminology is bedevilled by the use of the word 'tonal', with supposed antonyms such as 'modal', 'atonal' and the like. What 'tonal' usually means is the major–minor system of the Baroque to early modern periods, better called 'duotonal'. The restriction to two keys and scales, and the concomitant, especially delimitative, usage of accidentals is part and parcel of the styles of these periods. Older (together with more modern) music is usually outside this system, and therefore does not have the same restrictions regarding the use of accidentals: it is 'diatonal'.

Because of its usage of accidentals, Renaissance music sometimes has an equivocal tonal balance which might result in final cadences unexpected to the modern ear: pieces often appear to 'end on the dominant'. Duotonal music, on the other hand, has a particularly strong sense of tonic: this is strategically important since its tonal design includes digressions to other tonal levels whose relation to the main key must nonetheless remain obvious. The evolution towards this duotonal system from the diatonal freedom of the Renaissance took longer than is imagined (spanning roughly the century 1575 to 1675), but an important transitional stage can be seen, well advanced, in the music of the English virginalists. As Gerald Hendrie and others have shown,[24] the virginalists employed a system of 'tones' similar to those used in certain types of continental instrumental music: these tones were not dissimilar to the later keys, into which they evolved. An important feature of such tones was that each was bounded by predetermined accidentals at the sharp and flat extremes, whose limits would not normally be exceeded: thus the tonal balance was more carefully poised than in earlier diatonal music.

In the second decade of the seventeenth century, Coprario and Campion wrote treatises on music which both take for granted the notion that the bass is the seat of the harmony; and both mention the concept of key without giving any impression of novelty. Campion says that 'key, or Moode, or Tone . . . all signifie the same thing' and goes on to explain them more clearly than in the old vocabulary 'that which many in large and obscure volumes have been made fearefull to the idle Reader'.[25] Campion shows that the 'maine and fundamentall close' of the key 'is that which maintaines the aire of the key'[26] but that there are other cadential positions

[23] Morley, *Introduction*, p. 147 [249].
[24] See the chart and further discussion in Wulstan, *Tudor Music*, p. 120.
[25] Walter R. Davis, ed., *The Works of Thomas Campion* (London, 1967), p. 344.
[26] *Ibid.*, p. 343.

which, properly used, can contrast with the tonic cadence, yet remain within the hierarchy of that key.

In describing the music of this period of tonal evolution, it is therefore unhelpful to use dubious 'modal' terminology. Nor should the significance of Byrd's written keys be pressed very far. Since versions of the same work exist a fourth or fifth apart, for example, and the printed key may be a fortuitous choice of two possibilities of written pitch, and since furthermore the written key in any case differs from the modern sounding pitch, the question of key is often irrelevant. In particular, I do not see any fearful symmetry in the key distribution, written or sounding, in any of the *Cantiones* collections.

## Appendix 2

The pitch corrections and transpositions here discussed are not peculiar to Byrd, nor indeed to English music. As the computer statistics have shown, Byrd's singular voice ranges operate within the regimen governed by the normal pitch of the period and the transpositions demanded by the clefs of the sources. This regimen applies as much to the music of Palestrina, Lassus and Victoria as to that of Sheppard, Tallis and White, not to mention earlier and later composers from Willaert to Schütz.

Yet despite this, and in the face of the obvious fact that pitch has demonstrably vacillated during the course of the seventeenth to twentieth centuries, there is often an incogitant assumption that, nonetheless, the notation of the sixteenth century somehow relates to a pitch standard identical to our own, $a^1 = 440$.

To my knowledge, only once has an attempt been made to justify this view in print: Roger Bowers (in 'The Vocal Scoring, Choral Balance and Performing Pitch of Latin Church Polyphony in England, c.1500–58', *Journal of the Royal Musical Association* 112, Part 1 (1987), pp. 38–76) presents a great deal of interesting and valuable documentary information, some of which is new; but in attempting to relate this to the musical evidence, he falls victim to well-worn fallacies.

So far as the subject of the foregoing article is concerned, it is significant that Bowers tries to avoid the period of Byrd and his contemporaries by his choice of dates, and attempts to ignore the obvious connection between the pitch of the English church music of Byrd, Tallis and Sheppard and the Latin church music by the same composers and of older sixteenth-century composers. That the pitch of the Duddington organ of 1519 is identical to that of Tomkins's organ at Worcester a century later seems conveniently to have been forgotten. It will not do to pretend that the religious changes consequent upon Queen Mary's death brought with them a fundamental change of pitch standards.

Yet while seeking to isolate Elizabethan and Jacobean pitch from earlier times, Bowers does not wish to push pre-Tudor music beyond the pale. He makes much of the supposed continuity between the limited-range polyphony (typically for three voices) of c.1400–50 (his dates) and later polyphony, such as the five-part music of the choirbooks. As I have pointed out earlier,[27] it seems at first sight that the earlier vocal forces simply expanded outwards, adding treble notes at the top of the texture and bass notes at the bottom of the total range. As I have further pointed out, however, this expansion cannot be interpreted other than vaguely, since the limited range of earlier music does not yield evidence that it was sung at one pitch only, nor yet what that might have been. Ludford's ferial masses, and certain pieces by Tomkins, are of limited range, and were clearly designed to be sung by more than one combination of voices, and therefore at different pitches. Earlier pieces of the same range might have been transposed facultatively, in the same manner; but this tells us nothing about the prevailing pitch. As Bowers's Figure 4 clearly shows, the similarities between the compasses of each voice make it difficult to tell whether a compass found in one work is to be compared with the same compass, but seemingly a fifth apart, in another work. With music for a greater overall range the outer limits solve the problem, quite apart from the known transposition functions of the clefs.

The expansion of overall range happened earlier than Bowers supposes. The four-part Egerton *Cantemus Domino* (see EECM 8/37) has a range of eighteen notes and has a treble clef in the uppermost part. If transposed up by a minor third, it would provide an early example of a treble compass; if transposed down by a tone, it would provide a nascent bass tessitura; either way (or indeed if the piece were sung at the written pitch) it does not conform with Bowers's Figure 4. Similarly, the four-part masses of EECM 22 (e.g. the anonymous *Veterem hominem*) and 34 (e.g. Frye's *Flos regalis*) have similar compasses to the York or Carver Masses with the same clef and which employ bass voices.

Turning to the three-part Egerton St Luke Passion (EECM 8/24) the ranges more nearly approximate with those given by Bowers (though as seen below, leger lines are more common than he imagines). These ranges look remarkably like those of Byrd's Passion printed in *Gradualia* I

---

[27] 'Vocal Colour in English Sixteenth-Century Polyphony', *Journal of the Plainsong and Mediaeval Music Society* 2 (1979), p. 41.

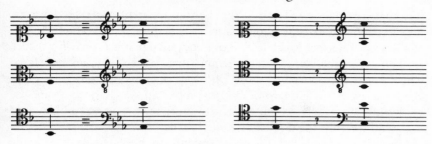

Example 4.2

Byrd, *St John Passion*          Egerton, *St Luke Passion*

(Example 4.2). It is plausible that the Egerton Passion might have been sung at the sounding pitch of the Byrd; but the similarity of ranges between the two pieces hardly proves this. If, however, the Egerton ranges are as significant as Bowers believes, then they show a 'continuity' with Byrd's ranges which Bowers has sought to deny. Similarly, the Egerton *Gloria laus* (EECM 8), if transposed up by the standard minor third, would reveal ranges identical with those of late mean, alto and tenor ranges. Bowers is disinclined to give boys an early role in polyphony, because of lack of documentary evidence. This silence probably extends to other practices, such as boys hitting each other over the head and swearing, but is hardly conclusive evidence for their behaviour. Moreover, since the Sarum *Gloria laus* specified *pueri* for the beginning and verses of this hymn, there seems no good reason why the choristers should be mute every time polyphony was sung.

Most of the points raised by Bowers are already answered in Chapter 8 of *Tudor Music*, where much of the same evidence is discussed, but with necessarily different conclusions. Many of Bowers's misinterpretations are strange. He seems to come to the conclusion that the mean was a boy's voice (p. 67), which is a welcome advance, but then tries to prepare the way for retreat by mixing up the mean *voice* with the mean *part*. Not content with this vacillation, he seems to think that I have misunderstood the significance of the word *contratenor*. On the contrary, the misapprehension is not mine: part-names were a different entity from voice-names, despite their nomenclature often being similar. To lessen the confusion, I have used the term 'alto' to denote the voice, lest the voice-name 'counter-tenor' in English should be confused with the part named *contratenor* in Latin. The choice of language does not always help, since 'meane' or 'cownter' appear as part-names in some sources and *medius* and *contratenor* denote voices in others. The difficulty is more apparent than real, however: the direction that a pianist should emphasise first the bass and then the alto of a Brahms Intermezzo carries no connotation of pianistic yodelling, since we know that the names refer to component parts of the texture. Even when we are introduced to those who sing the bass in a girls' choir, we need not avert our gaze from chin or upper lip, since, once again, the epithet does not refer to the voice, any more than when a stubble-faced Welsh miner sings the treble of *Cwm Rhondda*.

I regret having to labour the point, but it seems necessary to do so in the face of the misapprehensions under review. The main conclusion of Bowers's article seems to be that singers somehow picked their pitch out of mid-air, but yet that it was miraculously related to that of modern times. Transparently this was not the case, nor does the evidence suggest such a whimsical notion, either in relation to the music of the old tradition which Byrd knew as a chorister, nor in respect of his own music, whether it was written for the Chapel Royal or for recusant establishments.[28]

28 John Duffill's computer statistics will appear in a forthcoming issue of *Musicus*.

# 5

## 'Throughout all generations': intimations of influence in the Short Service styles of Tallis, Byrd and Morley

### CRAIG MONSON

It is well known that both William Byrd and Thomas Morley were given to compositional exercises in 'friendly emulation'. Several instances in which Byrd drew inspiration from his teacher Thomas Tallis have been observed in various genres.[1] Although Morley's most familiar musical debts are to continental musicians and in the secular realm, a few sacred borrowings from his own teacher, William Byrd, have also come to light.[2] It is not surprising that in the area of Anglican service music manifestations of the 'student–teacher relationship' should be strong. This was a realm in which tradition, precedent and decorum exerted greater influence than in other genres of composition. The restrictions of the so-called 'short' service style

---

[1] In MWB 3 Oliver Neighbour observes numerous stylistic and technical debts to Tallis, including a specific musical reference in Byrd's own keyboard setting of *Gloria tibi trinitas* (pp. 110–11) and the partial derivation of Byrd's keyboard fantasia a1 from Tallis's *Felix namque* of 1564 (pp. 236–7). Joseph Kerman cites similar instances for the Latin repertory in MWB 1, particularly in *Gaude Maria virgo* (p. 257). Hugh Benham has commented, on the other hand, that 'there are not many signs of the older man's influence in his [Byrd's] music'. See *Latin Church Music in England 1460–1575* (London, 1977), p. 220. On Byrd's debt to Tallis in his Preces, Responses and Litany, see my 'The Preces, Psalms and Litanies of Byrd and Tallis: another "Virtuous Contention in Love"', *Music Review* 40 (1979), pp. 257–71; on the relationship between Tallis's *I call and cry* and Byrd's *How long shall mine enemies* see my 'Authenticity and Chronology in Byrd's Church Anthems', *Journal of the American Musicological Society* 35 (1982), pp. 282–7.

[2] On Morley's debt to Gastoldi and Croce see Joseph Kerman, *The Elizabethan Madrigal* (New York, 1962), pp. 129–209. Morley's debt to Byrd in his Second Service was observed by Peter le Huray in *Music and the Reformation in England, 1549–1660* (London, 1967; Cambridge, 1978), pp. 249–50. Philip Brett noticed that Morley's early motet *Domine, Dominus noster* concludes with a quotation from Byrd's *Libera me, Domine, et pone me* from 1575. See 'Morley, Thomas', in *The New Grove Dictionary of Music and Musicians* (London, 1980), vol. 12, p. 580. Richard Turbet has suggested a link between Byrd's Second Service and the evening canticles of Morley's First Service: see 'Homage to Byrd in Tudor Verse Services', *Musical Times* 129 (1988), pp. 485–90.

were especially austere. It makes sense that when faced with this sober idiom the young Byrd, and Morley in turn, would have studied closely the efforts of their respective teachers, whose approaches to the artistic constraints of the short service, while still respecting the limitations of the style, managed to transcend the merely functional in a way some other Elizabethan composers failed to do.

When it came to short service writing, Tallis's own Short 'Dorian' Service[3] probably provided the inspiration for Byrd's own careful adherence to the unadorned short service idiom, in which chordal, note-against-note writing predominates, and where clear projection of the text is never obscured by extensive or extended melismas. Both composers largely resist the temptation to lapse into highly contrapuntal or imitative textures in this context, probably to preserve textual clarity and to avoid musical extensions of the phrase that might necessitate melismas or redundant repetitions of the words. In his Short Venite and to a lesser extent in the Te Deum, Byrd would move to the opposite extreme, offering drastically homophonic settings, with scarcely any animation or independence in the lower voices. Only in movements with shorter texts, the Kyrie, the Magnificat and particularly the Nunc Dimittis, does Byrd introduce imitation as a means to enliven the texture – but only momentarily.

Given the significant limitations on aspects of composition such as textural variety, word repetition, extension of phrases, etc. that Byrd had accepted, the harmonic element represented a primary means of maintaining musical interest in such a terse and concentrated idiom. Manipulation of vertical sonorities could provide variety and contrast without the need to abandon note-against-note style or to lapse into melismas or imitation which might obscure the text. Byrd's short- and long-range manipulation of the harmony has not gone unnoticed in the more elaborate idiom of his Great Service.[4] But it is the same sort of tonal sensitivity that sets his Short Service apart even from Tallis's or from those of his other contemporaries.

Tallis more commonly relies upon repetitive or sequential schemes to impose both some large-scale order and variety on his Short Service movements, and his insistence on the schemes occasionally imparts a

---

[3] Edition in EECM 13, p. 1. The Byrd works discussed in this essay are in BE 10a, pp. 59 and 136. Those by Morley will be included in EECM 38.

[4] See le Huray, *Music and the Reformation*, pp. 237–8. Oliver Neighbour has also noted that 'In his [Byrd's] own Short Service he had already made one notable advance on earlier services in his much freer use of every cadence degree available within the mode.' See Neighbour's review of *The Byrd Edition, vol. 10b: The English Services II: (The Great Service)*, in *Music & Letters* 65 (1984), p. 311.

mechanical aspect to certain passages.[5] Byrd emphasises instead clear chordal patterns and carefully varied cadences as a means to freshness and variety. This is perhaps the single most striking aspect of his Short Service, and one that would not be lost on Morley.

Certain correspondences between specific moments in the canticles of Tallis's 'Dorian' Service and Byrd's Short Service repeatedly suggest that Tallis's service served as the primary starting point for Byrd's equivalent effort, and provide a sense of what in Tallis's work may have caught Byrd's ear. The combination of such momentary correspondences and several more extended passages confirms how closely Byrd must have studied Tallis's original.

Correspondences between the Te Deum settings of Tallis and Byrd tend toward the sort which, taken in isolation from the Service as a whole, might appear coincidental. Some tonal similarities could be part of the abiding general tradition in vernacular settings of the Te Deum, described by John Aplin.[6] A cadence on A at the important articulation after 'Thou art the king of glory, O Christ' of Tallis's 'Dorian' Te Deum, for example, reappears not only in Byrd but also again and again in the Elizabethan and Jacobean settings tabulated by Aplin, regardless of their final. But it may be significant that Byrd, like Tallis, employs the distinctive, if not very uncommon, sonority of a juxtaposed sixth chord on F (F–A–D) and the final A major chord at this point (see Example 5.1a). Such a harmonic juxtaposition recurs a number of times at cadences throughout Byrd's Short Service. Byrd also begins the phrase with a C major chord, as Tallis had done.

Both composers' versions of the final verse of the Te Deum ('O Lord in thee ... let me never be confounded') begin by juxtaposing D minor and C major chords, employ similar chords and voicing for 'let me never be confounded', and conclude with a cadence on the final, D, which appears less commonly in other composers' settings (see Example 5.1b). After a general similarity in short-range repetitions with repeated cadences on A at 'Holy, holy, holy' (omitted from Example 5.1), both composers employ closely corresponding soprano lines falling from $c^2$ to $d^1$, above harmony that moves along similar paths from A major to D minor for 'Heaven and earth are full ... ' (Example 5.1c); and both composers repeat the music for the subsequent verse, 'The glorious company of apostles'. Yet, Tallis's

---

[5] See for example 'To give knowledge ... and to guide ... way of peace' from the Benedictus or 'And was crucified ... whose kingdom shall have no end' from the Creed.

[6] 'The Survival of Plainsong in Anglican Music: Some Early English Te Deum Settings', *Journal of the American Musicological Society* 37 (1979), pp. 247–75, and especially 275.

Example 5.1  Tallis/Byrd, Short Te Deum

* The musical examples are designed primarily to facilitate comparisons of melodic profiles, imitative points, and harmony in the various settings. The original partwriting of the inner voices has occasionally been condensed, especially when the original involved five or more parts. To facilitate the vertical alignment of the scores some rhythmic modifications have also been introduced (e.g., the occasional shortening of a semibreve to a minim, the omission of a rest in all parts, the suppression of some barlines).

largely stepwise bass line contrasts markedly with Byrd's consistent alternation of fourths and seconds to harmonise the descending stepwise soprano, a type of bass movement that remains relatively standard throughout Byrd's service. Such movement also throws into relief the carefully placed juxtaposition of D minor and C major chords in mid-phrase.

Similar correspondences between the two composers' Short Magnificats suggest, once again, that occasional striking sonorities from Tallis's original may have caught Byrd's attention. Tallis's initial juxtaposition of the opening D minor triad with C major at 'magnify', for example, may have provoked Byrd's similar gesture (Example 5.2a), where the contrast is intensified by the insertion of an A major chord between the first two D minor chords. Byrd also enriches the harmonic activity slightly in the remainder of the phrase before cadencing with Tallis on the fifth, A, at mid-verse.

At 'and his mercy is on them' both composers contrast their first harmony with another triad a third higher (Example 5.2b). Byrd also intensifies the contrast of sonorities by employing parallel motion in his outer voices and by returning to the first chord after the second. This putative correspondence is the sort most likely at first to seem coincidental since the choice of chords does not match precisely. But the use of comparable harmonic juxtapositions of third-related chords at 'He hath filled the hungry', this time at the same pitch and with similar voicings in both versions (Example 5.2c), strengthens the possibility that Byrd in both cases was working with Tallis's setting somewhere in mind.

CRAIG MONSON

Example 5.2 Tallis/Byrd, Short Magnificat

These correspondences from the Te Deum and Magnificat settings all focus on aspects of harmony. In isolation some of them might also be interpreted as coincidental, unconscious, or the result of setting the same texts in a determinedly simple style using D as a common final. Byrd's treatment of the shortest service texts, the Kyrie and Nunc Dimittis, on the other hand, removes the possibility of simple coincidence. Byrd's Kyrie represents a clear attempt to elaborate Tallis's model in a characteristic fashion observable in other comparably brief and simple works as well.[7] Byrd may adopt the melodic profile of Tallis's soprano, many elements of his bass, and some details of his inner parts so that the interrelationship is

7 See, for example, my 'The Preces, Psalms and Litanies of Byrd and Tallis'.

Example 5.3 Tallis/Byrd, Short Kyrie

clear (Example 5.3). But he enriches and complicates the model: harmonically by juxtaposing A major and C major triads between the first and
second phrase, where Tallis had employed A major and A minor, and by
enlarging the harmonic palette through the succession of C and F chords
and sixth-chords on Bb and D at the beginning of the second phrase;
contrapuntally, by first abjuring Tallis's note-against-note movement in
the first phrase, then staggering and modifying the entrances of the upper
voices at 'and incline our hearts' so that Tallis's dotted falling figure
in insistent parallel motion in the upper voices is modified to create

imitative entrances on the same figure, most obviously in alto and tenor.

In the Nunc Dimittis, on the other hand, Byrd's decision to turn quite consistently to more imitative textures and also to create a dialogue between the soprano and the lower voices may reflect once again the influence of his teacher, who marshals the voices in the same fashion in his own Nunc Dimittis. Tallis in fact constructs his entire Nunc Dimittis as a kind of 'free pseudo-canon', the most overt use of such polyphonically animated texture in his Short Service, which has not gone unnoticed by later scholars,[8] as it presumably did not escape Byrd. But Byrd introduces imitation only as the movement unfolds: he begins homophonically, then moves to more staggered vocal entries, and finally to quasi-canon. (See Example 5.4, where the settings by Tallis, Byrd and Morley are juxta-posed.)

Tallis introduces his simple canon at the outset, with alto and soprano in imitation at the fifth. Byrd remains independent of Tallis for this phrase, opting for his customary chordal texture. Instead of Tallis's more static symmetrical opening with its short-winded repetitive harmonic scheme as the canonic voices hover around D, Byrd is able to touch rapidly and effectively upon B♭ and F harmonies by the middle of the first phrase. Beginning at 'For mine eyes', while Tallis continues the close imitation between the top two parts, Byrd draws closer to him by adopting the dialogue between the soprano and delayed lower voices. Once again Byrd's harmonic palette is slightly enriched not only by the closely spaced false relations of an A⁶-chord (A–C–F) and A major, but also by another juxtaposition of an F⁶-chord (F–A–D) and A major of the sort that appears frequently in his service.

Only with the following phrase, possibly even inspired by the text, 'which thou hast prepared', does Byrd arrive at close imitation in Tallis's manner. Tallis switches his canon from the top two parts to outer voices at this point and Byrd follows his lead, though the younger composer

[8] See le Huray, *Music and the Reformation*, p. 198, and John Aplin, 'Cyclic Techniques in the Earliest Anglican Services', *Journal of the American Musicological Society* 35 (1982), p. 433. Other less extended passages of canon or quasi-canon in fact appear in other movements of the Dorian Service. See 'To perform the mercy promised to our fathers' / 'To perform the oath which he sware to our father' (soprano–tenor), 'And thou child shalt be called the prophet' / 'for thou shalt go before the face of the Lord to prepare his ways' (soprano–tenor), 'To give light to them that sit in darkness' / 'And to guide their feet into the way' (soprano–alto) – the last two examples perhaps inspired by the text – from the Benedictus. See also 'Begotten not made, being of one substance with the Father ... of the Virgin Mary' (soprano–bass) and 'Who proceedeth from the Father and the Son, who with the Father and the Son together' (soprano–tenor) from the Creed – again possibly intended to depict the text.

Example 5.4  Tallis/Byrd/Morley, Short Nunc Dimittis

Byrd

Morley

chooses a different point for the first half of the phrase, one which highlights the F and Bb harmonies that had already appeared prominently in the third bar of the movement. For the second half of the phrase, 'before the face', Byrd employs a rising point not unlike Tallis's, though he continues to use the outer voices as his imitative framework, while Tallis shifts to soprano and tenor. And by pitching his point a tone higher than Tallis, Byrd continues to exploit Bb and F, before returning to D at the cadence.

Byrd also follows Tallis's example in making 'To be a light ... people Israel' a variation on the previous verse. Byrd's earlier simple staggering of vocal entries at 'For mine eyes' now becomes overtly imitative for the varied repetition at 'To be a light', with outer voices in imitation, as Tallis also had done at 'To be a light'. (Byrd's imitation is at the twelfth, whereas Tallis's, after the opening leap in his outer voices, is at the octave.) When Tallis switches the imitation at the octave to soprano and tenor at 'and to be the glory' Byrd abandons his own quasi-canon.

As a short service composer, Thomas Morley apparently could not be quite content with the sobriety of Tallis or Byrd. But while he was usually ready to elaborate the texture and to extend the musical phrase beyond the narrow limits of one note per syllable, his attitude toward text setting still remained essentially cautious. Clearly, he also found Byrd's broader harmonic palette worthy of emulation. When it came to short service writing, Morley's indebtedness to Byrd is once again clearest in the Nunc Dimittis to his Short Service. Interestingly enough, several details of Morley's setting may also betray a close examination of Tallis's Nunc Dimittis. If the younger composer were looking for the Byrd Short Service canticle most akin to his own conception, with its more casual attitude toward the dictum 'for every syllable one note' and its more animated polyphonic textures, the Short Nunc Dimittis represented the clear choice, for as we have seen, it is the only Byrd movement that indulges at all consistently in a more imitative style. But though Morley reflects Byrd at several points, he is rarely content with Byrd's rather modest level of contrapuntal activity, and freely enhances the polyphonic complexity and expansiveness.

Although the opening of Morley's Nunc Dimittis (Example 5.4) does not quote Byrd's directly, both share similar tonal outlines, moving from D minor to A major and back again in their first verse and also employing the same soprano profile for 'according to thy word'. (Tallis, on the other hand, had moved from D minor to A.) But where Byrd's setting of 'according to thy word' is essentially homophonic, Morley delays the entry of the lower parts at 'according to ...' and modifies the bass slightly to create an imitation of the falling soprano line, before rejoining Byrd's plan more closely for the cadence. Such polyphonic animation or elaboration remains typical of Morley's Short Service as a whole, and represents his most characteristic way of reworking possibly borrowed details.

Beginning at 'For mine eyes' the interrelationship of the two settings becomes more specific: Morley adopts Byrd's soprano quite literally and also the delayed entry of the lower voices. Once again Morley alters the bass line and the harmonisation somewhat to create a clearer three-note hint at imitation. Morley's reharmonisation also substitutes simple fifth chords for Byrd's chords of the sixth. In doing so Morley loses the $F^6$ (F–A–D)/A major juxtaposition that Byrd (and Tallis before him) frequently had favoured at cadences. It is possible that such a cadence might have sounded a little too archaic to Morley, for he avoids it throughout the Magnificat and Nunc Dimittis.[9]

Where Byrd had concluded the verse on A major at 'salvation', Morley cadences on D minor, in a manner similar to Tallis at the equivalent moment. Morley's continuation for 'which Thou hast prepared' also employs an imitative point somewhat similar to Tallis's, with an opening drop of a fourth from $a^1$ to $e^1$ and with $e^1$ as the concluding pitch of the point. For 'before the face of all people', Morley chooses an imitative point that duplicates Tallis's still more closely, and joins him on A at the cadence. Like Tallis and Byrd before him, Morley makes 'To be a light' a variation on his own previous verse. He rejoins Byrd with a cadence on G before the doxology.

Having returned to Byrd's harmonic field, Morley continues to follow Byrd's model for important moments of the doxology: both composers begin on C with similar melodic profiles for the first few words, though Morley interchanges Byrd's alto and tenor parts; both also cadence on A at 'Holy Ghost'.

For the concluding eight breves of his own setting ('and ever shall be ...') Morley rejoins the last eight breves of Byrd's more closely. The soprano profile of Byrd's homophonic setting of 'and ever shall be' provides the material for Morley's more contrapuntal treatment of the same textual phrase, with imitation added between soprano and tenor. For the last few bars, as if to make his indebtedness more obvious, Morley returns

---

[9] Morley is not averse to using an $F^6$ before A major if the latter is followed in turn by an authentic cadence on D minor, however. Interestingly enough, Morley's version of the whole phrase also closely duplicates Byrd's own treatment of 'for mine eyes have seen' in his Verse Service.

to the specific outlines of Byrd's own outer voices quite unequivocally, but adds an extra semibreve in the antepenultimate bar to enhance a further final, clearer imitation between soprano and tenor, also already implied in the equivalent voices of Byrd's original.

Any relationships between Morley's Short Magnificat and Byrd's, on the other hand, are rather like the connections between Tallis's and Byrd's morning canticles, having to do with occasional similarities of sonority and cadential choices at important moments. The treatment of the opening verses offers but one example. Both Byrd and Morley follow similar tonal outlines for the first two verses of the Magnificat, for example: D minor – A major – D major, D major – A major (cf. Tallis: D minor – A minor – E major, E minor – A minor – E major). At 'For behold from henceforth' the two settings come together more precisely (Example 5.5): both composers move from their previous cadence on A major directly to F at the beginning of the phrase and cadence there via a 7–6 suspension at mid-phrase; Morley also closely follows the profiles of Byrd's soprano, alto and bass. Morley's continuation of the verse contrasts with Byrd, however, by turning to stretto imitation in all five voices of the sort that generally had found little place in either Byrd's or Tallis's short service style, but remains an essential feature of Morley's own. This turn to stretto imitation at 'all generations' may also have been guided by Byrd, however, who had introduced a brief stretto between soprano and tenor at that point. Byrd's point, consisting of two falling filled-in thirds linked by an upward leap ($bb^1$–$g^1$/$c^2$–$a^1$), might have suggested the basic shape for Morley's entries in his lower voices (tenor: a–g–f–$c^1$; alto: $c^1$–bb–a–$e^1$), while Byrd's lattice of consecutive thirds (G–B/F–A/E–G) in the lower two voices, with the repeated C above them in the soprano, parallels Morley's bass–tenor–alto entries, after which the fall from C in Morley's top part may allude to Byrd's soprano profile.

The doxology to Morley's Magnificat, on the other hand, and its second half in particular, is designed less as a link to Byrd than to the doxology of Morley's own Nunc Dimittis (Example 5.6). The rather briefer conclusion to the Magnificat introduces imitative figures similar to those of the Nunc Dimittis in the outer voices at the same pitches for 'as it was in the beginning', turns to the same rising point, but a third lower, for 'and ever shall be', then quotes the 'Amen' of the Nunc Dimittis quite literally.

If Morley turned to Byrd for his model, borrowing various gestures, tonal relationships and textures, he also chose to interrelate his own pair of movements through links less overt than the Amen quotation, and of a sort

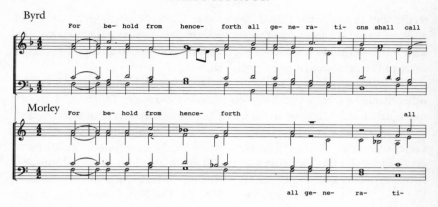

Example 5.5  Byrd/Morley, Short Magnificats

John Aplin has shown to have been well established by Morley's time.[10] Significantly, perhaps, parallels to Morley's own Nunc Dimittis are substantially closer than the links between Morley's Magnificat and Byrd's. It is as if Morley borrowed a number of prominent tonal gestures from the

[10] 'Cyclic Techniques'. At the end of verse 1 of the Magnificat, for example, Morley alludes to his own '[ac]cording to thy word', whose tenor and bass are quoted quite literally. A similar harmonic succession reappears at 'humble and meek', with tenor and bass quoted exactly and the soprano from the Nunc Dimittis transferred to the alto. 'The lowliness of his handmaiden', which, as mentioned above, cadences with Byrd on A, follows still more closely the outline of Morley's soprano from 'before the face of all people', and also reflects the shape of the three lower parts for the last several chords. Much the same series of harmonies recurs again for the A cadence at 'mighty hath magnified me'.

Example 5.6 Morley, Short Service Doxologies

equivalent Byrd movement, then interrelated the rest of his Magnificat more closely to the music of its own accompanying Nunc Dimittis.

Morley's Nunc Dimittis, on the other hand, seems to relate much more specifically to Byrd's as a model, as we have seen. Its final Amen quotes Byrd's concluding bass line almost literally and also seems to allude to Byrd's upper voices. Morley thus saves this overt reference to the work of the older composer until the very end of the Service as a whole. The turn from D minor to D major also stretches back to 'as it was in the beginning' in the Nunc Dimittis. In the Magnificat, on the other hand, the turn to the major happens rather abruptly at the appearance of the 'Amen' linked with the Nunc Dimittis. This all suggests that Morley began by composing the Nunc Dimittis, closely following Byrd's lead. He then worked backward to the Magnificat, which he linked closely to his own Nunc Dimittis, while also incorporating some gestures from the equivalent Byrd movement.

### Triple-time services

Peter le Huray was correct to mention Byrd's Third Service in the same breath with his Short Service.[11] Despite their differences in metre and mode, the two services show substantial affinity. It is even possible that the Third Service might antedate the Short Service, as I have suggested elsewhere.[12] The triple-time service once again appears to reflect the influence of Tallis. Indeed, to some extent Byrd's Third seems closer to Tallis than the Short Service does, particularly in its preoccupation with short-range repetitive schemes, both literal and varied.[13]

The most direct link to Tallis once again takes the form of an apparent quotation from an equivalent moment in Tallis's Magnificat, however. At 'throughout all generations' Byrd cadences with Tallis on D, the final of Tallis's 'Dorian' Service, the first appearance of that cadential pitch in Byrd's Third Service up to this point. For 'He hath shewed strength . . . he hath scattered the proud' Byrd largely follows Tallis's harmonic scheme, cadencing on A at mid-verse with threefold authentic or plagal cadences at that pitch, and also adopts Tallis's soprano for the second half of the verse (Example 5.7).

Shortly thereafter, 'He hath filled the hungry' seems to have prompted Byrd to take as a 'good thing' the simple sort of canon Tallis had occasionally introduced in the 'Dorian' Service (Example 5.8). Tallis's canon at 'To perform the mercy promised to our fathers' from the Benedictus

---

[11] *Music and the Reformation*, p. 235.     [12] BE 10a, p. x.

[13] The fourfold short repetitions at 'For he hath regarded' / 'For behold from henceforth' or 'and holy is his Name', the two-plus-two brief repetitions at 'As he promised' / 'and to his seed', or the threefold repetition at 'Glory be to the Father . . . Holy Ghost' of Byrd's Magnificat may be closer in spirit to short-range repetitions in Tallis's 'Dorian' Service than they are to Byrd's own Short Service. Compare, for example, 'The holy church . . . the Father of an infinite majesty' / 'Thine honourable, true . . . also being the Comforter' from Tallis's Te Deum, 'That we being delivered . . . might serve him . . . and righteousness' from the Benedictus. The nearest equivalents from Byrd's Short Service, e.g., 'Vouchsafe, O Lord, to keep us' / 'O Lord have mercy' from the Te Deum or 'And hath raised up' / 'As he spake by the mouth' / 'That we should be saved' / 'To perform the mercy' from the Benedictus are more expansive and more varied. Byrd's threefold sequential repetition at 'He remembering his mercy' from the Third Magnificat recalls Tallis's similar short-range sequences such as 'Forty years long . . . with this generation and said' from the 'Dorian' Venite, a reworking of the same passage at 'that takest away . . . have mercy upon us' from the Gloria, and slightly more expansive treatments such as 'Glory be to the Father . . . world without end. Amen' from Tallis's Magnificat.

Example 5.7 Tallis, Short Service Magnificat. Byrd, Third Service Magnificat

Tallis, Short Benedictus

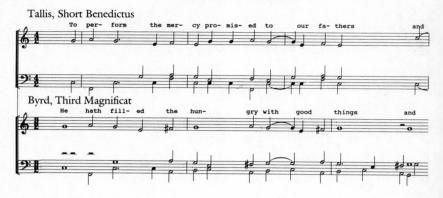

Byrd, Third Magnificat

Example 5.8  Canons

involves the same canonic voices at the same pitch, and a very similar melody. Interestingly enough, Byrd writes a somewhat different second phrase in order to keep the canon running; Tallis had abandoned the canon by this point.

As in the Short Service, what sets Byrd most apart from Tallis in the Third Service is his manipulation of the harmony. Byrd seems in fact to have constructed the Magnificat with a careful eye – or ear – towards tonal variety and contrast, and even large-scale structure. After the emphasis upon C, particularly in the fourfold cadences at 'For he hath regarded' / 'For behold from henceforth', Byrd begins to move away to a comparably emphatic fourfold G at 'and holy is his name'. Following a striking juxtaposition of G and F chords at the beginning of the next phrase he continues onwards to D, where, as we have seen, he joins up with Tallis, who leads him to A, but then back to D. Byrd then returns to G, which dominates the next several cadences, through the canon in the manner of Tallis, until C reappears momentarily at 'sent empty away'. 'He remembering his mercy' introduces a moment of ambiguity, cadencing on A (compare the earlier turn to E via A at 'for he that is mighty'), which is dispelled by the fourfold cadences on C before the doxology. A brief turn back towards G in the first half of the doxology is redirected by another emphatic F chord at 'as it was', which recalls the comparable harmonic juxtaposition at 'And his mercy', and C is clearly reestablished in the final phrases.

Thus, Byrd's overall tonal scheme is roughly palindromic, moving from C to G to D to A in a way bound to appeal to those searching for intimations of tonality in the late sixteenth century, then back to D, G and C, with several cadences in quick succession on these pitches at equivalent moments in each half of the work. The prominent juxtapositions of G and F in the first and second halves of the Magnificat, although they may not be placed in precise symmetry, are heard to balance one another. Perhaps the same might also be said of the brief A minor/E major ('For he that is mighty') and D minor/A major ('hath holpen his servant Israel') cadences. At the centre of the scheme appears Byrd's reference to Tallis's Magnificat, at the same pitch, an overt acknowledgement of Byrd's indebtedness, framed, however, by a carefully articulated tonal scheme – the feature that sets Byrd apart most obviously from his teacher.[14]

---

[14] A comparable scheme also appears in the much shorter Nunc Dimittis: C to A ('face of all people') to G ('people Israel . . . Glory be . . . ') to D ('and to the Holy Ghost'), back to G ('world without end. Amen') to C ('world without end. Amen').

By contrast with some of the putative relationships between Byrd and Morley's Short Evening Services, the connections between their triple-time services are quite unambiguous, as Morley obviously intended them to be. I have suggested that despite their different finals, Byrd's Third Magnificat had incorporated a tonal reference to Tallis's 'Dorian' Magnificat at its mid-point. Morley, on the other hand, takes his tonal inter-relationships to Byrd's Magnificat several steps further. Despite the fact that the younger composer's service has G as its final, the beginnings or the cadences of many of the verses of his setting reflect the tonal scheme of Byrd's version, which has C as its final. As if to make his indebtedness to Byrd's Magnificat as readily apparent as possible from the outset, after an opening G chord Morley moves to C major and largely duplicates the opening verse of Byrd's setting (Example 5.9a).

Morley's subsequent juxtaposition of G major and F major to begin the next phrase, 'For he hath regarded' (Example 5.9b), does not appear at the corresponding point in Byrd's Magnificat. But the identical move from G to F, followed by the same series of harmonies for several minims, does occur prominently at '[holy is his] Name. And his mercy is on them', and recurs less precisely at 'Ghost. As it was' in Byrd's version. As we have seen, this pair of harmonic moments had played a significant role in the large-scale shaping of Byrd's canticle. It seems not to have been lost on Morley, who introduces it as an effective way to emphasise the shift away from his own final toward Byrd's.

Morley's continuation of the phrase 'the lowliness of his handmaiden' resembles Byrd's setting, with its falling soprano line transposed up a tone. Like Byrd, Morley also makes 'For behold from henceforth' a repetition of the previous verse. But where Byrd had employed an essentially literal, basically chordal repetition, Morley turns to stretto imitation in all parts, based upon the previous falling soprano line and largely reproducing the harmonic matrix of the homophonic version once the voices have all entered.

Morley's 'For he that is mighty' returns literally to Byrd's model for many details, including pitch level (Example 5.9c). Morley's next phrase, 'And his mercy', again departs from the sequence of Byrd's ideas. (Reference to Byrd's setting of 'And his mercy' had already appeared earlier in Morley's setting at 'For he hath regarded'.) This time Morley may have had in mind Byrd's 'He remembering his mercy', where a similar soprano line had appeared at the same pitch, though Byrd had contrasted B♮ and B♭ as the phrase unfolded, in a way that Morley does not (Example 5.9d). At 'throughout all generations' Byrd had relaxed his chordal texture slightly to

Example 5.9  Byrd/Morley, Triple-Time Magnificats

d)

e)

f)

permit melismas in falling crotchets in the upper three voices as they approached this important cadence. Morley correspondingly lapses into the most expansive imitative section that he has introduced up to this point, though the imitative motives and harmony are independent of Byrd.

Morley's setting of 'He hath shewed strength . . . ' becomes considerably more elaborate, while Byrd adheres more closely to the homophonic idiom of his service as a whole, and also, as we have seen, to Tallis's model. Any relationships to Byrd's setting are therefore disguised in the more elaborate textures. Morley returns briefly to homophonic texture at 'he hath put down' (Example 5.9e), where it is possible that his 'IV–[V]–V' series of chords represents a response to Byrd's '[V]–V' at the same moment. More immediately obvious is the relationship between the cadences at 'the mighty from their seat', where both composers' bass lines move from A to G, with a 7–6 suspension above. Once again Morley complicates his model contrapuntally, with a threefold repetition of the 7–6 suspension, cadencing on G, D and again on G. (Only the last of the three statements appears in Example 5.9.) When Morley returns to homophony at 'and hath exalted' he likewise returns to Byrd's soprano, at the original pitch.

'He hath filled the hungry' recalls, not Byrd, but Morley's own setting of 'for behold from henceforth', with its repeated soprano $a^1$ harmonised by the same bass line leaping about the notes that make up a D minor chord. Morley's imitative setting of 'and the rich' may also refer back to his own falling point in imitation at 'all generations shall call me blessed', which likewise cadences on D, preceded by a series of stretto entries rising upwards from the bass voice, but with the soprano entering slightly ahead of the first alto in both cases. The motivic material of the concluding verse shows no obvious indebtedness to Byrd. The leaping point at 'as he promised', on the other hand, seems to recall Morley's own 'in the imagination of their hearts', where it appears at the same pitch level and likewise cadences on G.

It is also possible that Morley's previous cadence on A at 'his servant Israel' (Example 5.9f) may reflect Byrd's cadence on A at the same point. The cadence on C at 'his seed forever' very probably does too. The opening of the doxology recalls Byrd in all voices, as does the move to D harmony at 'to the Son' and the cadence on G at 'the Holy Ghost'.

Byrd had permitted some contrapuntal expansion as he approached his conclusion, beginning at 'and ever shall be', and Morley follows his lead (Example 5.9g). Predictably, however, the younger composer substantially complicates his version. Byrd had employed a double statement a 5 of a point falling from $c^2$ in the soprano, imitated at the fifth in the second alto. Morley instead employs a triple statement, also based upon a point falling from $c^2$. The first statement plays off the upper voices against the lower. In the second statement, which involves several voices in stretto entries with closer overlapping of parts, the rhythmic shape of the point more closely resembles Byrd's, and Morley's initial soprano–alto entries recall Byrd's own stretto in the equivalent voices. When Morley repeats the soprano a third time the soprano–alto stretto predominates once again, as it had in Byrd's setting.

Morley's triple-time Nunc Dimittis, on the other hand, was designed as a variation on the preceding Magnificat. For the verses before the doxology, however, Morley draws back from his own more expansive, polyphonic style to a simpler texture more akin to Byrd's ruffled homophony, abjuring the contrapuntal elaborations that had frequently occurred in the second halves of his own Magnificat verses. To conclude the Second

Service Nunc Dimittis Morley reverts to his own more elaborate style. He also makes the connection between the Magnificat and Nunc Dimittis explicit by interrelating the two doxologies quite specifically: one represents a reworking of the other.[15] For the final 'Amen', however, Morley abandons the Magnificat to create a more expansive imitative conclusion, with the outer voices in canon at a minim's distance. His imitative point might perhaps represent a final allusion to Byrd's setting, where we find a much less extended imitation on a falling dotted figure at the conclusion to the Nunc Dimittis. The shape of Byrd's simpler point, transposed up a tone, appears in the final bars of Morley's tenor quite exactly.

What Morley seems to have adopted most directly from Byrd was the musical element that had set Byrd's Short Service and Third Service apart most obviously from Tallis: harmonic planning and manipulation of cadences. The 'sense of direction and movement forward by the skilful manipulation of cadences[,] ... rather in advance of his time' that le Huray has observed in Morley's own Short Service[16] and which likewise appears in Morley's Second Service thus could represent a primary debt to his teacher.

Morley's persistent elaboration of the texture through simple imitation sets his services most obviously apart from Byrd's equivalent works. This penchant for complication of the plain short service idiom calls to mind, perhaps, Morley's artistic activity in the secular realm: his adaptation and expansion of the imported Italian ballet, canzonet and light madrigal, described by Kerman.[17] Such complication in the Anglican repertory is anything but new with Morley, of course. His frequent use of stretto in all voices is closely akin to what Oliver Neighbour has called 'English stretto imitation' in the more elaborate works of Mundy and Parsons.[18] Morley's achievement lies in his attempt to reconcile greater textural diversity with the restrictions of short service style. And he manages to strike a balance between simplicity and elaboration more successfully than many of his peers. His success derives partly from a willingness not to go on for too

---

[15] The invocation of the Trinity presents a homophonic version of the more polyphonic treatment from the Magnificat, largely preserving the soprano profile, cadence points and also the part writing of the chordal opening. 'As it was in the beginning' from the Nunc Dimittis reintroduces imitative texture; the shape of the imitative point, sequence of entries and pitch levels of the various voices all recall 'and to be the glory' of the Magnificat. The imitative points for 'and ever shall be' are likewise interrelated quite specifically, and many details of the imitative lattice appear in both versions, though in the Nunc Dimittis Morley limits himself to a double statement of the point in the soprano, first falling from $d^2$ and then from $e^2$, rather than employing the more extended $d^2$–$d^2$–$e^2$ sequence of statements from the Magnificat.

[16] *Music and the Reformation*, p. 249.      [17] *The Elizabethan Madrigal*, pp. 129–92.
[18] Review of *The Byrd Edition, vol. 10b, Music & Letters* 65 (1984), p. 311.

long. It also derives, however, from the broadening of the harmonic field which must have removed some of the constraints in the choice of imitative materials. The resulting freshness and attractiveness of his solution in this respect may represent a chief debt to his own teacher, William Byrd.

# 6

## 'Write all these down': notes on a Byrd song

### JOSEPH KERMAN

A song that is well and artificially made cannot be well perceiued nor understood at the first hearing, but the oftner you shall heare it, the better cause of liking you will discover. *Psalmes, Songs, and Sonnets*, 1611

The first major body of music by William Byrd that I came to know was the vernacular music of the English songbooks. I was studying the English madrigal, and students in those days took issues of stylistic taxonomy rather seriously. It seemed very important to distinguish Byrd's songs from madrigals, to separate them off more clearly than had been done by Fellowes, and with firmer musicological apparatus than had been deployed by Dent.

But Byrd's songs refused to be moved tidily aside. The chapter in which this was supposed to happen took on a life of its own. It even acquired a certain dense, knotty quality, possibly a result of enigmatic stylistic emanations from its subject matter.[1]

What impressed me first of all, as I recall, was the massive stylistic control of the texted consort songs published in the 1588 songbook. One of the songs, *La virginella*, which had already been featured in *Musica Transalpina* of 1587, was set to an *ottava rima* stanza from Ariosto – and this verse, Einstein assured us, was a favourite among the Italian madrigalists.[2] But *La virginella* was certainly not to be classified as a madrigal. On the other hand *This sweet and merry month of May*, published not much later, certainly was. The stylistic crux adumbrated here grows more intense in the later Byrd songbooks. The musician in me was fascinated, and the

[1] Joseph Kerman, *The Elizabethan Madrigal: A Comparative Study* [1950], Publications of the American Musicological Society 4 (New York, 1962), chapter 4.
[2] Alfred Einstein, 'The Elizabethan Madrigal and "Musica Transalpina"', *Music & Letters* 25 (1944), pp. 66–7 – in the first paragraphs of this seminal study.

musicologist a bit worried, by those songs which I thought I could see winding a precarious course between the stylistic norms of the consort song and the madrigal.

One song it appears I didn't see clearly at all: *Retire, my soul*, no. 17 in the *Psalmes, Songs, and Sonnets* of 1611. It needed hearing oftener. I can now see it as an entirely unprecarious Byrd masterpiece.

### *What genre?*

'Unprecarious', because intuitively the musical style of the piece feels entirely normal and right, straightforward, almost unremarkable. One does not have to be deeply knowledgeable about the music of Byrd or indeed any other music of his time to feel this, I think. But what can be said about the genre? In a note to his edition, John Morehen writes that 'The poor word-setting in some of the lower voices, combined with several avoidable melodic inelegancies, suggests strongly that this composition originated as a solo song.'[3] Inelegancies? sir! beyond a tenor octave and a limping alto line in bar 4, some odd underlay in bars 33–4, and perhaps the repeated $f^1$ in bar 30, I hear nothing to offend. On the other hand, the putative melody of this song – Morehen speaks of it as a 'conflate' of the song's two soprano parts – is not of a quality that would in itself inspire superlatives, as song melodies by Dowland or Gibbons (*Ah, dear heart*) might, for example.

In fact, no arguments are adduced in the editorial matter to place the piece within the tradition of the consort song, or, rather, the consort song with words adapted to the instrumental parts. (The sorts of changes that Byrd routinely made in the adaptation process can be studied by comparing the originals with their texted versions in the 1588 *Psalmes, Sonets, & Songs*.[4]) And *Retire, my soul* does not quite look like any other Byrd song. Not one of its eight musical phrases entails systematic 'pre-imitations' in Byrd's usual manner. When Morehen describes the piece elsewhere as 'close to the consort song in spirit' (p. ix) – not the same as proposing its genesis as an actual consort song – the ghost of the taxonomist in me rests more easy. At some places in the song the basic conception seems less melodic than genuinely polyphonic. At other places (and at some of the same ones) the text in the lower voices is too carefully declaimed to be understood as a later addition, however *ben trovato*. Surely Byrd composed this song – as he appears to have composed others – for five actual

---

[3] BE 14, p. 183.
[4] The original consort versions have been available since 1976 in BE 16.

voices, albeit with the stylistic norm of the consort song sometimes dimly, sometimes less dimly in mind.

As Byrd's song style developed, a second soprano is introduced more and more often in the five-part choir. This tended to break down solo texture in favour of more even-handed polyphony. However, *Retire* though scored for two sopranos is *less* polyphonic than the two-soprano songs of 1588 and 1589. More to the point, perhaps, it is more concise; in the earlier songs the composer seems to have used the two-soprano texture as a way to expand his pieces, as much as to vary their texture. We will touch on the question of genre again later in this esssay, when comparison with an actual consort song will suggest itself.

It remains to say at this point that if *Retire* is less expansive than many of Byrd's middle-period songs, it is also less madrigalian than some of the late ones. Neither its rhythmic nor its harmonic style, nor its treatment of the words, owes much to the madrigal. Yet Byrd's response to the words in this song is unusually deep and affecting.

### Sizing up the poem

*Retire, my soul* is an aphoristic *sizaine* stanza in which, as usual, the quatrain sets forth the conditions of the argument and the couplet points the moral. As poetry, this verse is considerably more accomplished than most song texts set by Byrd, characteristic as it may be in content:

> Retire my soule, consider thine estate,
> And iustly summe thy lavish sinnes account,
> Times deare expence, and costly pleasures rate,
> How follyes grow, how vanities amount.
> Write all these down in pale Deathes reckoning tables;
> Thy dayes will seeme but dreames, thy hopes but fables.

The poet draws upon the lexicon of accounting and finance to enjoin his sinful soul to prepare its spread-sheet: 'estate', 'sum', 'account', 'dear expense', 'costly', 'rate', and 'amount'. The couplet begins solemnly, as heavy monosyllables pronounce a new, summarising injunction: 'Write all these down'. Then at the end of line 5, though we are still hearing about 'reckoning tables' (a 'reckoning book' is a ledger), these tables are now 'pale Death's' – no great surprise, after mention of retirement and estate. Under death's shadow, line 6 urges the soul to consider the illusion (seeming, dreams, fables) of that which it has amassed, of its hopes.

When this song was published, by the way, Byrd was a fairly rich man of sixty-eight. From drawing up his will probably on more than one occasion, he would have become familiar with the long process of inventorying his material assets, no less than with that of weighing his spiritual ones.

*Sizaine* stanzas are typically set in two sections, with the second section (covering the final couplet) repeated so as to hammer home the 'point'. What I have called the summarising gesture in line 5, 'Write all these down', appears to have encouraged the composer to plan for especially heavy parallelism between the beginnings of the two sections. Acting on this hint, he also made them parallel in other ways. Both go to F in their second phrase and to V/D minor in their third. And both contain four musical phrases, each ending with clear cadences, even though the first section sets four lines of verse and the second sets two.

The overall plan for the song is nothing if not economical (lower case letters here denote minor keys):

| text line | 1 | 2 | 3 | 4 | | 5a | 5b | 6a | 6b | |
|---|---|---|---|---|---|---|---|---|---|---|
| musical phrase | 1 | 2 | 3 | 4 | | 5 | 6 | 7 | 8 | |
| cadences | (d?) | (1/2g?) | F | 1/2d | g ‖: | d,F,1/2d | F | 1/2d | d | :‖ |
| length (semibreves) | 13 | 9 | 9 | 15 | | 6 | 6 | 8 | 14 | |

If I am right to think Byrd wanted four phrases in each section of the song, his strategy was simple enough. He fashioned his phrases in the quatrain out of full lines, and then in the couplet out of half-lines. The two sections of the song are symmetrical, then, though not proportional; no doubt he wanted more speed and intensity in line 5 than in lines 1 and 2. Between the two parts the ratio is approximately 4:3 or, rather, 2:3 when the repeat is included. While tallying of this kind can seem both mechanical and elementary, to the tallier as well as to the reader, the fact remains that such precompositional calculations underpin the form of the song and hence its rhetoric. It also seems to be a fact that systematic setting of half-lines in this fashion distinguishes *Retire* from any other of Byrd's songs.[5]

In the present case, of course, reducing the text-setting unit in the couplet to the half-line makes every kind of rhetorical sense. The caesura in line 6 practically demands such setting. And although line 5 does not have a caesura, when the composer in effect creates one of his own – he even supplies the text in all the voice-parts with a comma – the rhetorical effect is to delay and hence dramatise the evocation of death.

In the quatrain, setting each whole line to its own rather long melody

[5] The closest is *Penelope that longed*, no. 27 of the *Songs of Sundrie Natures*, though there is no real cadence or change of style between the half-lines of its final couplet. Also as in *Retire*, the second section of this song lasts longer than the first, thanks to the addition of a codetta:

| Retire | lines 1–4: 23 breves | lines 5–6: 34 (2:3) |
|---|---|---|
| Penelope | lines 1–5: 62 | lines 6–7: 75 (5:6) |

might have lead to diffuseness; this is often a danger in Byrd's consort songs. Possibly with this in mind, it seems that the composer looked out for lines that break into two parts with caesuras, once again; he still set these lines as single musical phrases, unbroken by cadences, but he set both parts of the line to the same motif. The phrases in question, then – lines 1 and 4, 'Retire my soul, consider thine estate' and 'How follies grow, how vanities amount' – are rather densely knit motivically, and far from diffuse. With line 4, where the caesura marks off two parallel 'how' phrases, the effect is immediately plausible as rhetoric. The text-repetitions in this line also extend the phrase so as to end the section strongly: after four appearances of the motif adapted to each of the two half-lines 'how follies grow' and 'how vanities amount', there are two freer entries at the end. The added soprano entry – a sort of free augmented stretto – is particularly expressive, and the motif also undergoes expansion of its interval structure. This is a detail that we can return to at more leisure later.

With line 1, however, was it somewhat arbitrary of Byrd to have used one and the same motif for both parts of the line, 'Retire, my soul' and 'consider thine estate'? There is no parallelism here. This too is a point that I should like to defer and return to later.

### Mapping the form

First, since form has to do with tonality, a word about the modal situation. The music is in a D mode with one flat in the signature, transposed Aeolian;[6] a standard high-clef combination is used, treble/treble/mezzo-soprano/alto/baritone. The D-Aeolian mode with this cleffing – a combination of features that Harold S. Powers calls a 'tonal type' – occurs more often than any other in the *Gradualia*, notably in the large group of Marian Masses of Book I.[7] It should be noted that one modal pattern expected in this tonal type is the cadential figure F–E–D–C♯–D. Byrd must have been quite conscious of never having his trebles sing this figure anywhere in the first part of the song (it is sung twice in the tenor).

What Byrd writes instead is B♭–A–G–F♯ and he writes it three times: not just as a pattern, but as a motif. His setting of line 1 consists of three

---

6 The music does not draw on the characteristic Dorian resource of using both natural and flat forms of the sixth degree. The alteration B♮ occurs on only three occasions, once as a *tierce de Picardie* (bar 23) and twice in non-harmonic situations (auxiliary, passing notes) involved with A major harmony (bars 16 and 21).

7 See Harold Powers, 'Tonal Types and Modal Categories in Renaissance Polyphony', *Journal of the American Musicological Society* 34 (1981), pp. 428–70, and Joseph Kerman MWB 1, pp. 68–72, 218.

Example 6.1

similar musical cells employing this motif: 'Retire, my soul' twice, plus 'consider thine estate' once. See Example 6.1a. (It is a nice point whether the listener actually hears this, and if so how, though I take it there is less of a problem of perception for the singers themselves. We hear first the prominent upper counterpoint, D–C–Bb–A. Then, as the texture increases from three voices to four to five, and the rhythm grows progressively more complex, we notice Bb–A–G–F# in the bass range, where there is nothing to hide the diminished-fourth outline. The motif is heard most clearly when it is adapted to the new words 'consider thine estate' with a dotted rhythm – and when the upper counterpoint disappears.) The whole opening leans towards the subdominant, and presages the rather elegiac close of the song's first section on G.

The same motif is employed in diminution for the beginning of the song's second section, at line 5. As I have said, Byrd planned a heavy parallelism here (see Example 6.1). Besides the common motif, the two phrases have in common their triple reiterative character, also their use of the F♯/F false relation in adjacent D major and B♭ chords (a sound not heard elsewhere in this piece). The cells that start Part 2 are of course shorter – two breves long, rather than four and five – and clearer – all in three voices. This underlines a new urgent tone to the poet's new injunction. And while the first cell replicates the B♭–A–G–F♯ line of the earlier cells, a new C♯ (over the G) already dilutes the subdominant feeling. Then the second and third cells modulate.

### Setting 'dreams'

The third cell modulates decisively to a half-cadence in D, on an A major chord, and finally brings the expected modal formula F–E–D–C♯ in the treble range. This formula now seems to permeate the rest of the song. It comes several times in the last phrase as the kernel of the melodic cadences. It also comes in the penultimate phrase, when the alto sings the word 'seem' on $c\sharp^1$, forming the third of another A major chord. This place, the song's expressive climax, deserves our close attention.

There is one and only one line in the poem where the caesura or the natural line-break comes after the third metrical foot, rather than after the second. This climactic effect is saved for the poem's last line; an inner rhyme which Byrd certainly heard – 'Thy days will *seem* but *dreams*, thy hopes but fables' – stresses the new metric situation. In setting the half-line 'Thy days will seem but dreams', Byrd does not devise a motif covering all six of the words. He sets up a little ostinato just for the words 'Thy days will seem', C (or F, or B♭)–F–D—(?) – which has the effect of stressing the word 'seem' – changing the ending harmony each time to 'modulate'. The music modulates back from F (the cadence point of the previous phrase 'in pale Death's reckoning tables') via C to another A major chord, as already mentioned. See Example 6.3b, *infra*.

Perfectly placed, in close position, this A major chord turns out to be Byrd's trump card for the word 'dreams'. Four suddenly converging voices sing 'dreams' for the first time on this chord. The word glistens (and we surely want it sung by four voices, not by one voice accompanied by viols). This is the word that articulates the fresh caesura. Of all the words in the poem, too, it is probably the most remote in feeling from the original fiscal vocabulary, with its accounts and reckoning tables.

Let us listen oftener, more closely. The first voice to sing the ostinato motif is soprano 2; being the voice that initiates the text fragment, it is also the one voice to utter the word 'dreams' before the others converge upon it. Although soprano 2 sings the word very beautifully on a descending fourth $d^2$–$a^1$, it is somewhat obscured by soprano 1 beginning the ostinato motif in the same high range. And soprano 1 treats the key word in its own new beautiful way, with a pregnant rest before it: 'Thy days will seem – but dreams'. The slow-down continues. On the cadential A major chord, soprano 1 and the tenor sing a breve (as does, a moment later, soprano 2). After this weighty cadence is sounded, free imitations on the motif (and words) of the first half-line continue for five minims more before there is any sign of the second half-line commencing.

Given Byrd's time-scale, this certainly counts as a profound caesura. Previously he has never interposed more than a single minim's space between one phrase and the next. Occasionally he has arranged for an overlap.

Most gorgeous, of course, is the false relation formed when soprano 2 returns to the words 'but dreams', making a kind of subdued echo, an afterbeat to the extraordinary focus of declamation on the 'dream' chord (bars 32–3; to *play* the $c\natural^2$ here and not sound the word would be a great pity, once again). It was certainly unusual to end the point 'Thy days will seem but dreams' with murmuring imitations on the main motif *after* the ostensible final cadence. It was even more unusual to allow the aphoristic notes $a^1$ and $c^2$ of the second soprano's 'but dreams' to anticipate the motif for the next point, 'thy hopes but fables': for as first presented, the motif for that point begins with the identical pitches $a^2$–$c^2$. Unusual, because a non-motif for a loose word does not ordinarily presage a true motif for the next phrase.

### Ending the song

Of all the phrases in the song, the last one is the least clearly 'melodic', and not only because the second soprano voice now jostles more seriously with the first. There are really two soprano motives which fit together contrapuntally as a cadential unit (the less sharply defined motif involves the characteristic modal pattern F–E–D–C♯–D). What is more, imitations in the lower voices are more numerous and more closely organised here than in any of the earlier phrases, as I shall now try to show. I hope I shall not also try the reader's patience; the analysis necessarily becomes more dense at this point. There is value sometimes in looking quite closely at refinements of contrapuntal structure.

While the five-part texture of this last phrase is imitative, and therefore essentially homogeneous, a rather clear distinction exists between the high and the low voices. The tenor and bass are always simpler, because they never sing motif 2, with the repetition of the words 'but fables'; they are also stronger, because of their long high notes: 'Thy *hopes* but FA---bles'. The tenor's long high note is his melodic peak, the only high $a^1$ in the entire part. As for the alto, that evinces less distinctive character, but makes up for it by providing a scrumptious dissonant flurry for the final cadence.

The first entry, in soprano 1, establishes an attractive hemiola cross-rhythm repeated by soprano 2: 'Thy *hopes* but FAbles, but *FAbles*'. If we were to listen downward, as it were, from the soprano lines, we would catch a large 3/1 metre defined by appoggiatura-like accents that are occasioned by strong feminine cadences in bars 36 and 37. This is where the motifs come together – an effect adumbrated in bar 34. However, it is the strong low voices that define the large metrical organisation. We can perhaps hear them organising the total point of imitation into three similar cells, built around a stretto of motif 1 at the upper fifth. Each of these cells is a little more fully scored than the last, and each ends with a strong cadence. The cadences fall into a i–iv–i pattern. Motif 2 also figures in these cells, kept in its appropriate range – including high $f^2$ – by means of double counterpoint at the twelfth where necessary.

Cell 2 overlaps with cell 1, forming a large 3/1 pulse. Cell 3 restores a leisurely duple pulse, as traces of soprano cross-rhythm evaporate and the piece eases into its final slow-down. We can track this slow-down in various subtle details: soprano 1, by means of an absent-minded rest, delays the second, climactic part of her line and dilutes the hemiola feeling; soprano 2 declines to sing 'fables' in the established cadential rhythm, instead dragging the last syllable forward; and the tenor, after arriving on cue in bars 37–8, gets involved with the alto and bass in a sort of stammering stretto, with the result that his line is completed only a beat later (and an octave lower, in the bass). What the stammer prepares or emphasises is the pitch (pitch-class) F, which is about to put in its last appearance in the soprano. Compare the opening of the point, where two 'amorphous' lines stressing C – without, however, giving away the word 'hopes' – prepare the $c^2$ in the first entry of the new text, sung by the soprano.

Example 6.2 shows the structural cells in this point. The 'extra' motifs are bracketed.

Byrd scrupulously refuses to extend the final amphibrach 'but fables'; in fact, he emphasises the feminine rhyme-word in bars 36 and 37 by means of off-beat cadences. He might have allowed the anomaly to evaporate in cell 3, where the slight augmentation has the effect of changing the

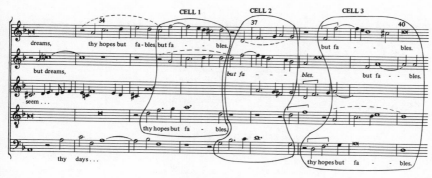

Example 6.2

feminine cadence to a masculine one. But at the very end of the song the second soprano insists on the feminine afterbeat – a sort of metrical reversal of her action in bar 36. The effect is a little bleak.

Is it fortuitous that the accented high $f^2$s in the second section of the song all come to *a* sounds: 'pale', 'day', and 'fables'?

### Why do I use my paper, ink, and pen

Of the various phrases of *Retire, my soul*, the second, third, and sixth are most easily construable in terms of Byrd's earlier work. Half-homophonic phrases of this kind would not be out of place in the more concise of the *Psalmes, Sonets, & Songs* of 1588. Phrases 1 and 5, with their repetition of brief cells, will strike us as most remote from the consort song repertory. But while such cells cannot be found in earlier songs by Byrd, they can be understood without too much difficulty as refinements of resources that had already been drawn upon in those works. A case in point occurs in one of his best-known songs, *Why do I use my paper, ink, and pen*, set to a poem on the martyrdom of Edmund Campion in 1581. The consort version was adapted to words in the 1588 songbook.

Byrd was probably anxious to do something special with the lame couplet that ends this highly-charged poem's first stanza (Example 6.3a):

> Why do I use my paper, inck, & pen
> and call my wits to counsel what to say,
> Such memories were made for mortal men,
> I speak of Saints, whose name cannot decay,
> An Angel's trump, were fitter far to sound
> their glorious death, if such on earth be found.

Example 6.3a *Why do I use*

Example 6.3b *Retire, my soul*

With the words 'an Angel's trump', Byrd's route to rhetorical emphasis was no doubt conventional enough – a sequential repetition of the motif in the 'first singing part' (the alto), and a flurry of stretto entries fitted into the other voices. This mildly climactic effect is capped by the emphatic setting of the phrase 'Their glorious death'. Here the words are repeated as an ostinato. The motif comes three times at the same pitch: twice in the first singing part, pre-imitated by the contratenor, and once at the upper octave, with the other voices deployed not imitatively but half-homophonically, so as to form slightly fuzzy semichoir cells. As the texture fills out from three to four voices to five, the rhythm marches, accelerates, then stops for a moment, to underline the word 'death' at its terminal appearance.

A composer who had written a reiterative structure of this sophistication could probably go on and write the beginning of *Retire, my soul*. The last line of *Why do I use* can also be usefully compared with the later song's ending (see Example 6.3b). As a rhetorical effect, singing 'death' again and again on A major chords in the ostinato passage, as in *Why do I use*, may or may not be preferred to saving both the word and the chord for one main moment, as in *Retire*. But in any case, the effect of the last 'death' in the ostinato is vitiated by the declamation in the other voices – not a weakness

Byrd seems to have minded when he texted the earlier song, but also not one that he condoned when he composed the later one. Notice, also, how in *Why do I use* the false relation performs a purely technical function, cancelling the C♯ so that some B♭s can be worked in easily before the final cadence. In *Retire*, where the false relation is introduced in much the same way, the texting makes it uniquely expressive.

The generic point to be made about *Retire* is that it is a single-stanza song. No extra stanzas are provided, and just because consort songs are strophic we must not postulate extra stanzas of *Retire* which have somehow got lost and which could not possibly fit the music. It is true, and it is well known, that later stanzas of Byrd's strophic songs often do not fit the music very well. His setting of *Why do I use*, determined by the poem's first stanza, makes amiable nonsense out of most of what turns up at the end of later stanzas (compare 'An Angel's trump ... Their glorious death' with 'As his Apos(tles) ... With many more ...' and 'That we therefore ... Pray we to Christ'). But this is as nothing compared to the carnage that new words would occasion added to lines 1, 4, 5 and 6 of *Retire*.[8]

### Some harmonic details

It has already been mentioned that the false relation in line 1 – F♯/F between D major and B♭ triads – is used structurally, as a way of linking the two sections of the song through their opening phrases (phrases 1 and 5).

Line 2 could be described as a loose, hastily syncopated canon between tenor and soprano 1. Here the word 'lavish' caught Byrd's ear, as well it might. When the tenor's high $f^1$ for '*la*vish' is imitated by the soprano $f^2$, a momentary dissonance (an augmented triad) supplies a touch of irony, perhaps. Then an even more biting dissonance is sounded against the second soprano's B♭ for this syllable; the graceful *echappée* that resolves the dissonant ninth sounds like a little gasp of relief. In line 3 it is the word 'pleasure' – continuing the irony? – that is first sung hastily, as before, before supporting rich dissonances in three of the other voices.

Another fleeting dissonance appears in line 3, in bars 17 and 18. Once again, comparison with *Why do I use* shows a growing refinement of technique (Example 6.4). What was used routinely in the early song is used

---

[8] Over and above this, the song's sectional proportions (2:3, as tallied above) suggest a one-stanza song. Such proportions are found only in such other sectional songs by Byrd as survive with only one stanza, such as *Compel the hawk* and *Penelope that longed* from the 1589 *Songs of Sundrie Natures*, and manuscript elegies such as *In angel's weed*.

Example 6.4a *Why do I use*

Example 6.4b *Retire, my soul*

here to initiate a formal process, for in *Retire* the dissonance arises in the first stage of a motivic expansion: beginning as a unison, the first interval of the motif grows to a minor second, a third, and a fourth.[9] Growing out of this motivic expansion, a little rush of upward leaps in the sopranos in bar 22 – a sort of snowballing diminution – imitates the trope by which several of the voices paint the word 'amount'. This lone madrigalian conceit contributes to the power of the expansion process and also has its own formal value, in that it helps destabilise the central cadence (on G minor rather than G major).

The third and last augmented sound in this song delicately colours the word 'pale' on its first appearance (bar 26). 'Pale Death' probably counts as

[9] Unisons – S2 and S1, bars 16–17; minor seconds – T, bar 17; S1, 18; A, 19 (here the new words are given to the motif, and the music itself is progressively inverted); thirds – S1 and S2, 20; and a fourth – S2, 21 (compare B, bars 18 and 20–1, and T, bar 19).

the poem's most stereotyped image, but that very fact makes it curiously momentous.[10] There is something faintly ominous, perhaps, about the bland near-homophony used by Byrd for this whole phrase, and the slightly slowing harmonic rhythm.

The common melodic progression 6–5 over a stationary bass occurs in only a few places (for example, F–E in bars 9, 21, 34). The most striking case is the most delicate: the progression A–G (and back to A) in bar 31. The anomalous sixth was Byrd's exquisite way of lingering on the word 'dreams' in its first presentation – the obscured soprano 2 entry that I referred to above. The contrast between the open scorings of the 6-chord (c c$^1$ a$^2$ e$^2$ and c a$^1$ c$^1$ c$^2$ e$^2$) and the close-position A major chord (a a$^1$ c#$^1$ e$^1$ a$^2$) adds yet another nuance to the setting of 'dreams' in bar 32.

### 'Write all these down'

*Retire, my soul* inscribes all that we have come to admire most in Byrd's art. Especially admirable is the balance between rhetoric and structure. This is a quality that I and others have pointed out frequently in Byrd compositions, frequently enough to prompt questions whether this critical category may not be anachronistic and even illicit. It may have been smuggled in to the sixteenth century by the twentieth-century observer; who can say if our mental metal detectors are sensitive enough to ideological baggage bearing the name-tags of other composers in other centuries? Yet observe the music. Does not the heavy parallelism between the two parts of the song – a unique feature, it seems, in the repertory of Byrd songs – establish an unusually strong shape to the music, and does it not also establish the basis for the rhetoric on the largest level?

For while phrases 1 and 5 are closely linked by their triple repetitive quality, the repetitions have quite a different effect in each case. In phrase 1, the unchanged fundamental pitch structure of the cells gives a feeling of mulling over, meditation, consideration. In phrase 5, that the faster-moving cells modulate gives a feeling of action, urgency, drama. It was perhaps exactly in order to magnify this contrast that Byrd used the same motif in setting the two different text fragments (the half-lines) of phrase 1. The progress between the two cell-organised phrases of the song from

---

10 Some of the imagery of *Retire, my soul* occurs in a lute song by Robert Jones:

    Life is a Poets fable,
    And all her daies are lies
    Stolne from deaths reckoning table . . .

Byrd's poem would appear to be the model for Jones's, though the latter was published earlier, in Jones's *First Booke of Songes & Ayres* of 1600.

meditation to action – from 'retire' to 'write' – is mirrored also by the different feeling of its two polyphonic phrases: elegiac in phrase 4, energetic in
phrase 8.

'Write all these down': one can say that with the three cells he composed
here Byrd was inscribing, repeating, accounting for everything that had
been said in the piece so far. Positioned by the G minor of the central
cadence, the first cell reinstates the *motif* of phrase 1. The second cell
resumes the *harmonic goal* of phrase 2. The third cell recalls the *melodic
outline* of phrase 3, which starts on high $f^2$ and works down through
canonic chains of thirds to a half cadence in D (an A major chord, bar 16.
This cadence should be heard as the strongest in the piece up to that point:
note the 6–8 progression between soprano and bass).

I have spoken of the formula F–E–D–C♯ which is introduced at this
point. The important new note is C♯, and Byrd makes $c\sharp^2$ doubly fresh by
prefacing it with a $c\natural^2$ at the start of a superbly inflected counterpoint in the
second soprano: '*Write* all – these down'. The rhythmic intensification
works powerfully for the rhetoric, once again. (Byrd has not finished with
the C♯–C♮ crux; it returns again in the next line at the word 'dreams', and
echoes repeatedly in the song's conclusion.) First articulated by the soprano
to mark the rhetorical climax of phrase 5, F–E–D–C♯ now echoes through
the rest of the song as an element of its form. With this figure the song clari-
fies or achieves its true modality, which is perhaps to say its true identity.

The figure also marks the rhetorical climax of the entire song, as we have
seen, when the alto sings 'Thy days will seem' on the notes $c^1\ f^1\ d^1\ c\sharp^1$, and
$c\sharp^1$ becomes the third of the 'dream' chord. The preparation of this chord,
its declamation and sonority, the way it is cancelled when the words 'but
dreams' are sung again, on the notes $a^2\ c\natural^2$ – all this has been discussed
above. C♯ paints the seductiveness of dreams, then the false relation registers their vanity, then comes a three-minim wait . . . Not many madrigalists
could match this for subtlety and impact.

John Ward could not, in his setting of a poem rather similar to Byrd's:

> Retire my troubled soule, rest, and behold
> Thy dayes of dolour, dangers manifold.
> See, life is but a dreame . . .
> Begun with hope . . .[11]

Like Byrd, Ward moves to a striking chord on the word 'dream' – a C major
triad, in a madrigal that stays largely in a Dorian A minor region. He
returns to C major for 'hope', again following Byrd, whose figure $a^1\ c^2$ for

[11] *The First Set of English Madrigals*, 1613, no. 19.

'but dreams' anticipates the motif for the words, 'thy hopes . . .'. But Ward reserves his most dramatic gesture for the vocative 'See' – a mannerist move, privileging the form of an assertion over its substance. Byrd, more classical, focuses upon the dream, and his associating of dreams with hopes also fulfils a formal function. In line 4 he had underlined the parallelism between the half-lines that are separated by the caesura in a rather direct fashion. By equating dreams and hopes in line 6, he found a richer way of doing the same thing.

The rhetoric in these two phrases – the two polyphonic phrases which end the song's two parts – is a rhetoric of reiteration: but reiteration comes in many varieties with many shades of affect. In phrase 4 the repetitions of 'how follies grow' and 'how vanities amount' are rather placid in themselves, elegiac, even bleak, but the motif that repeats them is varied so that the feeling deepens. As a result of the manipulations of the motif, which I have traced above, we can hear the words of this phrase declaimed in four ways: 'How follies grow', '*How* follies grow', 'How *van*ities amount', and 'HOW – *van*ities amount' (soprano 1, bars 20–2). Not often is rhetoric that is as quiet as this so urgent. Nor can it be accidental that Byrd arranged for a similar variety of declamation in the next phrase, too: 'Write all these down', 'Write *all* these down, '*Write* all – these down'.

As for phrase 8, that is the first to be truly blanketed by reiterations. The word 'fables', which Byrd had to interpret (fairly enough) as the poem's clincher, is pressed on our consciousness ten times; within each of the three cells, the word occurs in a complex concatenation on several overlapping levels:

> Thy hopes but *fa*bles, but FA – – – – – – bles
> thy hopes but *fa*bles
> Thy hopes but *FA* – – – – bles

In the final cell, there is also the stammering effect of 'thy hopes' sung in close stretto. Density of imitation, extension of register, augmentation – these are classic devices used by sixteenth-century composers to add weight to the cadential sections of their pieces. These formal devices can also be used expressively. With a little help from Byrd, the technique of imitation itself is used here to point up the obsessive yet confused persistence of hopes, their wispiness and ultimate futility.

It is the trajectory, finally, that is so impressive. A formal archetype for Byrd and his time was to begin a piece in a relatively homophonic style and close with relatively rich polyphony; one hears this in works ranging in time from *Emendemus in melius* to *Ave verum corpus* and from *Come to me, grief, forever* to the song that we have just now been admiring. Byrd has the capacity and the imagination to reuse such archetypes in widely different expressive contexts, in much the same way that later composers could manipulate archetypes such as sonata form. Or, to venture a closer analogy – for it is the text that inspires – the way Mozart could manipulate sonata-like procedures in opera ensembles. Byrd seldom absorbed an English text and transmuted it into music so profoundly as he did in *Retire, my soul*.

*Textual note*

Byrd's last songbook, the *Psalmes, Songs, and Sonnets* of 1611, contains eight compositions each in three, four, five, and six parts; *Retire, my soul* opens the five-part section.

The editions by E. H. Fellowes (The English Madrigal School, vol. 16, 1920 = BW 14) and Thurston Dart (revised edition of the Fellowes editions, 1964) have now been superseded by that of John Morehen (BE 14, 1987). *The Byrd Edition* differs from its predecessors in skipping editorial accent marks, dynamics, piano reduction, etc., and in barring the piece in 4/2 rather than 2/2. The barring I prefer is irregular (vertical strokes indicate the cadence points):

$$4\,4\,4\,4\,4\,4\;\left|6\,4\,4\,4\right|4\,4\,4\,6\left|4\,4\,6\,6\,4\,4\;\;\right|4$$

$$\|\!:\;\;2\,4\,4\;\;\left|4\,4\,4\;\;\right|4\,4\,4\;\;\left|4\,4\,4\,6\,4\,4\,4\right|4\;:\!\|$$

In bar 10, Fellowes liked the beautiful alto *echappée* $c^2$, it seems, for he let it stand, even though he believed that 'C in the original edition is probably a misprint for A', in the words of his note. Dart's addition to this note was 'though the printing is generally accurate'; still, he endorsed Fellowes's conclusion that the C was probably a misprint – and kept it anyhow. Morehen thinks the *echappée* is an error and emends it away, though unlike Dart he does not suspect a misprint, concluding instead that the error was in the compositors' copy.

In bars 36–7, all editors take the obvious course and expand the *iterum* (ij) in the second soprano to 'thy hopes but fables'. But for motivic consistency, and also to preserve the *a* sounds on high $f^2$, the underlay here ought to be:

but   fa – – – –   bles

# 7

## *Byrd and Jacobean consort music: a look at Richard Mico*

### JOHN BENNETT

The author of a modern study of William Byrd's consort music remarks how little it affected the course of English musical history, despite its originality and distinction, and adds:

In some of his consort fantasias Gibbons did echo Byrd, distantly but distinctly ... But no other younger composer of consort music showed Byrd's influence in any significant way ... The new fantasias were madrigalian ... and composers soon began to indulge the English propensity ... to cultivate texture at the expense of form.[1]

Another Jacobean composer, younger than Orlando Gibbons, seems to deserve notice in this context: Richard Mico (c. 1590–1661).[2] He was named by both Simpson and North as one of the leading consort composers of his time.[3] But his music stands somewhat aside from the Jacobean mainstream – still more from the age of William Lawes.

Mico is known to have been in contact with Byrd. Before the turn of the century Byrd had settled at Stondon Massey in Essex, only a few miles from his patron Sir John Petre (later first Lord Petre) of Thorndon and Ingatestone Halls. In 1608 Richard Mico, then aged about eighteen, entered the service of John Petre's eldest son William (1575–1637) as resident household musician. William Petre was at that time living at Thorndon Hall with his widowed father, on whose death in 1613 he succeeded to the title and estates. Mico remained in the service of the Petre

---

[1] Oliver Neighbour in MWB 3, pp. 265–6.
[2] John Bennett and Pamela Willetts, 'Richard Mico', *Chelys* 7 (1977), pp. 24–46.
[3] Christopher Simpson, *A Compendium of Practical Music in Five Parts*, reprinted from 1667 edition, ed. P. J. Lord (Oxford, 1970), p. 78; and John Wilson, ed., *Roger North on Music* (London, 1959), p. 343. Both name Ferrabosco (II), Coprario, Lupo and Mico. Simpson adds White, Ward, Colman, Jenkins and Locke. North omits these (though he would obviously have ranked Jenkins with the original four) but adds East.

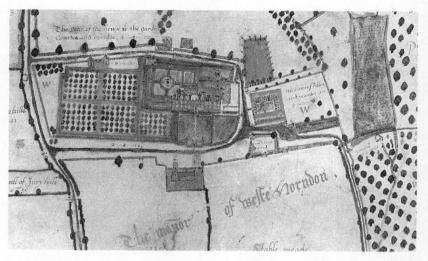

Plate 7.1 Thorndon Hall, West Thorndon, Essex, from a map by James Walker, 1598. (Essex Record Office D/DP P5.) Reproduced by kind permission of The Lord Petre, and of the Essex Record Office

family until well after Byrd's death in 1623, eventually moving to London in 1630 as organist to Queen Henrietta Maria.

The two musicians must have seen a good deal of one another during Mico's first fifteen years in Essex. Byrd was on close terms with the Petre family, and is known to have interested himself in the musical life of the household.[4] As well as late Elizabethan evidence, there is a Thorndon Hall inventory dating from 1608 which includes 'Mr. Byrd's chamber' (and 'Richard Mico's chamber').[5] Byrd was evidently a regular visitor. Among other connections it seems likely that he would commonly have heard mass in Lord Petre's private chapel. Mico too was a Catholic. Sharing a mistrusted minority religion might have helped bridge the age gap between the two men.

Thorndon Hall was well stocked with Byrd's music, particularly his Latin works. A list of household music books placed in Mico's charge on arrival consists mainly of Byrd's published works, down to Book II of the *Gradualia* (1607, dedicated to John Lord Petre).[6] There was also a set of

---

[4] A. C. Edwards, *John Petre* (London, 1975), pp. 61, 73, 85; and Essex Record Office (ERO) T/A 174, William Petre's account book 1597–1610, recording payment in June 1608 'to Mr. Birde for his riflings for song books' (f. 170v).

[5] ERO, D/DP F. 218.     [6] ERO, D/DP E. 2/1.

manuscript part-books containing music by Tallis and earlier sixteenth-century composers as well as some Byrd motets.[7] Byrd's masses are not listed, perhaps as a political precaution, but it is inconceivable that they too were not available in this recusant house. A list from 1616 adds Byrd's *Psalmes, Songs and Sonnets* of 1611, which included two of his consort fantasias.[8] Mico had charge of the Petre chest of viols, doubtless used for household recreation, perhaps with Byrd sometimes taking a part.[9] The Petre chapel would have been a regular feature of Mico's duties, with Byrd's music as the staple fare and the composer himself sometimes present. The young household musician must even have been familiar with Byrd's views on the interpretation of his own works. In effect Mico lived with Byrd's music for over twenty years. It would be surprising if nothing had brushed off.

Mico's surviving compositions are all consort music, clearly intended for viols although no instrumentation is specified. They are unusual for their period in being confined solely to the more serious kinds – fantasias, pavans and one In Nomine. He left no string music in the lighter styles then coming into fashion: no galliards, almains, corants and so on, nothing for lyra viol, nothing suggesting the range and manner of the violin. Nor is there any keyboard music of his, although he must have been an accomplished organist and virginal-player. (The organ parts accompanying some manuscripts of his consort music seldom go beyond the skeleton of the viol parts, and may well not be his own composition, since there are no organ parts with the autograph set of his four-part consorts.[10]) The 'whole atmosphere' of Mico's music has been called 'much darker and more introspective' than that of his contemporaries generally.[11] These features combine to imply a musical temperament disposed, like Byrd, to 'gravity and piety', and perhaps more likely to be responsive to Byrd's art than to react against it.

Comparisons need not be limited to Byrd's consort works. A recent Byrd editor remarks that his Latin motets 'were apparently regarded as

[7] ERO, D/DP Z. 6/1.    [8] ERO, D/DP E. 2/8 (probably in Mico's own hand).

[9] For Byrd as viol player, see for example the punning reference 'Byrds on bowes are playing' in Marenzio's *Sweet hart arise*, no. XIV of Thomas Watson's *First Sett of Italian Madrigals Englished* (London, 1590). The spelling with a Y and the capital B (which also occur in nos. VIII and XXVIII, Byrd's own settings of *This sweet and merry month of May*: 'And Byrds do sing, and beasts do play') together suggest a personal allusion. Watson's collection was in use at Thorndon Hall, presumably by Byrd among others: see Bennett and Willetts, 'Richard Mico', p. 31.

[10] GB-Lcm 1197.

[11] W. Coates, 'English Two-Part Viol Music, 1590–1640', *Music & Letters* 33 (1952), p. 143.

vocal chamber music ... and, no doubt, performed in ways appropriate to
the secular repertory ... the accompaniment of viols would not have been
considered out of place'; and it has been said that 'the model for such
*Gradualia* choirs would ... have been ... the informal madrigal groups of
the 1580s and 1590s ... an essentially chamber-music effect'.[12] Instruments are known to have been sometimes used in recusant chapels.[13] The
Petre accounts show no trace of a professional chapel choir. The family and
their handful of Catholic retainers and neighbours might well have wel-
comed instrumental support in the more intricate parts of Byrd's masses
and motets. The house possessed an organ; but support on a suitable
chamber music scale would have been ready to hand in the household chest
of viols. Hence there was no lack of opportunities for Byrd's vocal idioms
to leave some mark on Mico's instrumental vocabulary. The age of music
'apt for voices or viols' was not yet over.

In the following paragraphs, references to Byrd's compositions are to
the Byrd Edition, and those to Mico's follow the numbering used by the
Viola da Gamba Society.[14] Since some of Mico's music still awaits publication, examples have as far as possible been taken from his published
work. Mico's notation tends to halve Byrd's normal note values – perhaps
no more than the result of several decades of 'deflation' and sounding much
the same. In the comparisons discussed below, this notational adjustment
is taken into account.

Two strands are perceptible in Mico's consort music. Some pieces do
reflect the fashionable madrigalian style, with its reliance on contrasts of
mood and texture rather than on form or thematic development. This
applies notably to his five-part fantasias and to a few of those in four parts.
One of the latter (no. 17) also exists in a revised, more instrumental
version, incorporating some divisions;[15] and his *Latral parte seconda*, a

[12] Alan Brown in BE 3, Preface, p. viii; and Joseph Kerman in MWB 1, p. 52.

[13] A. C. Southern, ed., *An Elizabethan Recusant House* (London, 1954), a contemporary life
of Lady Magdalen Montagu (d. 1608, for whom Byrd wrote a consort song elegy,
BE 15/40). In her chapel 'on solemn feasts the sacrifice of the mass was celebrated with
singing and musical instruments' (p. 43).

[14] G. J. Dodd, *Thematic Index of Music for Viols* (London, 1980). In this Index pieces in free
form are described as 'fantasies' rather than 'fantasias'; the title 'Fantasy' is more usual in
recent Mico editions. Mico's consort music has recently been edited by Andrew Hanley in
'Richard Mico: Complete Works' (M.A. (Mus.) diss., U. of Bristol, 1990). In this edition
the fantasias follow the order of *Lcm* 1197, rather than that of the Viola da Gamba Society.

[15] In the source *Lcm* 1197 one version of Fantasia a 4, no. 17 appears in sequence in the
part-books, in the same hand as the other entries there. The other version is on an extra leaf
roughly pasted in (and in some cases now loose), and in a different hand. It may
reasonably be inferred that this is a later revision.

textless parody-sequel to a Monteverdi madrigal, stands apart from his other works in all the sources. Both features suggest the possibility of an early date for the madrigalian works as a whole.

This madrigalian element in Mico's work can scarcely have owed anything to Byrd, who took little interest in madrigals, and counts against the otherwise attractive hypothesis that Mico came into the Petre household through having been a pupil of Byrd. It may probably be inferred that he arrived already grounded in the current madrigalian style. It is not known who originally taught him. Certain thematic affinities with Ferrabosco II have been noticed.[16] But in general Mico's music lacks the distinctive 'drive' of Ferrabosco.

Mico's other manner is less episodic or rhetorical than the madrigalian style and characterised by greater economy of material and attention to form, as well as by an apparent predilection for certain compositional devices discussed below. These features are observable to different degrees in at least one of his five-part fantasias, a number of his four- and three-part fantasias and most of the two-part ones. Perhaps we have here the marks of a maturing individual style, presumably developed during his long service with the Petres. Something seems to have turned him away from the madrigalian fashion. Could contact with Byrd have had anything to do with this? It cannot be claimed that Byrd's influence is demonstrably a dominant factor, but there are signs that it might have played some part.

First, two apparent 'trademarks' of Mico's fantasia style both suggest possible affinities with Byrd. Oliver Neighbour has remarked that 'subjects hinging on an expressive semitone step are important in Byrd's work, and decidedly rare in earlier English music'.[17] Subjects of that nature are particularly prominent in Byrd's *Cantiones Sacrae* of 1589, over half of which use them extensively to evoke the prevailing tone of lament and supplication. A common version is the pattern 5–b6–5, a shape which might be compared to a low-peaked Tudor arch, with its inversion 8–#7–8; sometimes a minor third replaces the semitone in one or other limb of the arch. Such patterns with similar emotive content occur in some of Byrd's consort song elegies, e.g. *With lilies white* (1608) and *Fair Britain isle* (1612), both dating from Mico's early years at Thorndon Hall.[18]

Semitone patterns of this type are characteristic of Mico too. He makes

[16] G. J. Dodd, 'Richard Mico' in *Chelys* 2 (1970), p. 45.

[17] MWB 3, p. 37, quoting Joseph Kerman, 'Byrd, Tallis and the Art of Imitation' in Jan LaRue, ed., *Aspects of Medieval and Renaissance Music: a Birthday Offering to Gustave Reese* (New York, 1966), p. 532.

[18] BE 15/34 and 40.

Example 7.1  Mico, Fantasia a 5, no. 2, third section

considerable use of them to build up pensive slow-moving passages,
usually as an interlude in an otherwise more lively work (Example 7.1).
Instances occur sufficiently often to imply deliberate preference; fantasia
a 4, no. 19 opens with a striking extended version.[19] On the other hand

---

[19]  See fantasias a 5, no. 2; a 4, nos. 4, 8, 10, 12–15 and 19; and a 3, nos. 1–3. Fantasia a 4,
     no. 19 was published in the English Consort Series (ECS, ed. Richard Nicholson), vol. 7
     (London, 1979). In the writer's opinion there are no serious grounds for questioning the
     attribution of this piece to Mico, despite the note against it and no. 19 in the Viola da
     Gamba Society Thematic Index. Both pieces figure in *GB-Och* 517–20 in sequence with
     the rest of the known Mico four-part fantasias, the whole set bearing only a single
     attribution at the beginning of the sequence. Their absence from *Lcm* 1197 could be due

this usage seems by no means a commonplace among English consort composers generally.

Byrd's 1589 *Cantiones Sacrae* figured among the Petre music placed in Mico's charge in 1608. The set had been dedicated to Edward Earl of Worcester, whose daughter Catherine married Mico's employer William Petre. It was 'my Lady' who actually handed over the partbooks and instruments to Mico. Evidently she took a special interest in the household music. Her will (1624) shows that she was a devout Catholic.[20] Thus Byrd's 1589 collection would probably have held a prominent place in the Petre chapel, both because of the dedication and because it gave poignant expression to the feelings of English Catholics. Might familiarity have impressed one of its characteristic musical devices on Mico's imagination?

Another device which seems to have had particular attractions for Mico is tight imitation between pairs of voices. He uses it frequently, usually to underline the entry of a new point, and often as close as a crotchet's distance. Examples occur in nearly a third of his four-part fantasias, over half the three-part ones, and all but one of those in two parts – enough to establish it as a distinctive Mico 'fingerprint'.[21] The process sometimes leads to quite extended passages of loose canon with reversed accents.

While imitation as such is of course one of the fundamentals of fantasia style, such intensive use of tight imitation seems by no means characteristic of English consort composers generally. For instance, a comparative study of the two-part fantasias of Morley, Orlando Gibbons, Coprario, White, Ward, Mico and others (published in the 1950s) found that Mico's stood out as regards the use of tight imitation.[22] Nor does the device seem to be conspicuous in textbooks of the period which Mico might have studied. Instances occur among the examples in Morley's *Plaine and Easie Intro-duction*, but Morley's text draws no special attention to them. Coprario's *Rules how to compose* (c. 1610) advise that 'the sooner you bring in your parts with the fuge, the better it will shewe', but the examples in his treatise contain no imitation at closer than a minim's distance.[23] One of his examples happens to use the same tag as Mico's (unpublished) four-part

to their having been written later. Both show stylistic affinities with other Mico four-part fantasias.

[20] ERO, D/DP Z. 30/13.

[21] See fantasias a 4, nos. 1, 2, 4, 6, 8 and 14 (all unpublished except 4 and 8, see fnn. 28 and 30); a 3, nos. 3–6 (ed. M. Bishop, Belmont, Mass., 1986); and a 2, nos. 1–3 (ed. D. Beecher, Ottawa, 1978).

[22] Coates, 'Two-part Viol Music', pp. 142–7.

[23] G. Coprario, *Rules how to compose*, facsimile edition, ed. M. F. Bukofzer (Los Angeles, 1952), ff. 36v–40.

Example 7.2a  Coprario, 'Rules how to compose', f. 37

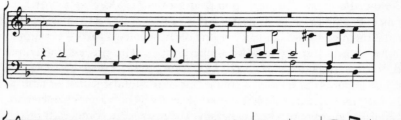

Example 7.2b  Mico, Fantasia a 4, no. 1, second section

fantasia no. 1, with the same note values, but Mico halves the distance
between Coprario's entries (Example 7.2). Contemporaries may perhaps
have thought devices of this kind rather old-fashioned, but for Mico
himself they were evidently still a living part of the musical language.

Against that background it is noteworthy that Byrd uses the same device
freely. It figures in both the consort pieces from his 1611 set, which we
know Mico had. Byrd's four-part fantasia no. 1 concludes with a long
masterly display of the tightest sort of imitation, mostly using the voices in
pairs. The device is prominent too in Byrd's Mass for Three Voices – a
dozen examples all told, almost always at the entry of a new point (as in

Mico).[24] Other instances can be found in Byrd's Mass for Four Voices and in some of the *Gradualia*, late works known to have been in the Petre music collection.[25]

Sometimes Mico seems to be almost quoting Byrd. For instance, a passage near the beginning of Mico's five-part fantasia no. 2 features canons at the fifth a crotchet apart, closely resembling those in the latter part of Byrd's four-part fantasia no. 1 cited above, and in the same key; and in Mico's three-part fantasia no. 3 the second and third sections respectively echo, again in the same key, the first and second sections of Byrd's six-part fantasia from the 1611 set.[26] Again, Mico's four-part fantasia no. 3 is built on a changing-note figure used by Byrd, in the same key though with slightly different rhythm, for the second part of his three-part fantasia no. 1.[27]

Another case combines near-quotation with a general attention to form and economy of material reminiscent of Byrd: Mico's four-part fantasia no. 4 considered alongside Byrd's well-known five-part canonic fantasia.[28] Both are in the same key. Mico's opening point follows Byrd's exactly for the first five notes, and the rest of the point has a similar contour (Example 7.3). It has been said of this Byrd fantasia that he 'takes the principle of motivic development further ... than in any other consort work except the 3-part fantasias'.[29] While Mico attempts nothing like Byrd's continuous strict canon, he does, like Byrd, use motivic development. His second section (of four) grows out of the opening point, rather than presenting a madrigal-style contrast, and his final section uses a theme derived from the opening point by crab-motion, presented antiphonally in close canon between pairs of voices (Example 7.4). Both works end by stating the theme in augmentation, in very similar terms. It is hard to believe that Mico could have been quite unaware of the Byrd model.

Similar economy and un-madrigalian attention to form can be noted in another Mico four-part fantasia, no. 8.[30] The opening point is modified by motivic development and worked at some length by the 'learned' methods

24 Gloria, at 'adoramus te', 'Qui tollis' (second time), and 'ad dexteram patris'; Credo, at 'Et ex patre', 'per quem omnia', 'Qui propter nos homines', 'de Spiritu Sancto', 'simul adoratur', and 'Et exspecto'; Sanctus, at 'Dominus Deus', 'Pleni sunt coeli', and 'Osanna'.
25 E.g. *Puer natus*, at 'cuius imperium'; *O magnum misterium*, at 'et admirabile'; *Venite comedite*, at 'comedite panem meum'.
26 Mico fantasias a 5 published ECS, vol. 2 (London, 1977); fantasias a 3, see fn. 21. The Byrd pieces are in BE 14/15 and 26.
27 The Mico piece published in ECS, vol. 7, the Byrd in BE 17/1.
28 Mico a 4, no. 4 ed. P. Grubb as no. 9 (London, 1959); the Byrd in BE 17/8.
29 MWB 3, p. 75.        30 Mico a 4, no. 8 ed. Grubb as no. 13 (London, 1959).

Example 7.3a  Byrd, Fantasia a 5, opening

Example 7.3b  Mico, Fantasia a 4, no. 4, opening

of canon, inversion and diminution. It culminates in a stretto whose entries are at distances halved by each successive voice – a device used at a moment of climax in Byrd's Mass for Three Voices, 'cum sancto spiritu' at the end of the Gloria. Mico's concluding section makes ingenious use of pairs of canons in which the lower voice raises the tension by accelerating half-way through the phrase and reversing the accents. Both this and fantasia no. 4 also each include a sustained emotive section based on the 'Tudor arch' theme found in Byrd.

Mico tends to avoid overlapping cadences. In this respect Mico (apart

Example 7.4  Mico, Fantasia a 4, no. 4, last section

from his conspicuously madrigalian pieces) follows Byrd rather than the
Jacobean mainstream. Indeed, he develops Byrd's ideas. More systematic-
ally even than Byrd's, Mico's cadence-schemes feature key-related patterns
such as tonic–dominant–mediant–tonic. And the sections thus demarcated
are usually in some balanced mathematical proportion to one another like
16–12–8 or 18–15–12 breves. Byrd's tend to be marginally irregular; he
usually prefers a broad canvas, while Mico is more of a miniaturist.

Possibly by extension of the same ideas, Mico favours two-section
fantasias more than his contemporaries. Over a third of his four-part
fantasias (seven out of nineteen) are thus constructed, without overlap.
Two of them (nos. 1 and 19) are further unusual in each falling into two
sharply contrasted sections of approximately equal length, separated by a
double bar: a slow rhapsodical harmonically-rich movement followed by a
brisk fugal one. Another (no. 12) uses the same pattern in reverse
sequence. Jenkins's two-section fantasias, for all their skill, do not show
such sharp internal contrasts. Some of Locke's suites do, but the proportions are different: a brief slow introduction before a long fugal piece. In
effect Mico has some claim to be regarded as an early experimenter in
prelude-and-fugue form. In the present context this prompts the question
whether his choice of form might have owed anything to Byrd's 'prelude
and ground' for viol consort, an isolated experiment which otherwise
seems to have had no musical progeny.[31]

Another instance of possible influence on general structure, rather than

[31] BE 17/9.

on specific stylistic features, is Byrd's six-part pavan, which has the two treble viols in loose canon throughout: Mico's five-part pavan no. 3 does the same.[32]

Each of these cases could, by itself, be simply coincidence. Cumulatively they seem to suggest something more. The apparent points of resemblance, however, are too few and specialised to fit readily with any idea of regular systematic instruction by Byrd. Proximity would no doubt have enabled Mico to pick up occasional hints or criticism if he had wished, but some more positive process seems to be indicated. Another possibility is that growing familiarity with Byrd's work aroused Mico's interest and led to his devoting some private study to the large body of high-class but now rather old-fashioned music left in his charge. Such a study could have continued after Byrd's death. Allowance must also be made for the possible subconscious effects of prolonged exposure to the music of a single great composer in the isolation of a Jacobean country house. Some of Mico's apparent borrowings or imitations might have been 'in his head' rather than directly attributable to close study of particular pieces. Perhaps a combination of the last two hypotheses is the least unlikely explanation. One way or another, traces of Byrd's methods seem to have been kept alive – albeit for a limited public – until the end of Mico's active musical life some time after the mid-century.

[32] BE 17/15a; ECS, vol. 2.

# 8

# Byrd and Tomkins: the instrumental music

## JOHN IRVING

With the death of Thomas Tomkins in 1656 the school of English virginalists comes to a close ... [His] earlier works show the influence of the chromatic style and make certain demands upon the virtuosity of the player. The music of his later years is written in a more conservative style which resembles that of his teacher William Byrd. Here in the years of the mid-century the circle has closed. Tomkins, the last of the school, returns at the end of his life to the style of his master, the first, and perhaps the greatest, of the virginalists.

Since 1954, when Stephen Tuttle made this stylistic comparison,[1] much has changed in Byrd scholarship. We now know far more about the various influences on Byrd's development as a composer, in particular the debt he owed to Taverner, Tallis and Alfonso Ferrabosco I in the sphere of sacred vocal music; to White and Parsons in his consort pieces; and to the generation of Redford and Preston in the formation of an idiomatic keyboard style.[2] Not much change is noticeable at the other end of the spectrum, though.[3] That Byrd was the most powerful native musical intellect faced by composers such as Morley, Tomkins, Gibbons, Coprario and Ferrabosco II is not in doubt. But what was the *nature* of Byrd's appeal? Was his music 'influential' in precise compositional ways or merely as a general, perhaps only loosely defined, model? Quantifying these composers' debt to Byrd is complicated somewhat by the presence of

---

[1] TK, p. xiii.
[2] See for instance: Joseph Kerman, 'Byrd, Tallis and the Art of Imitation' in Jan LaRue, ed., *Aspects of Medieval and Renaissance Music: a Birthday Offering to Gustave Reese* (New York, 1966), pp. 519–37; Craig Monson, 'The Preces, Psalms and Litanies of Byrd and Tallis: Another "Virtuous Contention in Love"', *Music Review* 40 (1979), pp. 257–71; Philip Brett, 'Homage to Taverner in Byrd's Masses', *Early Music* 9 (1981), pp. 169–76; Oliver Neighbour in MWB 3.
[3] See Richard Turbet, 'Homage to Byrd in Tudor Verse Services', *Musical Times* 129 (1988), pp. 485–90.

competing stylistic forces: for instance, the Italianate style was evidently a much stronger pole of attraction for some (Morley, Coprario, Ferrabosco II). On the other hand, Tomkins and Gibbons belong firmly in the tradition of Taverner, Tallis and Byrd, although a further complication here is the position of John Bull, who, for both Tomkins and Gibbons, shone as a rival star in native skies. His influence on Tomkins was considerable[4] and a few of the latter's keyboard pieces do 'make certain demands on the virtuosity of the player' (though Tuttle does not explicitly name Bull as an influence in the passage quoted above). It was Byrd, however, to whom Tomkins owed most. Indeed, in a list entitled 'Lessons of worthe' on pp. ii and iii of his well-known holograph keyboard volume, *F-Pn* Rés. 1122, Tomkins formulated an appealing distinction – not necessarily a value judgement – between the merits of Byrd's Quadran Pavan and Galliard ('for matter') and Bull's Quadran pair, ('for the Hand'). What mattered most to Tomkins was 'matter'.

If we are to enlarge on Tuttle's assertion that 'the music of [Tomkins's] later years is written in a more conservative style resembling that of his teacher William Byrd' then *Fortune my Foe*, a folksong set as keyboard variations by both Byrd and Tomkins, is a good place to begin since Tomkins's piece dates from 1654, right at the end of his composing career.[5] There are some obvious dissimilarities of size (Byrd has only four variations, Tomkins eight – to which the beginning of a ninth was added on p. 185 of the holograph) and mode (transposed Dorian on G for Byrd, Aeolian for Tomkins who ventures further flatwards within his mode at bar 75 than Byrd does anywhere in his). Elsewhere, the two settings exhibit some close parallels. Tomkins decorates the initial statement of 'Fortune' at exactly the same place as Byrd (the start of bar 3 in the top part of each piece) and in a similar rhythmic manner: for Byrd the dotted ♩. ♪♩♩ is an important feature of his opening, as is ♩ ♫♫ in Tomkins's, being used not only for melodic decoration but as an accompanimental figure and rhythmic 'filler' at the main cadence points. In addition to broadly similar shapes and styles of keyboard figuration both composers apply imitative counterthemes against the folksong, increasing their frequency towards the end of variation 1 (from bar 9 of both settings). Tomkins's countertheme – which generates much of the material in subsequent variations – outlines ascending or descending tetrachords, perhaps

---

[4] Tomkins's keyboard In Nomines (all from the last decade of his life) are a case in point. See John Irving, 'Keyboard Plainsong Settings by Thomas Tomkins', *Soundings* 13 (1985), pp. 22–40.

[5] BK 6; TK 61.

suggested by notes 7 to 10 of 'Fortune' itself. Byrd studiously avoids this tag in his opening variation (except at the upbeat to bar 5), probably to limit early rhythmic growth and allow the tune to assert itself. By comparison, melodic impact is weaker at the corresponding point in Tomkins, where rhythm and counterpoint are certainly the two most potent elements. Byrd's unhurried approach contrasts clearly with Tomkins's impatience here. Having surrendered imitation to melodic exposition at the start, Byrd proceeds in his three subsequent variations to add progressively to his range of melodic and rhythmic patterns, so that the antiphonal semiquaver dialogue in variation 4 arrives as a natural culmination. Tomkins's variation 4, which exploits the same semiquaver texture, makes a less decisive point (even allowing for its position at the centre of a larger set than Byrd's) precisely because of the greater diversity employed earlier. Perhaps the most significant point of contrast is one of phrasing, clearly displayed in both pieces by consistent structural placing of keyboard patterns within variations. Byrd evidently heard 'Fortune' as follows[6]

$$\|: A \text{ (4 semibreves} : \|: B \text{ (8 semibreves)} : \|$$

since in each variation he makes no attempt to draw attention to the tune's implied half-close after four semibreves of either B or its repeat. An example of this practice occurs in variation 4, bars 46–7, where Byrd straddles B's mid-point (a static Mixolydian seventh chord) by passing the same figure antiphonally from left hand to right. Conversely, Tomkins tends to introduce *new figures* at these half closes, marking out the following alternative division

$$\|: A \text{ (4 semibreves)} : \|: B \text{ (4 semibreves)} + B' \text{ (4 semibreves)} : \|$$

exhibited, for example, at bar 35 (variation 3), and bar 78 (variation 5). Tomkins only rarely borrows thematically from Byrd in *Fortune*, but, like his master, he is at pains to stamp the whole piece with its own motivic integrity. The intervallic shape (perfect fourth and adjacent step) of Byrd's quaver counterthemes at bars 34–6 (variation 3) recalls motives that close variation 1 (bars 9–12); a less explicit link, admittedly, than that made by Tomkins between his fourth and fifth variations (bars 35 and 44), and the inversion of this latter point at the start of variation 8 (bar 132), but likewise symptomatic of a concern for overall design.

As might be expected in free variations on a popular tune, Byrd and Tomkins exhibit affinities and idiosyncrasies of approach in roughly equal

[6] 'Fortune' is related to the Passamezzo Antico and La Folia; see John Caldwell, *English Keyboard Music Before the Nineteenth Century* (Oxford, 1973), pp. 94–6.

*a)*

*\* is lacking in the Sarum Version of this antiphon*

*b)* Byrd

*c)* Tomkins

Example 8.1

measure. In their settings of the plainsong antiphon *Clarifica me Pater* adherence to the chant's shape imposes greater uniformity.[7] It is clear that Byrd's second setting was Tomkins's model: he uses the same, slightly modified, version of the antiphon as Byrd (Example 8.1a), transposed up a fifth from D to A final and disposed in even semibreves in the highest part. Tomkins copies Byrd's canonic opening also, even designing his theme along similar lines, though whereas Byrd spans the interval of a sixth directly, Tomkins opens out more gradually (Example 8.1b and c). Tomkins imitates at the fifth (Byrd does so at the octave) but sticks quite closely to the general outline of his model, bringing in a second imitative point quite soon (chant note 5 in Byrd; note 7 in Tomkins), halving the time-distance between the free canonic parts from a semibreve to a minim and relating it loosely to the first point by inversion. Both settings share similar harmonic thinking: at chant note 16 they cadence on D (Byrd, bar 16; Tomkins, bar 7), at note 23 on A minor (bar 23; bar 10), and at note 31 on E minor (bar 31;

---

[7] BK 48; TK 4, in which note-values are halved. Original note-values are referred to throughout the present study.

*a)* Byrd

*b)* Tomkins

Example 8.2

bar 13). On the other hand, *sesquialtera*, which dominates the character of Byrd's piece from note (bar) 23, is entirely lacking in Tomkins; so, too, is Byrd's culminating 9:4 proportion, replaced in Tomkins by a flourish of semiquavers (in original note-values). The cadences on E minor (note 31) provide an interesting insight into Tomkins's relationship to his model. At this point Tomkins 'breaks' the plainsong, involving it in a three-part contrapuntal exchange (a texture wholly absent from Byrd's setting). But on close study a further resemblance emerges, exposing the younger man's continued susceptibility to Byrd's influence: Byrd's counterpoint to notes (bars) 31 and 32 features contrary motion across the main beats, and a parallel case can be found in Tomkins's *Clarifica* slightly later on (notes 36–8; bars 15–16) in which the device of sequence is added to that of metrical overlay (Example 8.2a and b).

The question remains why Tomkins chose this particular setting of the antiphon (Byrd composed two others, of which the third is the most developed motivically).[8] Presumably Tomkins was restricted to some extent by his knowledge of, and access to, sources of Byrd's keyboard music. That Tomkins indeed had access to such sources is confirmed by the

---

[8] BK 47 and 49. The choice of antiphon is curious. Only seven settings survive in the English canon, three each by Tallis and Byrd, dating from between c.1540 and c.1570, and Tomkins's setting (dated September 1650). A resemblance might be pointed out between the imitative style of Byrd's second *Clarifica* (the one examined here) and that of Tomkins's In Nomine TK 9, in which the general shape of the imitations at notes 11 (bar 4), 22 (bar 8) and 30 (bar 11) evokes Byrd's at notes (bars) 9 and 16. Once again the chant is set in even note-values in the top part and transposed up a fifth from D to A final.

fortunate survival in his keyboard holograph, *F-Pn* Rés. 1122 of six pieces
– including three *unica* – by Byrd:

| | | |
|---|---|---|
| p. 1 | Ut, Re mee, Fa, Sol, la: | BK 58 |
| p. 16 | A Fancy Fantasy* | BE 17/4 |
| | | EK 55 |
| p. 19 | M$^r$ Birdes Fantasi Two pts in one in the 4$^{th}$ above* | BK 26 |
| p. 30 | A fantasi of m$^r$ Birds | BK 13 |
| p. 36 | Two pts. gloria Tibi trinitas | BK 50 |
| p. 38 | A verse of Two pts Byrd | BK 28 |

* indicates a keyboard score of a consort fantasia

Unfortunately, we do not know what Tomkins's copytexts for these pieces
were. But his knowledge of a significant portion of Byrd's keyboard output
is shown by a list entitled 'Lessons of worthe', found on pages ii and iii of
Tomkins's holograph, which includes, in addition to those listed above,
the following keyboard compositions by Byrd:

| | |
|---|---|
| Two Fantasies of M$^r$ Byrdes in A re | uncertain (see MWB 3, p. 222) |
| M$^r$ Byrde grownd in A re [Hugh Aston's Ground] | BK 20 |
| M$^r$ Byrdes: Walsingham in gamut/: | BK 8 |
| A Fantasi of M$^r$ Byrdes in gamut | BK 62 |
| A grownd of M$^r$ Byrdes, on these notes | BK 86 |
| Birdes Ut,re,my,Fa,Sol,la: ⎫ in gamutt | BK 64 |
| Birdes Ut,mee,Re: ⎬ | BK 65 |
| M$^r$ Birdes goe From my windowe | BK 79 |
| [M$^r$ Birdes] O mistris myne I must | BK 83 |
| Another pretty grownd of M$^r$ Byrds/ in the clasped Booke | BK 36 |
| Two pavens of M$^r$ Birdes & galliards to them: | |
|    The one sir Charles Summersetts in F.Fa ut | |
|    The other my lo. peeters in gamut | BK 3a, 3b |
| Eccho paven & galliard, M$^r$ Byrde in the Black Clasped Booke: in gamut | BK 114a, 114b |
| mounsiers Allmayne ⎫ M$^r$ Byrds: gamut | BK 87 or 88 |
| Sellengers Rownd ⎬ | BK 84 |
| M$^r$ Byrds quadran paven & galliard Excellent for matter | BK 70a, 70b |

Byrd's pieces either copied or listed by Tomkins cover quite a wide stylistic and chronological range, including the evidently early *Gloria tibi trinitas* antiphon (of which Tomkins's text is the only survivor), the two early fantasias on 'A re' and G,[9] the didactic *Ut re mi fa sol la* in which the pupil (Tomkins?)[10] played the hexachord in breves while the master played the 'wayes', and some of his most mature pieces, such as 'Hugh Aston's Ground' and the 'Petre' pavan and galliard (both of which are found in My Ladye Nevells Booke of 1591) along with the Quadran Pavan and Galliard and the variations on 'O Mistress Mine' which possibly postdate that source.

Neither of Byrd's *Ut re mi fa sol la* hexachords bears much relation to Tomkins's own disappointingly mechanical settings in the manuscript. The most extended example, TK 35, owes everything to Bull and little, if anything, to Byrd, who was not above incorporating popular melodies in these teaching pieces.[11] This practice was never adopted by Tomkins, who perhaps had more to learn from Byrd's *Ut mi re*, a curious artificial hexachord of which the only other keyboard version is by Tomkins himself (TK 38). Although Tomkins never transposes the hexachord pattern from G final (Byrd transposes it to D at statement 3 and to C at statement 10) the settings share some common techniques. The clearest parallels involve texture: both composers pair statements 7 and 8 by reversing the disposition of parts between the hands, and at this point Tomkins copies Byrd's close canonic overlap of the *Ut mi re* pattern (in ♩. ♪ rhythm rather than Byrd's straight minims).[12] On the other hand, Tomkins eschews *sesquialtera* proportion, which occurs at statement 10 of Byrd's piece. If the quality of Tomkins's figuration here is mainly derived from Bull, he demonstrates, nevertheless, one important technical advance perhaps acquired from his master: namely, how to avoid spinning out unappealing, mechanical patterns from one hexachord note to the next by injecting distinctive counterthemes into the surrounding polyphony. Byrd's third statement provides an especially attractive model, overlapping two counterthemes, the second decorating its predecessor by means of a catchy syncopation which might just have been Tomkins's inspiration for his own statement 10 (Example 8.3a and b). Byrd's rhythmic patterning of

[9] BK 13 and 62. The latter is entitled Byrd's 'old fancy' on p. 186 of Tomkins's manuscript.
[10] See Alan Brown, review of MWB 3 in *Early Music History* 1 (1981), pp. 354–65, esp. p. 362.
[11] The *Ut, re, mi, fa, sol, la*, BK 58 (for which Tomkins provides the only surviving text) quotes from 'The Woods so Wild' and 'The Shaking of the Sheets'.
[12] In statement 8 Tomkins introduces his canon on G and d, rather than Byrd's c and g; Tomkins pre-empts this texture in his statements 5 and 6.

Example 8.3

the hexachord is rather flexible, achieving at times absolute parity of movement with the other polyphonic parts (bars 30–43 offer an extended case). This contrasts sharply with Tomkins's 'rigid' approach in which the only (partial) exceptions to a uniform disposition of the *Ut mi re* in either semibreves or minims occur during statements 9 and 10.

Among Tomkins's 'Lessons of worthe' are four of Byrd's pavan–galliard pairs – 'sir Charles Summersetts in F. Fa ut', 'my lo. peeters in gamut', 'Eccho paven & galliard … in gamut' and his 'quadran paven & galliard'. The identity of the first of these is in doubt, since none of Byrd's surviving pavans or galliards bears any dedication to Sir Charles Somerset.[13] The 'Echo' and Quadran pairs are quite specialised types which Tomkins never cultivated. There remains Byrd's 'Petre' pavan in which Tomkins clearly took great interest, since not only did he incorporate some of its compositional features into pavans of his own, but he included a quotation from its associated galliard towards the end of his early variations on 'Barafostus' Dreame'.[14]

A typically 'late' feature of Byrd's 'Petre' pavan is the extent of motivic interrelationships between strains. An obvious case is the opening of the first and last strains, related by inversion, while the secondary idea of strain III (bar 72) develops sequentially the interval of a third latent in some of

[13] The pavans BK 59 and 60 are Byrd's only examples in 'F Fa ut'.
[14] Byrd, BK 3b, bars 41ff; Tomkins, TK 62, bars 89–90. Tomkins's piece survives in the Fitzwilliam Virginal Book. Alan Brown pointed out this resemblance to me some years ago.

Example 8.4

the previous material (Example 8.4a–c). Byrd's strain I is likewise typical of his late practice in its foundation upon what Oliver Neighbour has aptly called the 'twin-cadence' pattern.[15] 'Twin' cadences are positioned in bars 7 and 15 of a sixteen-bar strain, and act as clear dividers. Within each division Byrd frequently applies contrasting themes (strain III of 'Petre' provides one example). In strain I, however, he relates the balancing halves thematically by separating off the consequent part (—x—) of Example 8.4b, and working it independently from bar 9. A similar procedure is adopted by Tomkins in the final strain of his pavan TK 54 in which the secondary theme is the antecedent part of the first, worked alone (Example 8.5). This is one of six pavans by Tomkins with no associated galliard.[16] To these may be added the single early pavan TK 56 from the Fitzwilliam Virginal Book[17] and nine five-part consort pavans.[18] Evidently the single pavan was a genre Tomkins favoured, and in examining Byrd's influence in this sphere these single pieces require consideration along with those to which he did append galliards.[19] Tomkins's attitudes to the pavan differ in a couple of quite important respects from those of his teacher: first, their foundation is on imitative counterpoint, taken to extreme; secondly, and perhaps consequently, Tomkins's pavan strains are sometimes longer by far than

[15] MWB 3, p. 182.     [16] TK 51, 52, 53, 54, 55 and 57.

[17] Originally published as a consort pavan in *Opusculum neuwer Pavanen, Galliarden, Couranten unnd Volten* . . . compiled by Thomas Simpson (Frankfurt-am-Main, 1610) [1610[22]], no. 7.

[18] MB 59/21–9.     [19] TK 43/44, 45/46, 47/48, 49/50.

Example 8.5

Byrd's.[20] In Byrd's pavans imitation plays its part (not necessarily the major part) alongside other defining elements, such as the cadence, in creating an elegant, stylised dance; in Tomkins's examples the metrical point and poise of the dance are lost, supplanted by the impersonality of the polyphonic fantasia.

One of the chief characteristics of Byrd's 'Petre' pavan is its sophisticated treatment of theme. Its opening melodic syncopation ♩ ♩ | ♩ ♩ ♩ | ♩. ♪♩ ♩ | ♩ neatly avoids the mechanical effect that would have resulted from literal diminution ♩. ♩ | ♩ ♩ | ♩. ♪♩ ♩ | ♩ ; equally, Byrd's imitation in the tenor voice avoids too great a feeling of symmetry by expanding the rhythmic values in the centre of the phrase (while retaining its melodic profile exactly). Also interesting is the way Byrd extends the secondary theme of his final strain intervallically from a third (bar 72) to a fifth (bars 74–5), an idea reworked in the subsequent varied repeat where a rising fifth motive is extended to an off-beat scale figure reproducing the melodic opening of the

20 For example, Tomkins's pavan TK 52 has the following irregular strain lengths (in semibreves): I:16  II:21  III:33. Byrd only once exceeds his usual sixteen-semibreve length, in the pavan BK 23a, whose final strain runs to eighteen semibreves.

Example 8.6

pavan at bar 90.[21] Tomkins never achieves such subtle melodic control (though the first two strains of his pavan TK 47 are rhythmically similar) and the composer links together the figures ⌐x¬ and ⌐y¬ to form the imitative point ⌐z¬ in bar 7 (Example 8.6a–c); this convincingly prepares the busier texture of strain III, whose melodic identity is itself a combination of the openings of I and II (Example 8.6d). Such procedures impart a degree of thematic coherence, reinforced by the retention of a similar melodic aspect in each strain, peaking about the middle with $g^2$ or $a^2$ (bars 2, 7, 13) approached either directly or indirectly from below. A corresponding concern for contour may be noticed in strain III of the pavan TK 52 in which the placement of $f^2$, $g^2$ and $f^2$ (bars 19, 21, 23) is highlighted by semiquaver roulades (original notation).

Both the Tomkins pavans singled out so far lack written-out repeats, as do the majority of his efforts, perhaps on account of their complex, densely-packed imitative textures, which might render subsequent patterned decoration ineffective. On occasion, though, Tomkins did append varied repeats, somewhat in Byrd's style. Byrd's examples always seem to contribute some new dimension to their originals. That of the 'Petre'

---

[21] A further delightful touch is the augmentation of this line in the tenor part at bar 92; this latter technique occurs in Tomkins's pavans from time to time, for example in TK 47, strain II, bars 6–7 (bass); TK 53, III, bars 20–1 (tenor and bass); TK 55, III, bar 27 (bass).

pavan's final strain actually simplifies the contrapuntal scheme of the original at bars 88ff, omitting an entry in the right hand from bar 72 and reducing its span to form interlocking fifths. In his most imitative keyboard pavan, 'Kinborough Good',[22] Byrd's decoration to the second strain standardises the originally flexible shape of the imitation beginning in bar 33 (though the placement of ornaments here is quite random). In Tomkins's incomplete pavan 'Lo[rd] Canterbury',[23] a similar type of clarification is attempted. The rather tenuous quality of imitative overlap at bars 23–7 (strain II) is brought into sharper focus by the ♩♪♪ rhythm at bars 33ff. At the beginning of the decorated repeats to both surviving strains of this piece, Tomkins inserts an antiphonal dialogue not present originally (bars 8, 9 and 29). The same technique is applied in the pavan TK 45: the start of the decorated repeat of strain II (bar 25) commences with a new antiphonal figure, colouring the original F major chord (bar 17) with an Eb.[24] If Tomkins's inspiration here and at bars 5–6 of the associated galliard TK 46 was Byrd, then he modified his master's technique somewhat, for Byrd does occasionally admit extra imitations in decorated pavan strains, but not at their openings.[25] A good example occurs in the second strain of the pavan 'Ph. Tregian' (BK 60a) whose repeat includes imitations not present at first as well as alterations to the original position and order of entries (Example 8.7). Whereas Byrd normally retains the intervallic and rhythmic features of his imitative points consistently,[26] Tomkins takes a more flexible approach. Partly this has to do with the construction of most of his points in an antecedent–consequent format, either element of which may be modified or omitted during the course of a strain. Such a case exists in the middle strain of his pavan TK 51 where the syncopated antecedent ♪ ♩    ♩ is retained while its consequent is modified rhythmically from ♩ ♪♪♩ (bar 9) to ♪♪♩♪♪♪♪♩ (bar 10) and transformed entirely from bar 13 (Example 8.8). In the pavan TK 45 the first strain's antecedent appears in three forms, ♩.♩ (bars 1, 3, 5), ♩♩ (bars 2, 4, 5) and ♩♩ (bars 6, 8), while the consequent retains its ♩ ♪♪♩ ♩ rhythm but is transformed intervallically.[27]

Byrd's style of imitation in the keyboard pavans tends towards even

[22] BK 32a. The openings of strains I and II bear some resemblance to the corresponding strains of Tomkins's pavan TK 45.

[23] TK 57.

[24] Cf. the decorated repeat of strain III of Byrd's 'Kinborough Good' pavan (BK 32a), adding an eb[2] in bar 82.

[25] But examples of light antiphony are found in Byrd's pavan BK 31a at bars 26–7 and 56–7.

[26] An exception is the middle strain of 'Kinborough Good'.

[27] Other examples may be found in TK 52, strain II, and TK 53, strain II.

Example 8.7

* reversed order of entries (soprano/tenor)

spacing of entries on degrees closely related to the final. Tomkins is far less regular in both spacing and pitch, reflecting his more abstract, fantasia-like approach. The following diagrammatic representation of Byrd's imitative patterns in the pavan 'Kinborough Good' adopts a method devised by Joseph Kerman:[28]

[C Final]

Ia):     $C_2$ $G_4$ $C_2$ C   b): $G_2$ $G_2$ $D_2$ D

IIa):   G $D_3$ E $G_3$ F C C E G G D   b): $G_2$ $D_7$ A *

III:     $A_2$ $F_2$ $C_2$ $A_2$ $A_2$ $A_2$ $A_2$ $C_2$ $E_2$ $C_4$ G

* this entry is ambiguous but is clarified by its decorated repeat at bar 62

[28] Kerman, 'Art of Imitation', p. 521. Capital letters represent pitch entries (denoting no particular octave register); subscript roman numerals indicate the distance (in minims)

Example 8.8

Tomkins's pavans TK 52 and 54 show some elements of temporal regularity comparable with Byrd, but their pitch degrees are wayward:

TK 52 [G Final]
I:     $G_6$ $C_6$ $D_6$ G
II:    $E_4$ $E_6$ $A_2$ $D_4$ $D_6$ $B_4$ $B_4$ F♯
IIIa): $D_6$ $D_6$ $A_6$ A   b): $F_4$ $F_6$ $D_2$ G $D_3$ $G_4$ $F_4$ F

TK 54 [G Final]
I*:    $D_4$ $D_2$ $G_4$ $G_4$ $G_2$ $C_4$ A A
IIa):  $E_6$ B   b): D/$F_6$† G/B♭†
IIIa): $A_4$ C♯$_4$ $D_4$ F♯$_4$   b): $E_2$ $E_2$ $B_2$ $B_2$
* strain I's inconsistent upbeat length has been ignored in calculating the imitative delay
† paired entries

Comparison of Byrd's 'Kinborough Good' with Tomkins's pavan TK 51 effectively displays their different attitudes to the role of imitation. Byrd's final strain is completely even, its periodicity reinforced by the placement of every fourth entry in the treble (italicised in the above diagram). Tomkins admits a more complex symmetry:

TK 51 [G Final]
III: $G_2$ $D_2$ $D_2$ $G_3$ $E_2$ $E_2$ $E_3$ $A_2$ $A_2$ A $E_3$ $E_2$ $E_2$
       $E_3$ $E_2$ $E_5$ $B_2$ $B_2$ $B_2$ $D_2$ $D_3$ A

between successive entries (no numeral indicates a single minim's distance); a) and b) refer to first and second imitative points, where appropriate, within a single strain (I, II and III).

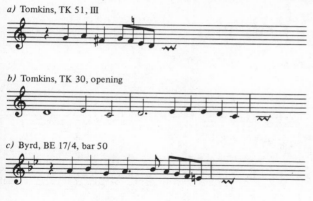

Example 8.9

The 'breathing spaces' between imitative groups are nearly always three minims, their immediately preceding entries ($G_3$ ... $E_3$ ... etc) occurring alternately in treble and bass parts.

In its 'obsessive' imitative style, this pavan strain is especially close to Tomkins's monothematic fugal keyboard pieces, such as the voluntary TK 30, to which it bears some thematic kinship (Example 8.9a and b). Closely related to both of these is an imitative point occurring towards the end of Byrd's first four-part consort fantasia, BE 17/4 (Example 8.9c), of which Tomkins made a keyboard score in his holograph volume (EK 55).[29] The closing portion of Byrd's fantasia might have appealed to Tomkins on account of its imitative 'saturation' – a technique that characterises much of his own work in a variety of genres. Likewise typical of Tomkins's own contrapuntal preference is the separate development of the consequent part of the 'point' which Byrd applies at bars 11–16 of his fantasia to form a transition between its first two sections (Example 8.10).

Surviving copies in Tomkins's hand show that he must have gained quite intimate knowledge of some of Byrd's consorts. Yet despite this, his own consort output does not closely resemble that of his master. The majority of his fifteen three-part consort fantasias (dating from the mid-1620s) are closer in spirit to the idiomatic string writing of Coprario and Ferrabosco II (alongside whose fantasias Tomkins's are also found in some surviving consort sources), especially in the formation of distinctive imitative themes from a wider mixture of note-values than generally obtains in Byrd's rather

[29] Keyboard scores of Byrd's six-part consort fantasias BE 17/12 and 13 occur on ff. 211 and 213v of another manuscript owned by Tomkins, *GB-Lbl* Add. 29996 (both are transposed up a tone).

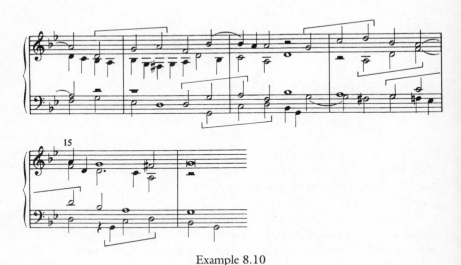

Example 8.10

'abstract' three-part pieces. Tomkins's three-part examples are developed at greater length than Byrd's, generally including three imitative sections, each extending to about the length of an entire Byrd fantasia. In two of these[30] Tomkins incorporates triple-time middle sections, clearly following Gibbons's lead in the last three of his printed *Fantasies of Three Parts* of c.1620.[31] In his choice of part ranges, too, Tomkins adopted the newer trend for two equal trebles (perhaps violins) and bass which became increasingly popular in the work of Coprario and Ferrabosco II after about 1600. One-third of his own three-part fantasias are for this combination, typically utilising clefs G2, G2, F3. Byrd, by contrast, employed C1, C4, F4 in his first two three-part fantasias, and C1, C3, C4 in the third. Only the first of these, BE 17/1, contains a point extended to a length comparable with Tomkins; the elegant imitative scheme of the point which enters in bar 24 is:

$$C_8 \; C_8 \; C_6 \, G_8 \; G_2 \, C_7 \; F \, G_6 \; C_4 \, C_3 \, C_8 \; F*$$
\* original note-values, counting in minims

[30] MB 59/5 and 9.      [31] MB 48/13–15.

making for an attractively unhurried close. Tomkins's closing sections are
altogether more hectic. Fantasia IX[32] (clefs G2, C3, F3) ends with an
imitative subject which, after an exposition for all three instruments, is
confined to the two outer parts, with occasional hints at the first four
notes of the figure in the middle voice. At bar 81 the rather flexible
consequent (typically, for Tomkins, in shorter note-values than its antecedent) strays into a shape similar to Byrd's at bar 24 of BE 17/1.
Tomkins's reaction is to continue in melodic sequence, a feature wholly
absent from Byrd's treatment of the figure. Sequence was a device which
held greater fascination for composers of Tomkins's generation than it
ever did for Byrd. It was frequently employed in the consorts of Coprario, Ferrabosco II and in Gibbons's printed fantasias (for example, MB
48/11), as a means of contrast with and movement between principal
imitative sections. That these same techniques also occur in Tomkins's
three-part fantasias suggests that Byrd's compositional techniques (in
consort music, at least) were less influential upon Tomkins at this stage
(c.1625). This point is perhaps reinforced by the style of Tomkins's
ascribed pieces in the roughly contemporary Fitzwilliam Virginal
Book,[33] which are wholeheartedly in Bull's idiom, and, as Tuttle puts it,
'show the influence of the chromatic style and make certain demands
upon the virtuosity of the player'. At any rate, Tuttle was clearly right to
point to Tomkins's renewed enthusiasm for Byrd's 'more conservative
style' in later life.

Evidently Byrd's music, though a model for Tomkins, was never the
subject of mere slavish imitation, but creative reinterpretation of a similar
kind to that applied by Byrd in his own early compositions to the procedures of a still earlier generation. Perhaps too much should not be read
into stylistic comparisons, though, since they can never hope to answer all
the fundamental questions we might wish to ask about Byrd and Tomkins
as master and pupil. The foregoing account attempts to highlight some
specific points of technical affinity that exist in their instrumental music.
While such detailed technical comparisons can usefully illuminate this
picture, the limitations are clear, too. They can effectively contrast Byrd's
techniques with, for instance, Tomkins's typical over-use of sequence in a
piece such as his prelude TK 3, but cannot satisfactorily explain what it was
about this piece which nevertheless led Will Forster to ascribe it to Byrd in

[32] MB 59/11.          [33] TK 39, 56, 58, 62, 65.

his keyboard manuscript of 1624.[34] Consider finally the dedication of Tomkins's five-part madrigal, *Too much I once lamented*, from his *Songs of 3, 4, 5, and 6 Parts* (1622),[35] which describes Byrd as 'my ancient, & much reverenced Master'. This madrigal features both chromaticism and perfectly prepared dissonance in large measure: were these two particular facets of style which Byrd had taught his pupil and which Tomkins now displayed for his 'much reverenced Master'? Or were they commonplaces of the age? We have no historical documentary evidence to provide any more than speculative answers to these questions (nor are we ever likely to discover any). All we have is the music.

[34] *GB-Lbl* R.M. 24.d.3 ('Will Forster's Virginal Book'), p. 386. Tomkins's prelude is there entitled 'A Parludam M^r Burd'.

[35] Edited by E. H. Fellowes in *The English Madrigal School*, vol. 18 (London, 1922), no. 14.

# 9

## Baldwin and the Nevell hand

### HILARY GASKIN

John Baldwin,[1] the copyist of My Ladye Nevells Booke, died in 1615. He was a singing-man at St George's Chapel, Windsor, where he is recorded in the Treasurer's Rolls as having been paid for copying music during the 1580s.[2] From 1598 until his death he was a Gentleman of the Chapel Royal. Three manuscripts in his hand survive: *GB-Och* 979–83 (a set of part-books of which the tenor book is missing),[3] which contains 172 pieces, most of them vocal and sacred; his Commonplace Book, *GB-Lbl* R.M. 24.d.2 (one of the very few surviving English score-books from this period),[4] containing a large variety (209 items) of texted and textless, sacred and secular, English and continental pieces plus musical puzzles and proportion exercises; and My Ladye Nevells Booke, an early, substantial and important source of Byrd's keyboard music.

In addition to these sources there are two (possibly three) manuscripts with which Baldwin was associated, and to which he made a contribution. The first of these is the Forrest–Heyther collection of masses, now in the Bodleian Library.[5] These part-books contain eighteen masses by Taverner, Burton, Marbecke, Fayrfax, Rasar, Aston, Ashwell, Norman, Sheppard, Tye and Alwood. For a detailed account of the books' structure and probable origins the reader is referred to John Bergsagel's article on the

---

[1] See Hilary Gaskin, 'Music Copyists in Late Sixteenth-Century England, with Particular Reference to the Manuscripts of John Baldwin' (Diss., U. of Cambridge, 1985).

[2] Baldwin is mentioned in the Treasurer's Rolls, St George's Chapel, Windsor, WR XV.59.13, 15, 16, 17.

[3] See Roger Bray, 'The Part-Books, Oxford, Christ Church, MSS.979–83: an Index and Commentary', *Musica Disciplina* 25 (1971), pp. 179–97, and Gaskin, 'Music Copyists', pp. 7–8, 17–21.

[4] See Roger Bray, 'British Library MS. Royal 24.d.2: an Index and Commentary', *RMA Research Chronicle* 12 (1974), pp. 137–51, and Gaskin, 'Music Copyists', pp. 8, 13–17.

[5] *GB-Ob* Mus.Sch.e.376–81.

subject;[6] the aspect of them which is of most interest and relevance here is the fact that they were completed by Baldwin. The first eleven masses are copied in an unidentified hand, and the remaining seven in the hand of William Forrest, described by Anthony à Wood as 'a priest ... who was well skill'd in music and poetry'.[7] However, Forrest died around 1581, leaving the last book incomplete from the Agnus Dei of Mass no. 15 onwards, and Baldwin finished that section and copied the last three masses into the book. This is the likely course of events, although, as Bergsagel notes,[8] it is possible that this last group of masses was inaccurately copied or met with some accident, and that Baldwin replaced rather than completed the section. Bergsagel contends that the books passed into Baldwin's possession after Forrest's death c.1581.[9] When Baldwin himself died, in 1615, the books came into the possession of William Heyther; both men were Gentlemen of the Chapel Royal. Heyther joined the Chapel in March 1615, and Baldwin died in August of that year.

The second of the three manuscripts with which Baldwin is associated is the set of part-books *GB-Och* 984–8. This anthology, which survives with all its books intact, was both owned and compiled during the 1580s by Robert Dow, whose source announces its owner on the title-page of each part-book with the legend 'Sum Roberti Dowi'. He has been identified by Philip Brett[10] as the Robert Dow who was a fellow of All Souls from 1577 until his death in November 1588 – a cultivated and learned man, as the inclusion of many interesting Latin inscriptions in the manuscript testifies.[11] The books have attracted much interest on account of their extensive repertoire of 'songs', but they also form an important concordance for a good deal of the sacred music which Baldwin included in his anthologies. Nos. 53 and 54, *O bone Iesu* and *Vestigia mea* by Parsons and Giles respectively, are in Baldwin's hand.

A third manuscript which has a possible connection with Baldwin (although its layout is more diminutive than other surviving examples of

---

6  'The Date and Provenance of the Forrest–Heyther Collection of Tudor Masses', *Music & Letters* 44 (1963), pp. 240–8.

7  Anthony à Wood, *Athenae Oxonienses*, ed. Philip Bliss, 5 vols. (London, 1813–20), vol. 1, col. 297.

8  Bergsagel, 'Date and Provenance', p. 248.        9  *Ibid.*

10  'The Songs of William Byrd' (Diss., U. of Cambridge, 1965), p. 20. For further information on Dow, see David Mateer, 'Oxford, Christ Church Music MSS 984–8: an Index and Commentary', *RMA Research Chronicle* 20 (1986–7), pp. 1–18.

11  For examples of these, see M. C. Boyd, *Elizabethan Music and Musical Criticism* (Philadelphia, 1962), pp. 312–17.

his work) is *GB-Och* 45, a sixteenth-century source copied in table-book form containing forty extracts from longer pieces. Joseph Kerman has suggested[12] that the hand which added an extract from Byrd's *Infelix ego* to the contents at no. 37 is Baldwin's.

Both the Forrest–Heyther and the Dow contributions are copied in what can be termed, for convenience, Baldwin's 'Nevell hand', which has lozenge-shaped noteheads and upright stems. (The hand which he uses in his Christ Church anthology and his Commonplace Book has more rounded noteheads; his italic-type text underlay hand, apart from some superficial variations, remains constant throughout his copying output.) The Nevell hand bears a noticeable resemblance to the two other hands in the Forrest–Heyther books (those of William Forrest and the unknown scribe), so it is possible that it actually originated in Baldwin's attempt to achieve continuity in this source. However, since only one of his copying projects in this hand carries a date (1591 in the Nevell book) it is not possible to establish a precise chronology of their copying. If, as Bergsagel contends, the Forrest–Heyther source came into Baldwin's possession after Forrest died, c.1581, and remained in his possession until his own death in 1615, Baldwin could have worked on it at any time within a possible time-span of about thirty-four years. The contribution to Dow's anthology probably involved a much shorter time-span in the late 1580s soon after Dow's death.[13] It is possible, therefore, that Baldwin developed the Nevell hand specifically for any one of these three projects, and thereafter selected it from his 'repertoire' of scribal hands to use it in the others. As a copying hand it was elegant and probably more laborious to produce than the hand which he used in his vocal sources; thus it was a suitable hand to use for the Dow and Forrest–Heyther contributions, which are short, and the Nevell book, which was to be an important presentation anthology.

My Ladye Nevells Booke, the most extended surviving example of Baldwin's Nevell hand, bears the following colophon:

finished & ended the leventh of September in the yeare of our lorde god 1591 & in the 33 yeare of the raigne of our sofferaine ladie Elizabeth by the grace of god queene of Englande: etc by me Jo: Baldwine of windsore: laudes deo.

The physical aspects of this source have been described by Hilda

---

12  MWB 1, p. 177.
13  See May Hofman, 'The Survival of Latin Church Music by English Composers, 1485–1610' (Diss., U. of Oxford, 1976), p. 40.

Andrews[14] and E. H. Fellowes,[15] and the quality of its texts assessed by
Alan Brown.[16] The main focus of the considerable interest which it has
attracted since it was first published in 1926 has been its value as a
keyboard source and as a source of Byrd's music, one which he himself is
thought to have overseen. If, however, we focus on the scribe, and examine
the Nevell book in the context of his other work, this opens up some quite
different lines of enquiry. Since Baldwin's surviving manuscripts, with the
exception of this one, contain predominantly vocal music, the main questions are: did Baldwin have to adapt his copying methods to music for this
different medium, and if so, how? And in what ways can his methods be
related to and compared with those used by the scribes of the other major
keyboard sources of the period?

The Nevell source consists entirely of music by Byrd. Therefore its major
concordances (although it predates them all) are keyboard sources which
transmit Byrd's music in some quantity. They are the 'Weelkes' manuscript
(*GB-Lbl* Add. 30485), Will Forster's Virginal Book (*GB-Lbl* R.M. 24.d.3)
and the Fitzwilliam Virginal Book (*GB-Cfm* Music MS 168). The first of
these, Add. 30485, has on its title-page a misleading note in a later hand,
which reads: 'Extracts from Virginal Book, Lady Nevil's: Tallis. Byrd. Bull.
etc.' There is in fact no historical or textual connection between the manuscripts,[17] although they share thirteen pieces. Alan Brown has convincingly
suggested that the copyist of the source is likely to have been Thomas
Weelkes.[18] Attempts to date the manuscript have been tentative, but a
completion date of 1601 or 1602 is a possibility. It contains over 30 pieces
by Byrd, and music by other composers. Will Forster's Virginal Book is
signed and dated '31 Januarie 1624. Will. Forster.' It contains 80 pieces, of
which about 45 are by Byrd. Thurston Dart suggested that Forster had
access to Byrd's papers, after the composer's death in July 1623.[19] According to the published research to date,[20] the Fitzwilliam Virginal Book was
compiled by Francis Tregian the younger during his imprisonment in the
Fleet for recusancy, from 1609 to 1619. The source Egerton 3665 and the

---

[14] See the Historical and Analytical Notes to her edition, *My Ladye Nevells Booke* (London,
1926; repr. New York, 1969), pp. xiii–xliv.

[15] E. H. Fellowes, 'My Ladye Nevells Booke', *Music & Letters* 30 (1949), pp. 1–7.

[16] See his dissertation, 'A Critical Edition of the Keyboard Music of William Byrd' (U. of
Cambridge, 1969), his article, '"My Lady Nevell's Book" as a Source of Byrd's Keyboard
Music,' *Proceedings of the Royal Musical Association* 95 (1968–9), pp. 29–39, and the
commentary and notes to BK.

[17] See Fellowes, 'My Ladye Nevells Booke', pp. 6–7.          [18] EK, pp. xvi–xix.

[19] *Ibid.*, p. xix.

[20] But see Ruby Reid Thompson's forthcoming dissertation, 'The Tregian Manuscripts: a
Study of Their Compilation' (U. of Cambridge).

'Sambrooke' manuscript have both been traced to his authorship.[21] The Fitzwilliam book contains nearly 300 pieces, including about 70 pieces by Byrd.

All these manuscripts contain a substantial amount of Byrd's keyboard music, much of it concordant with what Baldwin copied, and none of them is separated by more than twenty-five years or so from the completion of the Nevell project in 1591. Outside this main group, for different reasons, stand various other sources: the earliest source of Byrd's keyboard music, the manuscript *GB-Och* 371 (c.1570), which contains his two *Miserere* settings; a group of sources which provide only small numbers of pieces by Byrd, and which in most cases were copied well into the seventeenth century, many years after Baldwin completed the Nevell source; and the only printed English keyboard source of the period, *Parthenia, or the Maydenhead of the first musicke that ever was printed for the Virginalls* (1612/13), containing music by Byrd, Bull and Gibbons.

It is instructive to compare My Ladye Nevells Booke, as a source, with other types of source. As Alan Brown remarks,[22] it is the only surviving manuscript which was apparently a presentation copy for an aristocratic patron, although other extant sources are associated with a name, examples being Priscilla Bunbury's Virginal Book and Elizabeth Rogers' Virginal Book.[23] Another distinguishing feature of Baldwin's source is that of all these manuscripts it is the only one for which there is any evidence that the scribe had little to do with choosing the music copied. This is, of course, necessarily a matter of conjecture, but it is highly unlikely that Baldwin, the scribe, made a present of this manuscript to 'Ladye Nevell'. He must have compiled it at someone else's instigation, probably the composer's; and if that was the case, the composer surely supervised what was selected for inclusion in the book. The probability that the compiler of Nevell was carrying out someone else's orders is greater than for any of the other sources, even *Parthenia*. Some of them, indeed, are clearly commonplace books (in the general sense of being compiled in one hand, for personal use rather than presentation). The 'Weelkes' manuscript Add. 30485 is of this type, as Alan Brown has noted,[24] and so also (if it is the product of one

---

[21] See B. Schofield and T. Dart, 'Tregian's Anthology', *Music & Letters* 32 (1951), pp. 205–16, and E. Cole, 'In Search of Francis Tregian', *Music & Letters* 35 (1952), pp. 28–32.

[22] Brown, 'A Critical Edition', p. 30.

[23] This book, dated 1656, includes a piece entitled 'When the King enjoyes his owne againe' – an oblique reference to the hope of an eventual Restoration?

[24] EK, p. xix.

hand) is the Fitzwilliam book in its way, although it is an unusually lavish one.[25]

Baldwin is not alone in being a copyist of vocal as well as keyboard music: the other extant manuscripts in the Tregian group contain texted madrigals and motets, while Weelkes, as a composer of vocal music, was clearly involved in writing it down at some stage. Despite this common factor, however, Baldwin's keyboard manuscript is copied in an unusual and distinctive hand compared with those found in the other keyboard sources, including the print (which was produced by line engraving, not type). There is a complete lack of evidence as to why Baldwin's keyboard script should be so different from the others. We have already noted its possible origin in a copying project involving vocal music; if it was an earlier keyboard manuscript that influenced him, it has not survived. Nor does his manuscript seem to have influenced later styles, although there is no evidence that it disappeared into complete obscurity as soon as it was presented to the Nevill[26] family. The difference between his markedly more angular shapes and other scripts is, in any case, a cosmetic one, since – as the following discussion should demonstrate – the principles which governed his keyboard copying and that of the other scribes were basically similar.

In her Historical Note on the Nevell source, Hilda Andrews comments: 'The prevailing fashion of written music, shown at its best in the notation of *My Ladye Nevells Booke*, abounds in evidence of the transitional nature of the period.'[27] As she observes,[28] this transitional nature is particularly apparent in the use of bar-lines and accidentals.

At the time of the completion of the Nevell source (1591) the use of barring was largely confined to lute and keyboard sources, and Baldwin's own commonplace book, R.M. 24.d.2, is unusual among vocal and instrumental sources of the period in its partial use of a score-book format.[29] The barring found in the keyboard sources, including Baldwin's Nevell book, belongs to the period between its introduction and its eventual application in a consistent manner on the part of all copyists. This transitional period appears to have lasted about a hundred years. Denis Stevens remarks of the use of bar-lines in the Mulliner Book (the compilation of which he dates

---

[25] For a detailed division of manuscripts into eight suggested categories, see Thurston Dart's article, 'An Early Seventeenth-Century Book of English Organ Music for the Roman Rite', *Music & Letters* 52 (1971), pp. 27–38.

[26] Modern spelling.          [27] Andrews, ed., *My Ladye Nevells Booke*, p. xxix.

[28] *Ibid.*, pp. xxx–xxxi.

[29] See Gaskin, 'Baldwin's Commonplace Book: Problems of Space in a Sixteenth-Century Score-Book', *Soundings* 10 (1983), pp. 18–22.

Example 9.1  Fitzwilliam Virginal Book (*GB-Cfm* Music MS 168), p. 19.

from c.1547 to c.1559), 'there is no principle, and nothing is to be gained by pursuing the matter. Notation in England was at that time suffering from growing pains.'[30] Yet well into the seventeenth century regular barring was far from universal among keyboard sources. Benjamin Cosyn, in his virginal book (dated 1620), seems to have applied the principles according to which modern barring is used; and an instance of irregularity, such as that shown in Example 9.1 (from the Fitzwilliam Virginal Book), may well be connected with the deliberate emphasis of cross-rhythms. However *GB-Och* 431 – compiled, according to Thurston Dart,[31] between c.1625 and c.1635 – uses bars which are very variable in length. Nor does the transitional period show a steady progression from one method to another: a source such as *GB-Lbl* Add. 30486, c.1600,[32] is regularly barred while the printed *Parthenia* of 1612/13 is not.

The irregularity itself occurs in two forms. The first could be summed up by Stevens's phrase, 'no principle': passages in which the number of beats per bar shows random variation. An example of this is Example 9.2, a passage from Will Forster's Virginal Book, in which it could be said that internal rhythmic divisions take precedence over external ones. A more common type of inconsistency concerns the halving and doubling of the number of beats per bar. Hilda Andrews describes this practice as being 'of common occurrence in florid repetitions and quickly moving semiquaver variations, following slow sections in semibreves and minims'[33] – in other words, a means of pointing up contrast. Its use is not quite as systematic as this implies, since an alternation between two different bar lengths can still occur even when a florid (or slow) passage is well established. Nor is it connected to inflexible bar *size*: Baldwin's R.M. 24.d.2 with its pre-ruled bar-lines appears to have no parallel among the keyboard sources.

The keyboard sources, in short, show a good deal of variation on this

[30] Denis Stevens, *The Mulliner Book: a Commentary* (London, 1952), p. 20.
[31] See the notes to his edition of the keyboard music of John Bull, in MB 19, p. 225.
[32] Brown, 'A Critical Edition', p. 93.     [33] Andrews, ed., *My Ladye Nevells Booke*, p. xxxi.

Example 9.2  Will Forster's Virginal Book (*GB-Lbl* R.M. 24.d.3), p. 50.

point, not necessarily connected to their chronological order. Some of them achieve something close to modern use of the barring system; others, including the Nevell source and the print, show a more irregular division of the musical flow. All, however, respect the basic musical pulse – it is rare for a bar-line to cut through a minim beat.

There is as yet no clear relationship in these sources between barring and the use of accidentals. The latter are given the unsystematic, transitional treatment that they receive in vocal sources of the period: key/stave signatures (some of them very idiosyncratic, such as the one C♯ in Elizabeth Rogers' Virginal Book of 1656) are often duplicated in the text, and accidentals appear to operate only in an immediate sense, although as Hilda Andrews remarks, 'this rule seems to be but casually observed'.[34]

Accidentals are preplaced (that is, placed several notes in advance of the one to which they refer), distanced (placed immediately before the note, but at some distance, in a spacious layout) or placed under the note in many of the keyboard sources. Indeed they are presented in exactly the same way as in contemporary vocal sources, and the same priorities are apparent. Much emphasis is placed on the first accidental on a new line, by preplacing it at the end of the previous line and then applying it immediately before the note in question. It was clearly important to give advance warning of this accidental, not just for a scribe such as Baldwin, who copied vocal music and could have transferred this technique to keyboard music, but also for William Hole who engraved *Parthenia* (or those who

[34] *Ibid.*, p. xxx.

prepared the exemplars from which he worked). In the keyboard sources, as in vocal sources, there appears to be a variety of motivations behind preplacement. Some sources, such as the 'Weelkes' book (Add. 30485), show marked signs of the notes' having been copied first, after which the accidentals were added wherever there was space for them; sometimes this space occurred several notes 'early'. Other sources, such as the Nevell book, provide some preplacement in spite of a reasonably spacious layout – preplacement which is apparently deliberate rather than merely dictated by convenience, and which may therefore have been prompted by a desire to give the player advance warning of accidentals. There is also a 'hybrid' form, represented by the sources such as Will Forster's book, Benjamin Cosyn's book, and the sources Christ Church 431 and Add. 30486, in which the layout is spacious and accidentals are seldom preplaced or placed under notes except during quaver and semiquaver runs. Here it may well be that the copying of notes preceded the copying of accidentals, but there was usually plenty of room, and problems only occurred at running passages.

One possible motivation raised in connection with preplacement in vocal music – the theory that it is connected in some way with solmisation procedures – can be discounted. It is hardly likely that solmisation was envisaged as an alternative method of performance for this music. Furthermore, the fact that preplacement in keyboard sources manifests itself in exactly the same way as in contemporary vocal sources must raise serious doubts as to the plausibility of this explanation for preplacement in vocal music.

The placement of notes in keyboard sources falls into two distinct types: alignment (however approximate) and centralisation. The latter practice is seen most clearly in Baldwin's Nevell texts, and an example is given in Plate 9.1. The principle of centralisation is as follows: whenever a pair or group of moving notes is heard against a held note, that note is placed in the centre, relative to the moving notes, rather than aligned with the first note of the group. This can take place on several different levels in the same bar, as the principle is put into operation with notes of different values. The effect is one of great visual symmetry, and to modern eyes it seems that artistic considerations predominate over musical ones. Nevertheless, a sixteenth-century player familiar with the method may not have found it any more difficult to read than the system of alignment.

The two methods of note placement coexist in the keyboard sources. Benjamin Cosyn, like Baldwin, uses pronounced centralisation; Francis Tregian also uses it, but not quite so conscientiously or precisely as

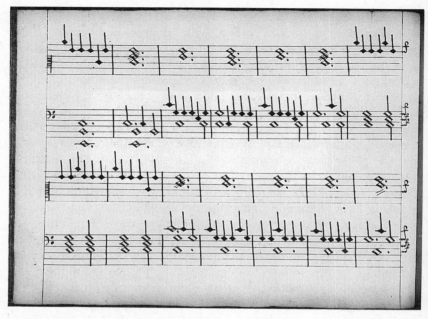

Plate 9.1 My Ladye Nevells Booke, f. 28v: the principle of centralisation in operation. (This photograph and the ones which follow are reproduced by kind permission of the Marquis of Abergavenny.)

Baldwin does. The scribe of Elizabeth Rogers' book uses alignment for the most part, but centralisation for left-hand semibreves.

As Howard Ferguson has observed,[35] the proportion signs most commonly found in the keyboard sources are C and ¢ for simple and compound duple time; ³⁄₂: C and ¢ for simple triple time; and 3 for brisk triple time. Baldwin occasionally gives a Ɔ sign, presumably with the same intended meaning as C . In addition, the signs 3/1, 6/1 etc. divide the minim beat into three and six respectively, and signal a change to brisk compound time.

Other types of sign occur in the sources with varying degrees of frequency. Repeat signs at the end of sections occur regularly, and are generally indicated (although individual practice may be inconsistent on this point)[36] by the use of dots either within, or on either side of, a double

---

[35] Howard Ferguson, *Keyboard Interpretation from the 14th to the 19th Century: an Introduction* (Oxford, 1975), p. 41.

[36] See Howard Ferguson, 'Repeats and Final Bars in the Fitzwilliam Virginal Book', *Music & Letters* 43 (1962), pp. 345–50.

bar. The sections are often numbered, and Francis Tregian goes so far as to append the abbreviation *Rep.* to some of his written-out repeats or 'divisions'. One or two sources, including Add. 30486 and the Nevell book, introduce extra stave lines for a high- or low-lying note or group of notes. Ornaments are very frequent, and although the more common double-stroke ones predominate, examples of single-stroke ornaments are to be found in several sources, including Benjamin Cosyn's book and the Nevell book.

Corrections in these manuscripts are achieved by erasing or crossing out the mistake. Baldwin is unusual in drawing the player's attention to an error and its correction; on f. 145v of the Nevell book there is the following annotation:

here is a falte, a point left out, w$^c$ ye shall finde prickte, after the end of the next songe, upon the .148.leafe:-

and on f. 148v:

this pointe bee longeth to the song before:- .145.leafe:-.

However Baldwin's source is also exceptional for a more significant reason: many of its corrections were apparently made by somebody other than him. Margaret Glyn has suggested[37] that the corrector was Byrd himself, and although it will probably never be possible to ascertain this, it is a plausible theory. Since her reason for proposing it lies in the nature of the corrections themselves, it is worth investigating them.

Many of the corrections are in fact additions – of accidentals, extra notes, and ornaments. Some are in the form of changes made to the layout and presentation of the notes: bar-lines are added; notes are tied together, or – the reverse procedure – a dot is changed to a repeated note. Only a minority of the corrections are clearly alterations of something that is wrong or inadequate: into this category come the deletion of notes, the addition and removal of beams on beamed groups of notes, the placement of directs on a different line, and the insertion of dots in a double bar or their removal from it. Also, on a few occasions, Baldwin had copied a note's stem but omitted the head, which the corrector filled in. Plates 9.2–9.5 illustrate some of these corrections.

It seems unlikely that Baldwin himself was responsible for these corrections. The inserted notes would appear to be written in a passable but not very good imitation of his hand. Moreover, Baldwin apparently did correct

---

37 Margaret Glyn, *About Elizabethan Virginal Music* (London, 1924; rev. and repr. 1934), pp. 38–9.

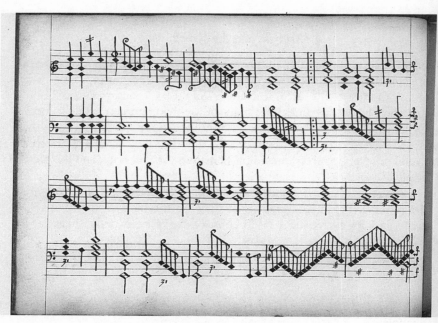

Plate 9.2  My Ladye Nevells Booke, f. 38v: added note in right-hand stave, second bar of page

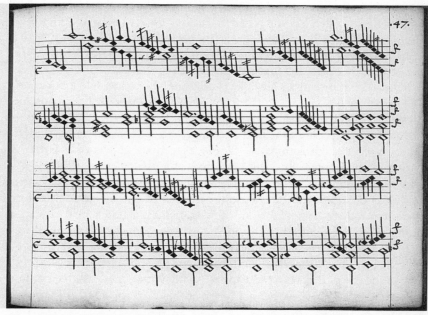

Plate 9.3  My Ladye Nevells Booke, f. 47: added notes, ornaments and accidentals; alterations to bar-lines

Plate 9.4  My Ladye Nevells Booke, f. 52: note added to penultimate chord

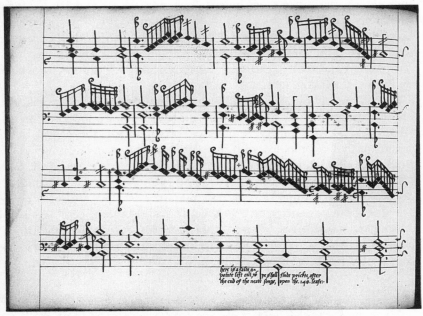

Plate 9.5  My Ladye Nevells Booke, f. 145v: Baldwin's own correction

his own mistakes on occasion, and the types of correction do not resemble each other. Apart from physical characteristics, however, the nature – one might say the 'spirit' – of these corrections has led Margaret Glyn and later writers to identify the composer as responsible: 'It is seldom a matter of correcting what is entirely wrong, but of inserting subtle little improvements that only Byrd's brain would have thought of.'[38] On the evidence of the corrections there seems no reason to question this. It should be noted, however, that it involves not one assumption but two: first, that the composer was responsible, and secondly, that his additions were themselves afterthoughts, and had not been present in his holographs. Nevertheless, on the evidence of the rest of Baldwin's output it does seem unlikely that he could have made so many omissions. It is probable that he made some, and that the rest of the 'corrections' are genuine improvements on Byrd's part.

It appears to have been a relatively straightforward matter for Baldwin to adapt his copying practices to the exigencies of keyboard music. There are two notable differences between his usual style of layout and that required for the Nevell book. First, there is a six-line instead of a five-line stave (probably used at this time because keyboard melodies moved through a wider range more quickly than vocal ones); indeed, Baldwin sometimes adds a temporary seventh line for low- or high-lying passages. Secondly, there are several directs, rather than one, at the end of each line, necessitated by the interplay of several parts on each stave. Baldwin also had to insert keyboard fingerings,[39] which are likely to have been provided by Byrd in the holographs.

On the whole, however, the differences are scarcely perceptible. Baldwin uses preplacement and cancellation of accidentals in the same way as in his vocal sources. As regards the question of alignment, the Nevell book cannot really be compared with the scored section of his Commonplace Book R.M. 24.d.2, in view of the very different types of music in the two sources, the greater number of parts per line in the Nevell book, and the peculiarities and cramped layout of R.M. 24.d.2.

There is one instance where Baldwin seems to become confused as to which hand to use: on f. 175 one of the notes is copied in the hand which he used for his two vocal sources. This abrupt reminder of a substantial source of very different music, also in his hand, points up not only the

---

[38] *Ibid.*, p. 39.

[39] For a study of these, see Ton Koopman, '"My Ladye Nevells Booke" and Old Fingering', *The English Harpsichord Magazine and Early Keyboard Instrument Review* 2 (1977), pp. 5–10.

astonishing variety to be found in his surviving output, but also its underlying unity. Whatever the stylistic differences between his Nevell hand and the hand he used for Christ Church 979–83 and R.M. 24.d.2, the characteristics of his copying are unmistakably recognisable in both.

# 10

## *My Ladye Nevells Booke and the art of gracing*

### DESMOND HUNTER

The purpose of this essay is to examine the application of grace signs in My Ladye Nevells Booke and to consider the implications of the gracing against the background of a more general discussion of virginalist ornamentation.

The problems posed by a study of the art of gracing in virginalist music need to be underlined at the outset. The evidence is provided largely in the form of the application of grace signs in the sources of keyboard music surviving from the period in question.[1] Those responsible for the gracing, however, whether composers, copyists or teachers, did not necessarily use the signs with similar intent. Few of the sources are holograph; even when the music may have been copied from composers' papers copyists possibly were responsible for some addition or modification of grace signs, and errors of transmission undoubtedly were committed occasionally. Furthermore, a manuscript may illustrate varied usage of grace signs in that its contents and the application of the signs could derive from more than one source. My Ladye Nevells Booke should provide a reliable focus for the study of virginalist gracing: it was compiled by an experienced copyist, John Baldwin, and the manuscript appears to have been checked and corrected by someone familiar with the music, possibly the composer, William Byrd.[2]

A reference to graces in English keyboard music, albeit little more than a parenthetical comment, is found in *Musicks Hand-maide* (1663). John Playford writes: 'But as for the true Fingering and severall graces used in

---

[1] The earliest explication of keyboard graces is Edward Bevin's idiosyncratic *Graces in play* (c.1630), given in *GB-Lbl* Add. 31403, f. 5.

[2] See Margaret H. Glyn, *Elizabethan Virginal Music* (2nd edn, London, 1934), pp. 35–9 and Alan Brown, 'A Critical Edition of the Keyboard Music of William Byrd' (Diss., U. of Cambridge, 1969), pp. 36–8.

the playing on this Instrument [the virginals], it cannot be set down in words, but is to be obtained by the help and Directions of the Skilfull Teachers, and the constant practice of the Learner.'[3] Undoubtedly this was sound advice although it provides little comfort to the modern performer of seventeenth-century English keyboard music. However, gracing was discussed in connection with other instruments. Thomas Robinson, in his *The Schoole of Musicke* (1603), treats the subject at some length with reference to the execution of graces on the lute. His comments are of interest and relevance, not least because he and Byrd were contemporaries. Although he refers to specific graces, Robinson's interpretation is very much in the spirit of improvisatory practice. He uses the term 'relish' generally to mean any grace, and when he states that 'a relish will help ... to continue the sound of the note his full time: but in a quicke time a little touch or jerke will serve',[4] he seems to be suggesting that according to context the relish may vary from an extended grace (a shake) to an appoggiatura. He draws attention to the expressive function of graces in referring to 'a strong relysh for loudnesse, or a milde relysh for passionate attencion'.[5] Early in the eighteenth century Roger North expressed a view in connection with 'the manner of artificiall Gracing' with which Robinson and Playford would probably have agreed when he stated that 'The Spirit of that art is incomunicable by wrighting'.[6] It seems probable that the lack of information on keyboard graces from the virginalist era reflects a concern for improvisatory realisation, a point which is perhaps underlined by the limited vocabulary of grace signs employed by the virginalists. Indeed, only one sign, the double stroke, enjoyed widespread currency.

The earliest application of the double stroke as an indicator of embellishment is found in one of the pieces of keyboard music recorded in the Evesham Abbey Bible (c.1540).[7] The context of the application, in a piece entitled *Non Exspextat*, suggests that the sign was used as an abbreviation for a form of shake. There is evidence that the sign was used also as an abbreviation, for various divisions, in the early layers of *GB-Lbl* Add.

---

[3] *Musicks Hand-maide* (London, 1663), [Preface].

[4] Thomas Robinson, *The Schoole of Musicke* (London, 1603; facsimile, Paris, 1971), Plate VIII.

[5] *Ibid.*, Plate IX.

[6] *Lbl* Add. 32533, f. 106v; *Roger North on Music*, ed. John Wilson (London, 1959), p. 149.

[7] For a discussion of the bible (location: Almonry Museum, Evesham) and the music recorded in it see M. D. Knowles and Thurston Dart, 'Notes on a Bible of Evesham Abbey', *English Historical Review* 79 (1964), pp. 775–8.

29996.[8] In later sixteenth-century sources, in particular in the c.1570 additions to the Mulliner Book (*Lbl* Add. 30513) and in the Dublin Virginal Manuscript (*Eire-Dtc* 410), the application of the sign suggests a freer association with embellishment.

The single-stroke sign has a somewhat different history. Its main function in sources which antedate Nevell is as a correction sign: it is drawn, usually horizontally rather than obliquely, through the stem of a note-value notated in error at a level too low. This method of correction was not associated exclusively with keyboard music; in *Lbl* Roy.App. 58 (c.1530) for instance, it was applied where necessary in the vocal music recorded in this manuscript source. It continued to be used in keyboard sources even when the sign also related to embellishment. Apart from exceptional usage of the single stroke in one of the pieces in the Evesham Abbey Bible (the sign is used once as an abbreviation for a division), it was not until around 1570 that the sign was used in connection with embellishment (in the additional section of the Mulliner Book and in the Dublin Virginal Manuscript) and the application is of some interest in that the sign is used only in combination with at least one other single stroke. In the Dublin Virginal Manuscript the consistent application of single strokes in pairs is striking. An explanation for this form of application is that it was adopted possibly to avoid confusion with correction.

A period of some twenty years separates Nevell from the Dublin Virginal Manuscript and the contemporary section of the Mulliner Book. This time-gap is underlined in Nevell by a much freer application of the grace signs in general and what appears to be a refinement in the use of the single stroke in particular.

It is evident that a convention was observed throughout the virginalist era concerning the positioning of grace signs. The strokes tend to be either drawn through or positioned at the end of the stem of a note-value lower than a semibreve. When a semibreve is graced, the sign is either drawn through the note-head or positioned above or below the note (a sign gracing a note in the higher or highest part on the stave would be placed in superscript position, one gracing a note in the lower or lowest part in subscript position). Positioning at variance with this convention can sometimes be attributed to careless copying or lack of space. Occasionally, however, positioning which is unusual is applied in such a way or with a

---

[8]  See John Caldwell, 'British Museum Additional Manuscript 29996: Transcription and Commentary' (Diss., U. of Oxford, 1965), p. 68, David Wulstan, *Tudor Music* (London, 1985), p. 126 and Desmond Hunter, 'The Application of Grace Signs in the Sources of English Keyboard Music c.1530–c.1650' (Diss., National U. of Ireland, 1989), pp. 71–2.

Example 10.1 *Ut Re Mi* (Nevell, f. 55; BK 64, bars 74–81)

degree of consistency which suggests that some special meaning may attach
to it. In the main Baldwin, the Nevell copyist, drew the signs through the
stems of note-values lower than a semibreve. Some double strokes are
positioned at the ends of stems, but this positioning seems to have been
determined either by lack of space (notes drawn close together at the end of
a system) or by the need for positional variation of signs on juxtaposed
graced notes close in pitch.

The application of the double stroke in Nevell suggests that the implied
embellishment will vary both in form and duration depending on the
context. In the short opening section of *The Battle* (Nevell, f. 18; BK 94)
double-stroke gracing affects note-values ranging from a quaver to a (void)
semibreve. In *The Hunt's Up* (Nevell, f. 46; BK 40) the range extends from
a semiquaver to a (blackened) semibreve. The editor of the 1926 edition of
Nevell, Hilda Andrews, considers the double-stroke sign to be little more
than an abbreviation by suggesting that it should be interpreted as a shake
with termination.[9] There are instances in which this form of realisation is
entirely appropriate: the passage quoted at Example 10.1 is a case in

[9] See *My Ladye Nevells Booke*, ed. Hilda Andrews (London, 1926; repr. New York, 1969),
p. xxxii.

Example 10.2  The Tenth Pavan (BK 3a, bars 45–7)
Nevell, f. 182
*Parthenia*, no. 2

point.[10] Each of the double strokes arrowed in bars 76 to 80 decorates a
strong harmonic progression which is similar to that embellished with a
shake at the beginning of the extract. The quaver prefix to the written-out
shake also prefixes each of the four arrowed double strokes in the example.
The prefix in question is the most commonly used formula before a shake.
The presence of this figure before each of the double strokes marked
suggests that a similar shake may be implied in each case. It is well known
that in different source-readings of the same piece a shake given in one may
be replaced by a double-stroke sign in another; and it is clear that the sign
and the notated division were considered analogous. A comparison of the
Nevell and *Parthenia* readings of The Tenth Pavan: Mr William Petre is
instructive on this point. The revised version in *Parthenia* has many more
double-stroke signs than the version in Nevell, although most of the signs
in the latter are retained. In two places in the second strain of the Pavan a
double-stroke sign in one of the sources is replaced by a written-out shake
in the other. In both instances the embellishment implied by the sign is

[10] The single dot given above the treble bb[1] in bar 75 and the pair of dots above the final
treble note in the passage quoted, markings which may derive from Byrd, identify
statements of the hexachord: a single dot at the beginning of an ascending statement, a
pair of dots at the end of a descending statement.

Example 10.3 The Galliard to the Second Pavan (Nevell, f. 66; BK 71b, bars 33–6)

undoubtedly a form of shake. In the latter of the two occurrences, however, it is clear that the sign in *Parthenia* implies a less elaborate shake than that notated in Nevell; this is suggested by the elaboration of the alto part in the *Parthenia* version (see Example 10.2).

Apart from its occasional embellishment of a strong harmonic progression, often in a cadential or quasi-cadential context, the written-out shake is used also in Nevell to provide incidental melodic decoration, sometimes above static harmony. It is important to note that most shakes involve semitone alternation. This is true in general and not only in relation to the examples in Nevell. Another common form of written-out embellishment, the turn, is found only occasionally in Nevell, but the frequent correspondence between a turn in one source and a shake in another suggests that the turn may have been used either as an abbreviation for, or an alternative to, a shake. In the Nevell version of The Galliard to the Second Pavan a turn is notated in a context similar to that in which the corresponding decoration is a shake (see Example 10.3, bars 33 and 35). In the other source-readings the turn is replaced by a shake. It is worth noting that a shake given in the Pavan in G, no. 3 (BK 72a, bar 46) in *Lbl* Add. 30485 (f. 3) appears to have been notated originally as a turn; two notes were added at a later stage and these are squeezed in at the beginning of the figure. Two bars later a similar passage occurs, but the turn has been left unaltered. The turn and the shake are similar in shape although the former lacks the basic ingredient of the latter, rapid note alternation. The broken turn (i.e. ♩♩♩♩ ) is more common than the plain form. It also substitutes occasionally for the shake. In The Galliard to the Sixth Pavan (Nevell, f. 84; BK 32b) for instance, the cadences concluding the first and third strains are each embellished with a shake; in the varied repeats of the strains the corresponding embellishment is a broken turn. Clearly the shake and the turn (both forms) were considered analogous and it is conceivable that the latter was also occasionally expressed in the form of the double-stroke sign.

It was noted above that most written-out shakes involve semitone alternation. Where a shake seems to be implied by a grace sign a semitonal relationship between the graced note and an auxiliary note, if applicable, may be a factor to be taken into consideration in determining whether realisation should involve upper- or lower-note alternation. Another possible factor is melodic direction: a grace sign on a note approached from below may normally indicate lower-note embellishment, one on a note approached from above an upper-note grace. In his discussion of the execution of graces the Spanish theorist Santa María refers to the realisation of crotchet *quiebros* in an ascending line (involving lower-note alternation) and also in a descending line (involving upper-note alternation).[11] Ammerbach's reference to ascending and descending *mordanten* is similar.[12] With reference to virginalist music melodic direction would seem to be important particularly where the implied grace is short and therefore incidental, but of less significance in the case of a more prolonged embellishment which is something of an event; indeed this is borne out to some extent by the notation of cadential shakes which commence invariably on the upper-auxiliary note regardless of the direction of the approach. In Example 10.1 each of the notes graced with a double-stroke sign has a semitonal relationship with either its lower- or upper-auxiliary note. Realisation of each grace sign, excluding those arrowed, as a shake involving semitone alternation would ensure that the embellishments were accommodated to the line. The type of shake and its duration would vary. The incidental embellishment realised on each of the graced quavers would inevitably be a very short, crisp one; indeed it might be simplified to what Robinson refers to as 'a little touch or jerke'. Some of the shakes would take the form of undershakes (implied in Example 10.1 on the graced $ab^1$ (bar 76) and $bb^1$ (bar 79) and on each Eb graced with the double stroke). In other sources undershakes are notated occasionally, usually in the bass, at the end of a strain.[13] The double stroke frequently graces either an octave leap or a broken octave notated on the lower stave at the end of a strain and in such instances an undershake seems to be implied (see *The March before the Battle*: Nevell, f. 13v; BK 93, bar 7 and *The Second Pavan*: Nevell, f. 64; BK 71a, bar 32).

[11] See Tomás de Santa María, *Libro llamado arte de tañer fantasía* (Valladolid, 1565; facsimile, Farnborough, 1972), f. 48v.
[12] See *Elias Nicolaus Ammerbach: Orgel Oder Instrument Tabulaturbuch (1571/1583)*, ed. Charles Jacobs (Oxford, 1984), pp. lxvii and lxxxvii.
[13] For an example see the *Praeludium* by Farnaby in *GB-Cfm* 168, p. 358 (MB 24/1, bar 17).

One form of evidence which occasionally confirms whether a grace sign will involve upper- or lower-note realisation is fingering. Nevell is the earliest source of English keyboard music which contains fingering indications contemporary with the music.[14] In all probability the fingering was provided by Byrd and includes indications on graced notes. None of the pieces with fingering indications (seventeen in total) is heavily fingered. In the main indications tend to be scattered and unrelated. Each of the graced notes fingered has a double stroke and the majority are fingered either RH3 or RH2; the other fingering indications given on graced notes in Nevell are RH4 (twice), RH5 (once) and LH3 (once). It must be said that there is nothing unusual about the application of the fingering, and indeed if there were no grace signs the fingering would make sense on the basis of its logic. There is no reason to suppose therefore that the indications refer to anything other than the graced notes. This point needs to be made because in other sources some of the indications on graced notes possibly refer to auxiliary notes in the implied graces, and in such instances the fingering qualifies the meaning of the grace signs in a particular way. This is suggested for instance by otherwise illogical fingering in the short verse *for Edward* by Tomkins, which is preserved in the composer's hand in *GB-Ob* Mus.Sch.C93 (f. 80).[15]

Perhaps the most interesting of the fingering indications listed above is RH5 (see Example 10.4). There is little doubt that lower-note embellishment is implied but the fingering indication suggests that an undershake is not the most likely form of realisation; the execution of an undershake would engage weak fingers (RH5 and 4). In view of the context a slide, from the third below, would be a convincing form of realisation. Although this grace is normally associated with the single-stroke sign there is no evidence of exclusivity of association.[16] Where RH4 is given on a graced note the implication also seems to be lower-note embellishment. In each case (in the Galliard Jig: Nevell, f. 43v; BK 18, bar 20 and *The Carman's Whistle*: Nevell, f. 152; BK 36, bar 82) the graced note is approached from

---

[14] For discussions of source fingerings see Julane Rodgers, 'Early Keyboard Fingering ca.1520–1620' (Diss., U. of Oregon, 1971), pp. 116–60 and Peter le Huray, 'English Keyboard Fingering in the 16th and early 17th Centuries' in Ian Bent, ed., *Source Materials and the Interpretation of Music* (London, 1981), pp. 227–57.

[15] TK (2nd edn) 74. For a discussion of the implications of fingering indications on graced notes in this piece see Hunter, 'The Application of Grace Signs', p. 29.

[16] The evidence associating the slide with the single stroke is in Edward Bevin's *Graces in play* and in Roger North's account of Prencourt's interpretation of graces, c.1700 (*Lbl* Add. MSS 32549 f. 11v and 32531 f. 24). It would seem that Prencourt was familiar with virginalist notation as he refers to the single stroke drawn 'thro yᵉ tail of a note', which was certainly not the practice at the end of the seventeenth century when he was in England.

Example 10.4 *Qui Passe* (Nevell, f. 10v; BK 19, bars 58–60)

below and realisation as an undershake would involve semitone alternation. The approach to the majority of the graced notes fingered either
RH3 or RH2 involves a melodic descent, a circumstance which suggests
upper-note realisation of the grace sign.

In a number of instances the note immediately preceding a graced note
has a fingering indication and where the note in question proceeds to the
graced note by step the implied fingering on the latter can be established
with reasonable certainty. It is no surprise that RH3, the indication of
greatest pivotal importance in virginalist fingering, emerges as the
fingering most frequently implied. However, this fingering admits the
possibility of either upper- or lower-note realisation of the accompanying
grace sign. Other evidence (e.g. melodic direction) must be adduced
therefore to determine an appropriate form of embellishment.

In addition to its importance as the earliest English keyboard source
containing fingering indications, Nevell is also the earliest source in which
a single stroke appears to be used on its own as a grace sign. Although
application in Nevell illustrates a marked change in approach to the use of
the single-stroke sign, the total number of signs in this category is relatively
small (twenty-four). There is similar application of the single stroke as a
grace sign in several of the near-contemporary manuscript sources which
postdate Nevell: Suzanne van Soldt's Book (*Lbl* Add. 29485), Duncan
Burnett's Book (*GB-En* 9447), *Lbl* Add. MSS 30486 and 30485, *Ob*
Mus.d.143 and Tisdale's Book (*Cfm* 782), all of which date from
around 1600. Only in Burnett's Book is the incidence of single strokes
high; indeed they outnumber double strokes by around 2:1. Burnett's
Book provides a concordance for one of the pavan/galliard pairs in Nevell,
the Passamezzo [antico] (BK 2); however, the two readings provide
contrasting approaches to the application of grace signs. The Nevell
version has 240 grace signs, all of them double strokes. There are thirty-
nine grace signs in the version in Burnett's Book; thirty-two of these are

Example 10.5 The Third Pavan (Nevell, f. 69; BK 14a, bars 83–8)

single strokes. Twenty-two of the single strokes correspond to double strokes in Nevell. Four of the seven double strokes in Burnett's Book are paralleled in Nevell. The application of the single stroke in Burnett's Book suggests that it distinguishes a grace which begins on an auxiliary note. Like the double stroke the sign is often given in contexts in which realisation as a shake seems to be required, the single stroke probably implying one with an upper-note start. This apparent analogy between the meanings of the two signs would seem to be important in relation to the application also in Nevell and later sources, particularly in view of the fact that throughout the virginalist era the single stroke is applied as a grace sign only in addition to the double stroke;[17] and to some extent therefore the former sign may have been used to isolate and identify a form of embellishment normally associated with the double-stroke sign.

The fact that the single stroke is used sparingly in Nevell is not surprising. The long association of the sign with correction may well have been an influential factor. Most of the single strokes are applied to either semibreves or minims. Only in *Walsingham* and The Third Pavan is the single stroke applied to a note-value lower than a minim. Alan Brown has suggested that the single stroke given in the Voluntary for my Lady Nevell (Nevell, f. 107; BK 61, bar 37) is possibly a copying error for a tie.[18] Some doubt must be expressed about several other single strokes. The application of both single-stroke signs in The Third Pavan displays some inconsistency. With reference to the first single stroke in Example 10.5, similar figuration on the lower stave elsewhere in the manuscript tends to be graced with a double stroke; and in the Add. 30485 reading the note in question is graced with a double stroke. The second single stroke in Example 10.5 may also be an error and the sign may have been misplaced:

---

[17] Other signs including the triple stroke were introduced also as additional signs.
[18] See Brown, 'A Critical Edition', p. 97.

*a)* bars 1–6

Example 10.6 *The Hunt's Up* (BK 40)

in the succeeding imitative figuration the double-stroke sign is used and it graces the dotted crotchet. However, the single stroke on f#$^2$ is given also in the Add. 30485 version. The application of one of the single strokes in

*Walsingham* is rather unusual (Nevell, f. 141; BK 8, bar 146): the sign graces the upper note of an octave notated on the lower stave (the sign is not given in any of the other source-readings of the piece). Elsewhere in Nevell the upper note of a broken octave given on the lower stave is graced occasionally with a double stroke, an application which suggests that an undershake is implied (see above, p. 180). There is one instance of a static octave graced with a double stroke, in *Sellinger's Round* (Nevell, f. 172; BK 84, bar 151), and the context is similar to that of the single-stroke gracing in *Walsingham* referred to above.

Most of the single strokes are found in *The Hunt's Up*. The corrector had a busy time in this piece: he completed/corrected the parts in several places and added a number of grace signs (double strokes). This is the only piece in Nevell which has single-stroke signs drawn through semibreve note-heads. Twelve semibreves are affected; three further single strokes are drawn through the stems of minims. *The Hunt's Up* appears to have been composed early in Byrd's career,[19] and Alan Brown notes that Baldwin 'seems to have copied this piece from a poor source'.[20] These facts could account for the nature and frequency of the application of the single-stroke sign on semibreves, which is exceptional in Nevell; moreover it is not paralleled in any of the other source-readings for the piece. The application of the single stroke in bars 2, 4 and 6 is puzzling (see Example 10.6a). In the first of the two versions of the piece recorded in the Fitzwilliam Virginal Book (*Cfm* 168), the only other source-reading with single-stroke signs, there are single strokes corresponding to those in bars 2 and 4 of the Nevell version, but in each case the sign is drawn through the stem of the minim in the treble part. This provides support for a misplacement theory. It is worth considering, furthermore, that if the single stroke drawn through the semibreve $e^1$ in bar 6 was given as a grace sign on $a^1$ in the treble part, the consecutive occurrence of the double stroke (on $g^1$) and the single stroke (on $a^1$) could imply a compound embellishment similar to that notated at the corresponding point in the second Fitzwilliam Virginal Book version (see Example 10.6a); that is to say, realisation of a single stroke on $a^1$ as a slide executed before the beat would form a termination to the shake implied by the double stroke on $g^1$. Implicit in this hypothesis is the suggestion that the function of the signs in bar 6 would be one of abbreviation, a function which, it has been noted, was associated with the signs in earlier sixteenth-century usage (see above, p. 175). Assuming that Baldwin's positioning of the signs is correct it is difficult to determine the

[19] See MWB 3, pp. 22 and 123–5.
[20] See Brown, 'A Critical Edition', p. 134, footnote.

implied function of the single stroke in the passage quoted at Example
10.6a. It is conceivable that, in this context, the sign drawn through the
note-head of a semibreve does not relate to embellishment, a suggestion
which is supported by a consideration of a later passage. In bar 29 the
combination of signs on the third minim beat is unusual (see Example
10.6b); these signs are not given in any of the other source-readings. The
simultaneous application of single- and double-stroke signs on different
notes occurs nowhere else in the manuscript, nor indeed in any near-
contemporary source. It is perhaps significant that the lower sign was
added by the corrector, as indeed was the sign on $b^1$. These double strokes
grace imitative figuration (similarly graced elsewhere in the piece) and
their probable function, underlining the imitation, would seem to be
important. The passage in bar 29 recurs in bar 45. In the latter the crotchet
$e^1$ in the tenor line has a double stroke which the corrector added, but the
corresponding $a^1$ in the alto line is expressed as a minim and without a
single stroke. In mid sixteenth-century sources the single stroke served
several functions unconnected with embellishment; and Benjamin Cosyn
seems to have employed the sign occasionally as a visual aid (drawn
through semibreve note-heads) in his virginal book (*Lbl* R.M. 23.1.4).[21]
Francis Tregian frequently notated semibreves as tied minims in the
Fitzwilliam Virginal Book (see Example 10.6a), a mannerism which con-
ceivably had some visual significance analogous with Cosyn's use of the
single stroke. The relevance of this to the application in question in the
Nevell version of *The Hunt's Up*, however, is a matter for conjecture.

   Later in *The Hunt's Up* (in the seventh variation) the application of signs
is equally intriguing (see Example 10.6c). Four blackened semibreves were
graced originally each with a single stroke drawn through the note-head.
The corrector subsequently added a double stroke and positioned it above
the note-head in each case. A few bars later, however, the corrector added
double strokes above blackened semibreves which had no single strokes.
With reference to the application in the passage quoted at Example 10.6c,
this is another instance of an unusual combination of signs; and although
similar application (i.e. of a single- and double-stroke sign on the same
note) is found in Anne Cromwell's Book and in Tisdale's Book, it is in
music which was entered in these manuscripts over forty years later.[22] It
seems unlikely that the corrector's intention was to replace the single stroke
with a double stroke as no attempt was made to cancel the original sign.

---

[21] For discussion see Hunter, 'The Application of Grace Signs', pp. 16–17.
[22] Anne Cromwell's Book, dated 1638, is owned by the Museum of London, Tangye
   Collection (shelfmark: 46.78/748).

Example 10.7  The Galliard to the Tenth Pavan (Nevell, f. 185; BK 3b, bars 24–5)

Example 10.8  The Second Ground (Nevell, f. 130v; BK 42, bars 113–14)

The conventional method of cancellation, first applied in the Dublin Virginal Manuscript, involved appending short vertical strokes at either end of the sign. Any significance which these single strokes might have had therefore is vitiated by the lack of supportive evidence.

Despite the fact that the application of combined signs in the passages quoted at Example 10.6b and c is probably unintentional, combined signs are given elsewhere in the manuscript. The instances are not numerous and the application involves double-stroke signs only: mainly in pairs, gracing notes which in performance would be taken by different hands. The graced notes are separated mainly by a simple or compound interval composed of either a third or a sixth. Simultaneous execution of these pairs as parallel shakes would provide a satisfactory form of realisation. One pair of double strokes graces notes given on the upper stave, and clearly both graced notes would be taken by the right hand (see Example 10.7). It seems unlikely that the signs indicate separate graces, although a pair of shakes with a common auxiliary note would constitute a practicable solution. However, the implication is possibly a shake involving the alternation of the graced notes. This form of application is not uncommon in other sources and the interval affected is usually either a third or a sixth, occasionally a fourth or a fifth. A shake with a third, the suggested form of realisation of the pair of signs in Example 10.7, is mentioned by Ganassi in his *Opera Intitulata Fontegara* (1535).[23] Oscillating figuration, involving thirds, fourths and larger intervals, is not uncommon in virginalist music and it is possible that a more rapid variety is represented by pairs of double-stroke signs. A further instance of a combination of signs in Nevell involves three double-stroke signs (see Example 10.8). The implied embellishment would seem to be rather elaborate. Realisation of the sign on $d^1$ as an undershake would seem appropriate; the signs on $f\sharp^1$ and $a^1$ possibly indicate a shake involving the alternation of the graced notes.

Where a double stroke is applied to a triad at the beginning or end of a strain it may indicate elaboration of the complete triad rather than a specific grace affecting one note (see for instance The Fourth Pavan, end of the varied repeat of the first strain: Nevell, f. 72; BK 30a, bar 16). The gracing of semibreve triads in Nevell varies: the sign may be positioned above, below, drawn through one of the notes or located between two of the notes. This variation in positioning seems to have been determined largely by the location of the third of the triad: in most cases the double stroke is drawn through or positioned close to the third. There is an interesting addition (in the corrector's hand) in The Galliard to the Second Pavan. At the beginning of the varied repeat of the second strain a triad notated on the upper stave has a double stroke drawn through the stem of the highest note (see Example 10.9). The lowest note of the triad was added by the corrector and it is perhaps surprising that he positioned it on the upper stave rather than locating it on a leger line above the lower stave (in the other source-readings the note is given on or above the lower stave indicating that it would be taken by the left hand). If the triad in Nevell is to be taken by the right hand it would seem that realisation of the double stroke as a shake is very unlikely. It is possible therefore that elaboration of the triad, including a slide (from $g^1$), is implied.

Although the treatment varies, the most frequent application of grace signs is in connection with incidental decoration, and in the main simple graces seem to be required. In certain instances, however, Byrd possibly associated the signs with specific functions. Cadential embellishment is an obvious one and has been mentioned already; and with reference to the passage quoted at Example 10.6b it was noted that the double stroke underlines the imitative writing. Occasionally the application appears to

---

[23] See *Sylvestro Ganassi: Opera Intitulata Fontegara (Venice, 1535)*, ed. Hildemarie Peter (Berlin–Lichterfelde, 1959), p. 87.

Example 10.9  The Galliard to the Second Pavan (Nevell, f. 65v; BK 71b, bars 25–6)

underline a cross-rhythm. This is suggested for instance at the beginning of the tenth variation of the setting of *The Woods so Wild* (see Example 10.10).[24] In *The Carman's Whistle* the double-stroke sign appears to have an important rhythmic function throughout. The application of the sign in this jovial piece suggests that it probably indicates a short, crisp grace. Certainly the application seems designed to underline the lilting quality of the tune and the rhythmic interest in several of the variations (particularly variations 4 and 5). The implied grace would also give impetus to the quaver figure which dominates variation 6 and characterise the sequential decoration in the penultimate variation. This varied usage highlights the integral part which the sign plays as a vital ingredient in the music.

A striking feature of the application of grace signs in *The Carman's Whistle* is the unusual positioning of several single- and double-stroke signs: the signs are drawn below blackened semibreves where one would expect them above. It seems probable that the positioning reveals the intention of the composer. In contrast to the application in *The Hunt's Up* there appears to be no reason to doubt that the subscript single strokes were applied as grace signs. In each case the graced note is approached from the third below (see Example 10.11a). A form of lower-note embellishment would therefore seem to be implied and the subscript positioning of the sign possibly indicates or confirms that the grace should commence on a note below the written note. The implied grace therefore could be a slide or forefall. The corresponding beats in Clement Matchett's Book (*En 9448*) in bars 10 and 22 are graced with double strokes (the only grace sign used in this source); however, the fingering suggests that a form of lower-note embellishment is implied and the positioning of the double stroke below $f^1$ in bar 22 is possibly of some significance. Add. 30486 is the

---

[24]  See also the Passamezzo Pavan (Nevell, f. 98v; BK 2a, bar 88).

Example 10.10 *The Woods so Wild* (Nevell, f. 111v; BK 85, bars 73–4)

only source which gives a corresponding single stroke for one of the bars in question (bar 22); the sign is superscript, positioning which is conventional in Add. 30486 (the single stroke is never drawn through the note-head of a semibreve in this source).

The first of the double strokes which are drawn below the note where superscript positioning would be more usual is given in bar 10 immediately following the first single stroke in subscript position (see Example 10.11a). In bars 46, 50 and 58 there are further subscript double strokes (see Example 10.11b); the positioning is supported by the reading in at least one other source, and in bar 46 the fingering indication (RH4) given in Matchett's Book on the note in question suggests lower-note realisation.

*a)* bars 9–10, 13–14, 21–2

Matchett, ff. 4–4v
Nevell, f. 149

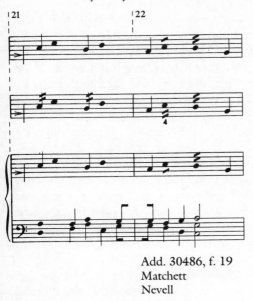

Add. 30486, f. 19
Matchett
Nevell

*b)* bars 46, 50, 58

Forster, pp. 131–2
Matchett, ff. 5v–6
Nevell, ff. 150v–1

Example 10.11 *The Carman's Whistle* (BK 36)

The subscript positioning of the first sign in bars 46 and 50 would seem unnecessary if it was usual to accommodate graces within the line, and in these instances an undershake would involve semitone alternation. The significance of the positioning therefore may be that it indicates a lower-note start to the grace. There are further instances in Matchett's Book and Will Forster's Book (*Lbl* R.M. 24.d.3) of the double stroke drawn below a blackened semibreve where one would expect it above; in conjunction with this positioning RH4 is indicated in bars 29 and 41 in Forster and in bar 62 in Matchett.

The use of the single stroke, the positional variation of signs and indeed the presence of fingering indications on graced notes are features which distinguish the application of grace signs in Nevell from that in earlier sixteenth-century sources. In view of the fact that the approach to the art of gracing in Nevell accords fairly closely with the approach in later virginalist sources, it could be argued that Byrd exercised some influence in this direction.

With certain exceptions the single stroke continued to be used sparingly in later sources.[25] Indeed, in some sources it is not used at all, and there are no single strokes in the pieces which Byrd contributed to *Parthenia*. It seems likely that at least some of the single strokes in Nevell bear the stamp of Byrd's authority; however, by the time of the compilation of *Parthenia* it appears that he preferred to express embellishment in the form of the double-stroke sign only.

The limited use of the single stroke in Nevell suggests that the sign had a more specific function than the double stroke. Clearly, the double stroke, which is applied in a variety of contexts, was regarded as an all-purpose sign. In certain instances it is possible to determine an appropriate form of embellishment. In the main however, the application of signs suggests a free association with embellishment, in keeping with the improvisatory approach which seems to have been encouraged during the virginalist era and indeed throughout the seventeenth century.

[25] Apart from application in Burnett's Book (referred to on pp. 182–3), the incidence of single strokes is high in *F-Pn* Rés. MSS 1185 and 1186 and in Cosyn's Book (*Lbl* R.M. 23.l.4).

# 11

## Some anonymous keyboard pieces
## · considered in relation to Byrd

### OLIVER NEIGHBOUR

The recent publication of EK, an important volume edited by Alan Brown,[1] provides the opportunity to review a question which has long exercised both the editor and the present writer. The new edition is largely composed of hitherto unprinted or uncollected pieces from two important Byrd sources which Brown discusses very fully in his preface. One, *GB-Lbl* Add. 30485, can be shown on the basis of the handwriting and a signature to be almost certainly the work of Thomas Weelkes. The Byrd texts in the first, self-contained section of the manuscript, in which his hand shows earlier characteristics, are exceptionally good, suggesting that he was in close touch with the composer; those in the later part are less reliable. The other source, *GB-Lbl* R.M. 24.d.3, was completed by Will Forster within eighteen months of Byrd's death and contains pieces of his, both early and late, which were not widely circulated; the texts may therefore have derived directly or indirectly from his papers. Forster transmits a number of pieces in unique texts, and others which, though given anonymously, are securely attributed to Byrd elsewhere; to a lesser extent the same is true of Weelkes. It follows that further pieces by Byrd may lie unrecognised among the anonyma in either book.

Brown and I have reached similar conclusions about four pieces in Forster: there need be little hesitation in assigning to Byrd two preludes and an alman (EK 3, 4 and 30),[2] for they are clear examples of his distinctive late manner, while an arrangement of Dowland's *Piper's Galliard* (EK 26),[3] though in many ways characteristic, presents a less clear-cut

---

[1] The Introduction and Critical Commentary to EK are the source for all references to Brown that follow.

[2] See MWB 3, pp. 169–70, 210, 223–4; also Oliver Neighbour, ed., *Three Anonymous Keyboard Pieces Attributed to William Byrd* (London, 1973).

[3] See MWB 3, p. 165.

case because arrangements are inevitably harder to assess than original compositions. In the same tentative category with this piece Brown places two pavans from Weelkes (EK 15 and 16). However, the difficulties of admitting these to the Byrd canon appear to me considerably greater.

The pavans are of the shorter kind with eight rather than sixteen semibreves to each strain. As Brown says, the best point of comparison in Byrd's work is provided by his early pavans on the same pattern, of which there are three: BK 4a, 30a and 73a. The last two of these occur in the later part of Weelkes not far from the pavans EK 15 and 16 and sandwiched between another two, EK 10a and 7a, which need to be taken into account. As a group the four pavans in EK, while not of equal quality, share a certain formal clarity that may appear to ally them more closely with Byrd than with some lesser composers, though it should be remembered that very little keyboard music contemporary with his earlier output survives. But other factors set them apart from BK 4a, 30a and 73a. Although these differ from one another in many respects they share two features with all Byrd's pavans up to the masterpieces of his middle years: virtually every strain contains some imitation or at the very least motivic exchange between the parts, and the melodic peaks of each strain are carefully coordinated (the three strains of the three pieces rise to $f^2$, $f^2$ and $g^2$ respectively, except for strain I of BK 73a, which only reaches $e^2$). By contrast imitation plays a very small part in the pavans from EK, what there is being mostly based on stock descending scale figures, and in none has any thought been given to overall melodic planning. Now while it would be perfectly possible for a composer to write pavans that made considerable use of imitation alongside others that did not, it is hard to imagine that once he had become sensitive to the question of melodic intensification he would ever neglect it, unless for some special technical purpose.

Thus, if any of the four EK pavans are by Byrd, they must represent an earlier stage in his development of the genre than do those hitherto accepted as his. That, of course, is possible, at least in theory, and it might be used as an argument to dispose of other untypical features, since no one can know what Byrd might have tried out at an early date and decided against repeating. All the same, they cannot be lightly dismissed. The opening in the major mode on D of EK 15 is not paralleled elsewhere in Byrd, nor is the doubling of the melody in thirds throughout a strain, as happens in strain II, nor the closely sequential writing of EK 16, strain III. There is nothing specially problematic about EK 7a, a piece not dissimilar to EK 15 and 16 but with less well distributed keyboard textures, a feature it has in common with EK 10a. It is ironical that this last meagre little piece,[4] paired with a galliard that contradicts Byrd's practice in fundamental respects, is the only one of the four to bear an ascription, and to Byrd at that; Brown quite rightly rejected it when editing BK. Of course, EK 15 and 16 are more accomplished pieces than 7a and 10a and may well be by different composers. They are also, if not more accomplished, at least smoother than BK 73a, but paradoxically that too may speak against Byrd's authorship. The pavan BK 73a presents an altogether more varied sequence of events than the anonymous pieces, for in his early cultivation of a genre Byrd often preferred to risk some roughness where ambition conflicted with inexperience, rather than play for safety. In the early section of the manuscript, where Weelkes's lines of communication with Byrd seem to have been particularly strong, there is one more pavan, EK 12a, which belongs to the same general stylistic family as the anonymous pieces while displaying greater imitative activity. It is ascribed to Marchant, no doubt correctly, but had it not been it would certainly have found a place in this discussion, a fact that emphasises the dangers of stylistic attribution at a stage in Byrd's composition of pavans that is only hypothetical.

No more anonymous original compositions in either manuscript lay claim to consideration in relation to Byrd, nor any of the arrangements of instrumental pieces beyond the version of *Piper's Galliard* already mentioned. Four chanson arrangements in Weelkes may also be passed over. The first (EK 45) occurs in the early part of the book, but Byrd, though sufficiently interested in the original composer, Van Wilder, to take a motet of his as a partial model on more than one occasion, was certainly not responsible for the wearisome busyness of the semiquavers or such untypical figures as quavers rocking back and forth on adjacent notes (bars 13, 30). Of the rest, all in the later part of the manuscript, one (EK 44) is known to be of continental origin and the other two (EK 46, 47) are highly elaborate indigenous productions that Brown is inclined to give to Weelkes.

Weelkes and Forster between them transmit arrangements of seven vocal pieces by Byrd himself, a motet and six consort songs (although five of the songs were published by the composer in fully texted form in 1588, the transcriptions all derive from the original consort versions).[5] The most elaborate of the song arrangements is a setting of the famous *Lullaby* (EK 53) in the later part of Weelkes. Decoration has been applied lavishly but fitfully with an inattention to the structure of the piece remote from Byrd's

[4] See MWB 3, pp. 178, 192, 197.
[5] For the original versions see BE 16/14, 22–5; for the remaining song see BE 15/6.

habits of thought. Three of the other Byrd transcriptions form a group in the early part of Weelkes; the rest occur close to one another at the end of Forster. Apart from the motet all are in a very simple style suited to domestic use, but the position of *Care for thy soul*, *If that a sinner's sighs* and *O God but God* (EK 52, 51, 54) in Weelkes, coupled with the fact that the first of these is common to both manuscripts, may indicate an origin for all of them not far removed from the composer. At any rate, it seems worth while to sort through them.

The simplest of all, *O God but God*, is mostly a straight intabulation of the full five-part texture, unadorned save for a sprinkling of ornaments; the result would have been much the same whoever undertook it. *Care for thy soul* and *If that a sinner's sighs* are treated a little more freely. The texture tends to be reduced to four parts, passing notes are removed or added in about equal measure, and there is decoration in the treble at important cadences. *My mind to me a kingdom is* and *Susanna fair* (EK 49, 50, both in Forster) differ from *Care for thy soul* and *If that a sinner's sighs* in two respects. The singing part in the originals is the top line, to which the arranger adds no more than some ornaments and passing notes. This precludes even the modest decoration noted in the other two songs, where the singing part is the second from the top and often loses its identity in the keyboard texture or drops out altogether. The second point is that *My mind to me* and *Susanna fair*, unlike the other two, are transposed: the first is copied twice consecutively, once at original pitch and once a tone higher, while the second is a tone below its original. All this strongly suggests that their purpose was accompanimental: it is hard to see any reason for writing out a self-sufficient piece at two levels, and the sound of a voice doubled by a slightly ornamented line on the harpsichord would surely have been perfectly acceptable. Moreover the version of *My mind to me* seems too sketchy, too damagingly impoverished harmonically and contrapuntally, to be meant to stand on its own (or to have been made by the composer for any purpose whatever).

On the other hand *Care for thy soul* and *If that a sinner's sighs* may well have been intended, as Brown proposes, as independent keyboard pieces, though presumably for those already familiar with the original songs. There is a striking passage in the latter (bars 18–19) where the gap between two high-lying phrases has been bridged by moving forward the melodic peak in the second to produce a lengthy decorated line in the run-up to the halfway cadence, with tenor and bass effectively finishing its work (bars 20–1). Just possibly Byrd's hand is to be detected here; the procedures are not uncharacteristic, but it is odd that nothing comparable happens in the second half of the transcription. Perhaps he left it to someone else to finish, or leant over a pupil's shoulder to make an improvement. Idle fancies, but they serve to bring home the fact that with such slender evidence nothing very useful can be said.

The rest of this essay will be concerned with the remaining Byrd transcription in Forster (EK 48), a work of an altogether different calibre. The original is the motet *O quam gloriosum est regnum*,[6] published in the *Cantiones sacrae* of 1589 but probably composed about 1580.[7] Brown does not include the transcription in his list of possible Byrd pieces in the introduction to his edition, but in the commentary remarks that 'it would be rash at this stage to attribute the arrangement to Byrd himself', thereby admitting that the idea has crossed his mind. And indeed the thought imposes itself, even if the stage at which such an attribution can be definitively accepted or rejected may never be reached. Byrd's highly imitative motet has, of course, little in common with the songs and chansons which form the basis of the transcriptions so far discussed, but the distance separating the keyboard versions is only partly dictated by the originals. The arranger of the motet could, after all, have contented himself with a simple intabulation, or he could have cut through the texture with toccata-like runs in the manner of the chanson transcriptions (though not without doing violence to the sobriety that decorum presumably demanded in a sacred setting). In fact, while in no way shunning elaboration, he had entirely different ends in view.

There is nothing distinctive about his choice of figuration in itself. It is drawn from the common stock employed in countless continental transcriptions from the mid sixteenth century onwards. The opening notes of an imitative point are usually left plain at each entry for ease of recognition, decoration being applied to its tail; this practice too was well established. What is uncommon is the consistent attempt to ensure that no entry is entirely lost, and that as far as possible each shall follow through to its decorated continuation where the model does not itself deviate. The resulting keyboard texture is dense, and the level character of the figuration, which consists for the most part of quaver groups in largely conjunct motion confined within a narrow orbit, contrapuntally determined. Having decided upon this mode of transcription, how far did the arranger simply work through the motet applying it more or less automatically until

6  See BE 2, pp. 187–201. The barring of the motet in this edition corresponds precisely with that of the transcription in EK, so that the same bar references serve for either.
7  See MWB 1, pp. 129, 155–6.

he got to the end? To answer that question it will be necessary to follow fairly closely in his footsteps.

The first and longer of the two parts of Byrd's motet divides into four sections, each marked off from the next by a strong cadence and the introduction of fresh words and music. The first section itself encompasses three text fragments and musical ideas, none of them dwelt on for long. The arranger keeps his elaboration relatively free: for instance he postpones decorating the entries in the opening exposition until the point where each takes its own course. In compensation he introduces motivic echoes between lines which are not connected by the imitative structure of the music, a procedure employed quite frequently throughout the transcription for additional coherence. In the same spirit he even introduces a new entry of a principal point on the analogy of one three bars later (bars 8, 11). The second section (at 'amicti stolis albis'), following a firm tonic cadence that the arranger saw no need to emphasise (bar 22), consists of an exposition and strettos on a single subject. This receives characteristic decoration close enough to the original line to stand almost unchanged at every appearance. Since the third section of the motet (from 'sequuntur agnum') is related in its cell-like structure and inexact imitation to the first, and the fourth (from 'laudantes Deum') shares strict imitation with the second, the arranger had only to continue as before.

But he did not do so. The first sign of change appears at the dominant cadence that closes the second section (bar 34), which overlaps the first entry of the next point. To clarify the break, which the absence of a sung text tends to obscure, the arranger draws attention to the cadence with a flurry of semiquavers. It is the first of a number of such passages, all resembling the quaver decoration in being largely conjunct and somewhat limited in range; all are confined to the top line of the texture and are carefully placed to define the structure. They play an important role in the third section. The motet employs two soprano parts of equal range, and its particular character derives in part from their antiphonal exchanges of phrases reaching up to $f^2$. The arranger seizes on this feature in the third section, throwing the four $f^2$s into relief by using a generally less elaborate keyboard texture than in the first section but introducing runs of semiquavers. The first of these decorates the first $f^2$ (bar 36), but the next two are low-lying passages placed between almost unadorned phrases containing $f^2$s, which stand out all the more prominently by contrast. Byrd has given the cue here: the descent from the second $f^2$ pauses on a long held $c^2$ a fourth lower (bar 39) which acts like a ceiling, keeping the other parts low. The transcriber translates this $c^2$ into low semiquavers, as he does the exactly comparable one (bar 57) that marks the trough between two more widely spaced $f^2$s (bars 53 and 59) in the fourth and final section of the Prima Pars. In other respects the strict imitations[8] of this section are decorated similarly to those in the second section except at the end, where three entries which in the motet take a slightly quieter form receive extremely exuberant decoration, twice with semiquavers. Semiquavers signal the final cadences of the last two sections, as of the second.

The words of the Secunda Pars begin with a list of the deity's attributes that Byrd sets in short cells with rising points of harmonic arrival (from the tonic opening to C, G and D), a tauter kind of construction well reflected in the transcription. The arrival on D initiates a long phrase circling round $d^2$ and $f^2$, answered antiphonally in very similar terms by the other soprano; the passage ends with a strong cadence on D (bar 90). In the motet this cadence is not especially emphatic, for the next section (to bar 100) continues with more antiphonal high $f^2$s and concludes with another cadence on D. Yet in the transcription the arranger converts bar 90 into a turning point: he ends the first phrase of the preceding antiphony with three minims' worth of consecutive semiquavers and the second with double that number, and since this is by far the longest such passage in the whole arrangement (and the last) it invests the cadence with enormous weight. Clearly he has a special strategy in mind.

In the motet the approach to the last of the D cadences (bar 100) is somewhat protracted, with the top line in slow values and held to a relatively low level. The quieter flow of the music prepares for the final section ('in saecula saeculorum. Amen'), where the entries of the new point are initially widely spaced and the top line regains height relatively slowly. What the arranger has done at bar 90 is to start this broadening process earlier. The long outcrop of semiquaver divisions does not merely create a stronger sense of caesura than exists in the motet at this point, but initiates a new technical procedure that plays a leading role right through to the end of the piece. Up to this point divisions have been mostly well distributed through the parts; single lines in even quavers have not exceeded four minims in length and there has been no precedent for the six minims of unbroken semiquavers leading to the bar 90 cadence. But from here on the principle of line assumes increasing prominence, starting immediately with five minims of quavers at the outset of the new section (bars 90–1), and the music lengthens its stride. The quaver line in bars 96–7, echoed an octave

---

[8] In bar 55 the arranger starts the bass entry correctly on F instead of on the A which Byrd was obliged to substitute in the motet because the range of the piece did not go lower.

lower at bars 99–100, leaves no doubt that the arranger has arrived at his linear concept by analogy with Byrd's treatment of the cadence at bar 100.

The looser sequence of entries in the final section of the motet would have made the application of a uniform decorative pattern a simple matter. But at this late stage the arranger is no longer interested in reflecting his model so precisely: he is intent rather upon achieving a comparable build-up towards the close in keyboard terms. In his concern for melodic continuity he even omits the odd entry (bar 111). This development reaches its culmination where the sopranos rise to their last exchange of $f^2$s before the coda and the musical texture lightens with a stretto on the tailpiece of the point (the word 'saeculorum') in bars 111–17. The arranger lets the $f^2$s stand out undecorated, but turns again to unbroken quavers to accompany them, first a line of four minims' length in the bass and then one of no fewer than eight minims in the tenor. Their powerful forward movement is absorbed by two bars of rising figures in even crochets which are likewise unprecedented in the vocabulary of the transcription and entirely replace the vocal stretto. Arrangement and model than fall into step again for the plagal coda, where the diminution earns a well-deserved special mention from Brown.

What evidence about the arranger has this investigation brought to light? He was thoroughly versed in keyboard writing and musician enough to apply decoration contrapuntally without detriment to the integrity of Byrd's workmanship; he was also remarkably sensitive to the subtleties of Byrd's formal articulation and consistent in his approach to interpreting them in keyboard terms. Yet the possessor of such qualities did not, strictly speaking, need to be a composer. It is the attempt to achieve greater clarity through changes in structural emphasis, especially in the highly imaginative treatment of the later sections, that is difficult to account for except as the work of the composer himself. Above all the extraordinary lucidity with which the linear principle that is to govern the end of the transcription is introduced and followed through is characteristic of Byrd, particularly in his instrumental work, and hard to match elsewhere.

How the piece is to be understood is another question, and one no less difficult than that of authorship. It is, of course, part of a wider one that may be asked about coloured intabulations in general. The successive stages of a through-composed vocal composition can make little sense deprived of the words that occasioned them; the listener is presumably supposed to know the model well enough to supply the missing element. The arranger of *O quam gloriosum* demands a great deal of his audience, unless indeed he was writing primarily for himself. Although the sixteenth-century ear may have been adept at picking out well-covered strands and the player at making them audible, there are contexts where the listener would need to know the model by heart to hear everything that the transcription retains in its denser textures. Where imitative entries are masked by more florid lines and other supporting voices they are hard to recognise till their decorated continuations bring them into prominence, and even then motivic correspondence with free parts sometimes makes their status difficult to disentangle. It may be argued that not everything that has been woven in is meant to be heard. Perhaps not, but only close listening to the structure of the music will save it from monotony, a danger which the arranger clearly appreciated and took ingenious and often successful measures to counteract.

The final impression is one of uncertainty in the mind of the arranger as to how the main lines of the musical argument should be defined. This state of affairs is extremely uncharacteristic of Byrd's keyboard music at any period, but since his entire instrumental output bears witness to his disbelief in vocal forms as valid models for textless composition and to his originality in devising self-sufficient structures, it does not necessarily argue against his authorship. He might well have been prepared to experiment with a genre of which he disapproved. He was not greatly attracted to the madrigal, yet he tried it out and learned from it. If his labours on the transcription served only to confirm a long-held conviction he might not have felt them misplaced.

# 12

## A Byrd discography

### MICHAEL GREENHALGH

#### Introduction

##### Order of entries

This Byrd discography is a chronological listing of recordings of individual works. It follows the order of Byrd's works in *The New Grove Dictionary of Music and Musicians* vol. 3 (London, 1980), pp. 545–52, as this is the most readily accessible comprehensive list with details of editions. However, for convenience, individual items within headed sections are here always listed in alphabetical order. Recordings are of complete works unless the title is prefaced by an asterisk (*), when the portion(s) recorded are cited after the title. Such recordings are entered in descending order of portions recorded, thereafter alphabetically. Where a work exists both in a version for several voices and in one for solo voice and consort of viols, i.e. an earlier consort song version, entries for recordings of this earlier form are prefaced by a dagger (†).

##### Key to entries

Recordings of every work are listed in chronological order of year of issue (not necessarily date of recording) and, within year, in alphabetical order of company or label. The initial entry is the identifying, though not always sole, performing artist, with the name of the director following an oblique stroke (/). In further identification of artists and the instruments on which they perform, the following abbreviations are used, with the suffix 's' always denoting more than one: (b) [for] bass; (bar) baritone; (c) contralto; (cha) chamber; (clvc) clavichord; (clvg) claviorganum; (cnr) cantor; (ct) countertenor; (hist) historic, i.e. sixteenth, seventeenth or eighteenth century; (hpsc) harpsichord; (ms) mezzo-soprano; (msr) muselar; (org) organ; (pf) pianoforte; (rec) recorder; (s) soprano; (spt) spinet; (t) tenor; (tr) treble; (virg) virginal; (vdb) viola da bracchia; (vl) viol.

The timing of the performance is then given, with a minute mark (') dividing minutes and seconds. Where timings are the discographer's they are enclosed in square brackets ([ ]), as are all such enrichments of entries. When no timing is given ([nt]), this is because the recording has not been heard by the discographer and was not in 1989 available for public listening at the British Library National Sound Archive, 29 Exhibition Road, South Kensington, London SW7 2AS, where the reader is reminded that most material listed here may be heard by appointment. Next in the entry, when known, the edition used for the performance is cited, prefaced by 'ed', as are thereafter the location and date of the recording, introduced by 'rec'.

The company or label, the technical characteristic of the recording [mono (monaural), or stereo (stereophonic), which may be quad (quadra-phonic), digital or digitally remastered] and the catalogue number is then supplied, followed by the designation of format. The following abbre-viations are used for formats: (cd) compact disc; (ep) extended playing [45rpm] 7–inch disc; (lp) long playing [33rpm] 12–inch disc; (mc) musicassette; (sep) short playing [45rpm] 7–inch disc; (slp) long playing [33rpm] 10-inch disc; (sp) short playing [78rpm] 12-inch disc; (ssp) short playing [78rpm] 10-inch disc. When the recording is part of an issue only available as a set, the numbers of the set are cited. The year of publication is stated following every catalogue number, with the label, numbers and dates applying to any reissues following the initial entry in chronological order. Thus a recording's publication history is readily apparent. It is to be assumed that reissues of mono and stereo material are stereo.

### Inclusion policy

This discography lists all recordings of Byrd's music which have ever been commercially available in the United Kingdom. Its terminal date is the end of 1988. Many recordings were not made in the UK but provenance is only cited for those not generally distributed and thus only obtainable from import specialists. Misattributed works are not included. Instru-mental arrangements of Byrd's keyboard music are also omitted, including contemporary transcriptions for lute, but performances of analogous scale on instruments other than those for which Byrd wrote (e.g. keyboard works played on the piano and works for consort of viols played by consort of recorders or broken consort) are listed.

### Further discographical sources

Releases after 1988 can be traced through the annual indexes to the *Gramophone* for the United Kingdom and the *Schwann Record and Tape Guide* for the United States. More extensive treatment of United States and European material will be found in:

Francis Clough and G. J. Cuming, *The World's Encyclopaedia of Recorded Music* (London, 1952, includes first supplement; second supplement, 1953; third supplement, 1957; reprint, 3 vols., Westport, 1970).

James Coover and Richard Colvig, *Medieval and Renaissance Music on Long-playing Records* (Detroit, 1964, includes first supplement; supplement 1962–1971, Detroit, 1973).

Trevor Croucher, *Early Music Discography: from Plainsong to the Sons of Bach* (2 vols., London, 1981).

Marilou Kratzenstein and Jerald Hamilton, *Four Centuries of Organ Music, from the Robertsbridge Codex through the Baroque Era: an Annotated Discography* (Detroit, 1984).

Timothy Day, *A Discography of Tudor Church Music* (London, 1989).

See also the selective critical discographies in Richard Turbet, 'Byrd on record', *Brio* 20 (1983), pp. 41–5 and the same author's *William Byrd: a Guide to Research* (New York, 1987), pp. 283–94.

# Discography

*Mass settings*

[3, 4, 5vv ordinary followed by Gradualia propers]

Mass, 3vv
1. Renaissance Singers/Michael Howard [17'36]. Argo mono RG 114 [lp 1958].
2. King's College Cambridge Choir/David Willcocks [21'28]; ed Willcocks; rec King's College Chapel. Argo mono RG 362, stereo ZRG 5362 (lp 1963); ZK 53–4 (2 lps 1979); 4117231 (lp), 4117234 (mc 1984).
3. Pro Cantione Antiqua/Bruno Turner 21'12; rec Schlosskirche Schleiden 4/1972. Archiv stereo 2533113 (lp 1972).
4. Deller Consort/Alfred Deller (ct) 20'34; rec All Saints Church Boughton Aluph. Bach Guild stereo HM6 (lp 1975); Harmonia Mundi France HM 40211 (mc 1977); HM 211–13 (3 lps 1979).
5. Hilliard Ensemble/Paul Hillier (bar) 20'32; rec St James Church Clerkenwell 10/1983. EMI stereo digital EX 2700963 (2 lps), TC-EX 2700969 (2 mcs 1984); CDS 7492058 (2 cds 1987).
6. Tallis Scholars/Peter Phillips 17'44; ed Phillips; rec Merton College Chapel Oxford. Gimell stereo digital BYRD 345 (2 lps), ZCBYRD 345 (mc 1984); CDGIM 345 (cd 1985).

*Mass, 3vv: Kyrie & Sanctus
*1. English Singers [2'24]; ed Fellowes. His Master's Voice mono E 290 [ssp 1923].

*Mass, 3vv: Gloria
*2. Liverpool Cathedral Choir/Ian Tracey [4'09]; rec Liverpool Cathedral 10/1987. Solitaire stereo digital SOLI 107 [lp 1988].

Mass, 4vv
1. Fleet Street Choir/Thomas Lawrence [26'30]; ed Lawrence. Decca mono LX 3046 [slp 1951]; LXT 2919 [lp 1954].

2. Renaissance Singers/Michael Howard [21'45]. Argo mono RG 42 [lp 1957].

3. Montreal Bach Chorale Choir/George Little 22'15. Vox mono DL 880 (lp 1962).

4. King's College Cambridge Choir/David Willcocks [26'24]; ed Willcocks; rec King's College Chapel. Argo mono RG 362, stereo ZRG 5362 (lp 1963); ZK 53–4 (2 lps), D148D4 (4 lps), K148K43 (4 mcs 1979); 4117231 (lp), 4117234 (mc 1984).

5. Westminster Abbey Choristers/William McKie [23'50]; rec Westminster Abbey 11–15/6/1962. Archiv mono APM 14301, stereo SAPM 198301 (lp 1964).

6. Deller Consort/Alfred Deller (ct) 23'07; rec All Saints Church Boughton Aluph. Harmonia Mundi France stereo HM 40212 (mc 1968); Bach Guild HM6 (lp 1975); Harmonia Mundi France HM 211–13 (3 lps 1979).

7. Christ Church Cathedral Oxford Choir/Simon Preston [27'14]; [rec Merton College Chapel Oxford 4/1976]. Argo stereo ZRG 858 (lp), KZRC 858 (mc 1977).

8. St Margaret's Westminster Singers/Richard Hickox [27'04]; [rec St Augustine's Church Kilburn 11/1976]. RCA stereo RL25070 (lp 1977).

9. Boston Church of the Advent Choir/Edith Ho 24'48; rec Boston Church of the Advent 1982. [Wilmington Mass.:] Afka stereo S 4676 (lp 1982).

10. Quink [21'07]. Etcetera stereo digital ETC 1031 (lp), XTC 1031 (mc 1985).

11. Pro Cantione Antiqua/Bruno Turner [24'41]; rec St John-at-Hackney Church 5/1979. Libra stereo LRS 143 (mc 1986).

12. Hilliard Ensemble/Paul Hillier (bar) 26'03; rec St James Church Clerkenwell 10/1983. EMI stereo digital EX 2700963 (2 lps), TC-EX 2700969 (2 mcs 1984); CDS 7492058 (2 cds 1987).

13. Tallis Scholars/Peter Phillips 22'00; ed Phillips; rec Merton College Chapel Oxford. Gimell stereo digital BYRD 345 (2 lps), ZCBYRD 345 (mc 1984); CDGIM 345 (cd 1985).

14. St John's College Cambridge Choir/George Guest 24'40; rec St John's College Chapel 3/1986. EMI stereo digital EMX 2104 (lp), TC-EMX 2104 (mc), CD-EMX 9505 (cd 1986).

*Mass, 4vv: Sanctus, Benedictus & Agnus Dei
 *1. King's College Cambridge Choir/Boris Ord [7'13]; ed Fellowes; rec King's College Chapel. Columbia mono LB 91 [ssp 1950].

*Mass, 4vv: Agnus Dei
 *2. English Singers [3'35]; ed Fellowes. His Masters Voice mono E 290 [ssp 1923].

 *3. Worcester Cathedral Choir/Christopher Robinson [3'31]; rec Worcester Cathedral 1966. BBC mono REB 97M (lp 1971).

 *4. King's College Cambridge Choir/David Willcocks 4'15; ed Willcocks; rec King's College Chapel. Decca stereo SPA 335 (lp 1974) [from 4].

Mass, 5vv

1. Fleet Street Choir/Thomas Lawrence [26'11]; ed Lawrence. Decca mono K 1058–60 [3 sps 1942]; LX 3060 [slp 1951]; LXT 2919 [lp 1954].
2. Renaissance Singers/Michael Howard [23'44]. Argo mono RG 75 [lp 1956].
3. King's College Cambridge Choir/David Willcocks 26'12; rec King's College Chapel. Argo mono RG 226, stereo ZRG 5226 (lp 1960); ZK 53–4 (2 lps 1979); 4143661 (lp), 4143664 (mc 1985).
4. Montreal Bach Chorale Choir/George Little 21'55. Vox mono DL 880 (lp 1962).
5. Elizabethan Singers/Louis Halsey [23'00]. Pan mono PAN 6204, stereo SPAN 6204 (lp 1967).
6. Christ Church Cathedral Oxford Choir/Simon Preston [26'43]; [rec Merton College Chapel Oxford 4/1976]. Argo stereo ZRG 858 (lp), KZRC 858 (mc 1977).
7. St Margaret's Westminster Singers/Richard Hickox [27'55]; [rec St Augustine's Church Kilburn 11/1976]. RCA stereo RL 25070 (lp 1977).
8. Deller Consort/Alfred Deller (ct) 22'58; rec All Saints Church Boughton Aluph. Harmonia Mundi France stereo HM 213 (lp 1978), HM 211–3 (3 lps 1979).
9. King's College Cambridge Choir/Philip Ledger [24'52]; rec King's College Chapel. HMV stereo digital ASD 4104 (lp), TCC-ASD 4104 (mc 1982).
10. 'Madrigal' Ensemble/Lydia Davydova (s) 25'32; rec 1980. [Moscow:] Melodiya stereo C10 19015000 (lp 1983).
11. Hilliard Ensemble/Paul Hillier (bar) 26'36; rec St James Church Clerkenwell 10/1983. EMI stereo digital EX 2700963 (2 lps), TC-EX 2700969 (2 mcs 1984); CDS 7492058 (2 cds 1987).
12. Tallis Scholars/Peter Phillips 22'17; ed Phillips; rec Merton College Chapel Oxford. Gimell stereo digital BYRD 345 (2 lps), ZCBYRD 345 (mc 1984); CDGIM 345 (cd 1985).
13. St John's College Cambridge Choir/George Guest 23'42; rec St John's College Chapel 3/1986. EMI stereo digital EMX 2104 (lp), TC-EMX 2104 (mc), CD-EMX 9505 (cd 1986).

*Mass, 5vv: Agnus Dei

*1. St George's Singers [2'47]; ed Fellowes. Columbia mono 5547 [ssp 1929].

*Mass, 5vv: Sanctus [sung in English]

*2. Coronation Choir [2'11]; ed Fellowes; rec King George VI coronation Westminster Abbey 12/5/1937. His Master's Voice mono RG 1–15 [15 sps 1937].

Assumption of the BVM

1. Chanticleer/Joseph Jennings (ct) 16'49; rec St Ignatius Church San Fran-

cisco 6/1986. Harmonia Mundi USA stereo digital HMC 5182 (lp), HMC
405182 (mc), HMC 905182 (cd 1987).

Easter Day
1.    Chanticleer/Joseph Jennings (ct) 18'18; rec St Ignatius Church San Franci-
      sco 6/1986. Harmonia Mundi USA stereo digital HMC 5182 (lp), HMC
      405182 (mc), HMC 905182 (cd 1987).

Nativity of the BVM
1.    Elizabethan Singers/Louis Halsey [14'36]. Pan mono PAN 6204, stereo
      SPAN 6204 (lp 1967).

Nativity of our Lord Jesus Christ
1.    Clare College Cambridge Choir/Timothy Brown [22'38]; rec Clare College
      Chapel. Meridian stereo E 77109 (lp), KE 77109 (mc 1985).

*Alphabetical list of Latin works*

Ad Dominum cum tribularer
1.    Tallis Scholars/Peter Phillips [10'25]; ed Phillips; rec All Hallows Church
      Hampstead. Fanfare stereo FR 2197 (lp 1977); United Artists UACL
      10005 [lp 1978].

Alleluia, Ascendit Deus
1.    Deller Consort/Alfred Deller (ct) 1'15; rec All Saints Church Boughton
      Aluph. Harmonia Mundi France stereo HM 40212 (mc 1968); HM
      221–13 (3 lps 1979).
2.    King's College Cambridge Choir/Philip Ledger [1'13]; rec King's College
      Chapel. His Master's Voice stereo ASD 3764 [lp], TC-ASD 3764 [mc
      1980].

Alleluia, Cognoverunt. Alleluia, Caro mea
1.    Deller Consort/Alfred Deller (ct) 3'22; rec All Saints Church Boughton
      Aluph 1970. Harmonia Mundi France stereo HM 213 (lp 1978); HM
      211–13 (3 lps 1979).

Aspice, Domine, de sede sancta tua
1.    New College Oxford Choir/Edward Higginbottom 4'56. CRD stereo
      digital CRDD 1120 (lp), CRDCD 4120 (mc), CRD 3408 (cd 1984).

Aspice, Domine, quia facta est desolata civitas
1.    Cantores in Ecclesia/Michael Howard [5'25]. L'Oiseau-Lyre stereo SOL
      311 (lp 1969).
2.    Deller Consort/Mark Deller (ct) 6'01; rec 4/1980. Harmonia Mundi France
      stereo HM 1053 (lp 1981).

Assumpta est Maria ... Dominum. Alleluia
1.  Renaissance Singers/Michael Howard [1'29]. Argo mono RG 42 [lp 1957].
2.  Saltire Singers [1'15]; rec London. [New York:] Lyrichord mono LL 156, stereo LLST 7156 [lp 1966].
3.  Chanticleer/Joseph Jennings (ct) [2'21]; rec St Ignatius Church San Francisco 6/1986. Harmonia Mundi USA stereo digital HMC 5182 (lp), HMC 405182 (mc), HMC 905182 (cd 1987).

Attollite portas
1.  Cantores in Ecclesia/Michael Howard [4'54]. L'Oiseau-Lyre stereo SOL 311 (lp 1969).
2.  Deller Consort/Mark Deller (ct) 4'50; rec 4/1980. Harmonia Mundi France stereo HM 1053 (lp 1981).

Ave Maria ... fructus ventris tui
1.  Renaissance Singers/Michael Howard [1'45]. Argo mono RG 42 [lp 1957].
2.  Deller Consort/Alfred Deller (ct) 1'55; rec All Saints Church Boughton Aluph 1970. Harmonia Mundi France stereo HM 213 (lp 1978); HM 211–13 (3 lps 1979).

Ave regina
1.  Westminster Cathedral Choir [2'54]. His Master's Voice mono C 1606 [sp 1928].
2.  Deller Consort/Alfred Deller (ct) 5'15; rec All Saints Church Boughton Aluph 1970. Harmonia Mundi France stereo HM 40211 (mc 1977); HM 211–13 (3 lps 1979).
3.  Chanticleer/Joseph Jennings (ct) 4'31; rec St Ignatius Church San Francisco 6/1986. Harmonia Mundi USA stereo digital HMC 5182 (lp), HMC 405182 (mc), HMC 905182 (cd 1987).

Ave verum corpus
1.  English Singers [2'54]; ed Fellowes. His Master's Voice mono E 305 [ssp 1925].
2.  Westminster Cathedral Choir [3'58]. His Master's Voice mono C 1606 [sp 1928].
3.  Fleet Street Choir/ Thomas Lawrence [4'17]. Decca mono K 1081 [sp 1942].
4.  King's College Cambridge Choir/Boris Ord [4'32]; ed Fellowes; rec King's College Chapel. Columbia mono LX 1380 [sp 1951].
5.  St Paul's Cathedral Choir/John Dykes Bower [4'29]. Columbia mono 33CX 1193 [lp 1954]; SCD 2195 [sep 1963].
6.  Renaissance Singers/Michael Howard [4'19]. Argo mono RG 75 [lp 1956].
7.  King's College Cambridge Choir/David Willcocks 4'24; ed Terry; rec King's College Chapel. Argo mono RG 226, stereo ZRG 5226 (lp 1960);

SPA 245 [lp], KCSP 245 [mc 1970]; ZK 53–4 (2 lps 1979); 4143661 (lp), 4143664 (mc 1985).

8.   Ely Cathedral Choir/Arthur Wills [4'15]; rec Ely Cathedral. Alpha mono AVM 015 (lp 1964).

9.   King's College Cambridge Choir/David Willcocks 4'35; rec King's College Chapel. His Master's Voice mono ALP 2094, stereo ASD 641 (lp 1965); CFP 4144811 [lp], CFP 4144814 [mc 1985].

10.   Westminster Abbey Choir/Douglas Guest [4'07]; ed Morehen. His Master's Voice mono CLP 3536, stereo CSD 3536 (lp 1966).

11.   Saltire Singers [3'20]; rec London. [New York:] Lyrichord mono LL 156, stereo LLST 7156 [lp 1966].

12.   Bourne Singers [4'17]; ed Grayson. Decca mono ADD 163, stereo SSD 163 (lp 1967).

13.   Deller Consort/Alfred Deller (ct) 4'21; rec All Saints Church Boughton Aluph. Harmonia Mundi France stereo HM 40212 (mc 1968); HM 211–13 (3 lps 1979).

14.   Llandaff Cathedral Choir/Robert Joyce [nt]. Welsh Qualiton mono QUAD 102, stereo SQUAD 102 [lp 1969].

15.   Liverpool Cathedral Choir/Ronald Woan [3'55]; rec Liverpool Cathedral. Abbey LPB 663 (lp 1970).

16.   New College Oxford Choir/David Lumsden [4'37]. Abbey stereo LPB 751 (lp 1976).

17.   All Saints Church Maidstone Choir/Reginald Hughes [3'28]; rec All Saints Church Maidstone. Abbey stereo LPB 763 (lp 1976).

18.   King's Singers [3'43]; rec EMI studios Abbey Road London 1976. His Master's Voice stereo/quad CSD 3779 (lp), TC-CSD 3779 (mc 1977).

19.   St Mary's Church Woodford Choir/Robert Munns [4'17]; rec St Mary's Church Woodford 1976. Wealden stereo WS 122 (lp 1977).

20.   Salisbury Cathedral Choir/Richard Seal 4'10; rec Salisbury Cathedral 3/1979. Meridan stereo E 77025 (lp), KE 77025 (mc 1977); digitally remastered CDE 84025 [cd 1987].

21.   Southwell Minster Choir/Kenneth Beard [4'36]; rec Southwell Minster 7/1979. Rainbow stereo RSL 126 (lp 1979).

22.   Wells Cathedral Choir/Anthony Crossland [nt]. Exon Audio stereo EAS 25 [lp 1981].

23.   Boston Church of the Advent Choir/Edith Ho 4'37; rec Boston Church of the Advent Choir. [Wilmington Mass.:] Afka stereo S 4676 (lp 1982).

24.   University College Durham Choir/Jonathan Newell [4'31]; rec Norman Chapel Durham Castle. Alpha stereo APS 327 (lp 1982).

25.   Gibraltar Cathedral Youth Choir/Michael Davis [4'08]; rec Gibraltar Cathedral 5/1983. Alpha stereo APS 347 (lp 1983).

26.   Hilliard Ensemble/Paul Hillier (bar) 3'57; rec St James Church Clerkenwell 10/1983. EMI stereo digital EX 2700963 (2 lps), TC-EX 2700969 (2 mcs 1984); CDS 7492058 (2 cds 1987).

27.   Wells Cathedral Choir/Anthony Crossland [4'30]; rec Wells Cathedral 5/1984. Alpha ACA 535 [lp], CACA 535 (mc 1985).

28.   Tallis Scholars/Peter Phillips 4'17; ed Phillips; rec Merton College Chapel Oxford. Gimell stereo digital BYRD 345 (2 lps), ZCBYRD 345 (mc 1984); CDGIM 345 (cd 1985).

29.   Quink 3'44. Etcetera stereo digital ETC 1031 (lp), XTC 1031 (mc 1985).

30.   Pro Cantione Antiqua/Bruno Turner [4'38]; rec St John-at-Hackney Church 5/1979. Libra stereo LRS 143 (mc 1986).

31.   Belfast Cathedral Choir/Andrew Padmore [nt]; rec St Anne's Cathedral Belfast 6/1987. Alpha stereo ACA 566 (lp), CACA 566 (mc 1987).

32.   Jesus College Cambridge Mixed Choir/David Swinson [4'28]; rec Jesus College Chapel 6/1987. Alpha stereo ACA 568 (lp 1987).

33.   Corpus Christi College Cambridge Choir/Mark Lee [nt]; rec Corpus Christi College 6/1987. Alpha stereo ACA 569 (lp 1987).

34.   Beverley Minster Choir/Alan Spedding [nt]. Banks Music York stereo digital HAR 842 [lp], HAC 842 [mc 1988].

35.   Cambridge Singers/John Rutter 3'39; rec Lady Chapel Ely Cathedral 10/1982. Collegium stereo digital COLC 107 (mc), COLCD 107 (cd 1988).

36.   Liverpool Cathedral Choir/Ian Tracey [nt]; rec Liverpool Cathedral. Solitaire stereo digital SOLI 102 [lp 1988].

## Beata es, virgo Maria

1.   Elizabethan Singers/Louis Halsey 2'44. Pan mono PAN 6204, stereo SPAN 6204 (lp 1967).

2.   William Byrd Choir/Gavin Turner 2'45. Philips stereo 9502030 (lp 1981).

## Beata virgo

1.   Renaissance Singers/Michael Howard [2'42]. Argo mono RG 42 [lp 1957].

2.   Deller Consort/Alfred Deller (ct) [3'37]; rec All Saints Church Boughton Aluph 1970. Harmonia Mundi France stereo HM 211–13 (3 lps 1979).

3.   Clare College Cambridge Choir/Timothy Brown [2'54]; rec Clare College Chapel. Meridian stereo E 77109 (lp), KE 77109 (mc 1985).

## Beata viscera

1.   Ambrosian Singers/John McCarthy [2'36]. Delyse mono ECB 3204, stereo DS 3204 (lp 1968); L'Oiseau-Lyre OLS 153 [lp 1973].

2.   Elizabethan Singers/Louis Halsey 2'36. Pan mono PAN 6204, stereo SPAN 6204 (lp 1967).

## Beati mundo corde

1.   William Byrd Choir/Gavin Turner 3'18. Philips stereo 9502030 (lp 1981).

Benedicta et venerabilis
1.      Elizabethan Singers/Louis Halsey [1'30]. Pan mono PAN 6204, stereo SPAN 6204 (lp 1967).

Christe qui lux es . . . praedicans/Precamur
1.      York Minster Choir/Edward Bairstow [3'01]; rec York Minster. His Master's Voice mono C 1334 [sp 1927].
2.      Renaissance Singers/Michael Howard [3'15]. Argo mono RG 75 [lp 1956].
3.      [London] Carmelite Priory Choir/John McCarthy [3'35]. His Master's Voice mono CLP 1895, stereo CSD 1617 (lp 1965).
4.      Deller Consort/Alfred Deller (ct) 4'55; rec All Saints Church Boughton Aluph 1970. Harmonia Mundi France stereo HM 213 (lp 1978); HM 211–13 (3 lps 1979).
5.      Jeremy Ovenden (tr), Guildford Cathedral Choir/Phillip Moore [3'51]; rec Guildford Cathedral 6/1982. Priory stereo PR 117 (lp 1982).
6.      Hilliard Ensemble/Paul Hillier (bar) 3'10; rec St James Church Clerkenwell 10/1983. EMI stereo digital EX 2700963 (2 lps), TC-EX 2700969 (2 mcs 1984); CDS 7492058 (2 cds 1987).

Cibavit eos
1.      Deller Consort/Alfred Deller (ct) 3'10; rec All Saints Church Boughton Aluph 1970. Harmonia Mundi France stereo HM 40211 (mc 1977); HM 211–13 (3 lps 1979).
2.      London Oratory Choir/John Hoban [3'10]; rec London Oratory. Abbey stereo ABY 818 (lp 1980).
3.      Quink 2'29. Etcetera stereo digital ETC 1031 (lp), XTC 1031 (mc 1985).

Circumdederunt me dolores mortis
1.      New College Oxford Choir/Edward Higginbottom 4'52; rec New College Chapel. CRD stereo digital CRD 1139 (lp), CRD 4139 (mc), CRD 3439 (cd 1986).

Confirma hoc, Deus
1.      William Byrd Choir/Gavin Turner 1'41. Philips stereo 9502030 (lp 1981).
2.      Quink 1'19. Etcetera stereo digital ETC 1031 (lp), XTC 1031 (mc 1985).

Cunctis diebus
1.      New College Oxford Choir/Edward Higginbottom 4'10; rec New College Chapel. CRD stereo digital CRD 1139 (lp), CRD 4139 (mc), CRD 3439 (cd 1986).

Da mihi auxilium
1.      Cantores in Ecclesia/Michael Howard [5'42]. L'Oiseau-Lyre stereo SOL 313 (lp 1969).

Deficit in dolore
1.  Tallis Scholars/Peter Phillips 6'18; rec Merton College Chapel Oxford. Gimell stereo digital BYRD 345 (2 lps), ZCBYRD 345 (mc 1984).

De lamentatione Ieremiae
1.  Renaissance Singers/Michael Howard [11'26]. Argo mono RG 114 [lp 1958].
2.  Ambrosian Singers/John McCarthy [10'27]. Delyse mono ECB 3200, stereo DS 3200 [lp 1968]; L'Oiseau-Lyre OLSR 145 [lp 1972].
3.  Hilliard Ensemble/Paul Hillier (bar) 12'55; rec St James Church Clerkenwell 10/1983. EMI stereo digital EX 2700963 (2 lps), TC-EX 2700969 (2 mcs 1984); CDS 7492058 (2 cds 1987).

Dies sanctificatus
1.  Clare College Cambridge Choir/Timothy Brown [1'20]; rec Clare College Chapel. Meridian stereo E 77109 (lp), KE 77109 (mc 1985).

*Diffusa est gratia: Propter veritatem [2nd section], Audi filia [3rd section]
*1.  Chanticleer/Joseph Jennings (ct) [3'41]; rec St Ignatius Church San Francisco 6/1986. Harmonia Mundi USA stereo digital HMC 5182 (lp), HMC 405182 (mc), HMC 905182 (cd 1987).

Diliges Dominum
1.  Cantores in Ecclesia/Michael Howard [2'38]. L'Oiseau-Lyre stereo SOL 313 (lp 1969).

Domine, non sum dignus
1.  New College Oxford Choir/Edward Higginbottom 2'33; rec New College Chapel. CRD stereo digital CRD 1139 (lp), CRD 4139 (mc), CRD 3439 (cd 1986).
2.  Pro Cantione Antiqua/Bruno Turner [3'07]; rec St John-at-Hackney Church 5/1979. Libra stereo LRS 143 (mc 1986).

Domine, salva nos
1.  King's Singers [3'17]; rec EMI studios Abbey Road London 1976. His Master's Voice stereo/quad CSD 3779 (lp), TC–CSD 3779 (mc 1977).
2.  New College Oxford Choir/Edward Higginbottom 3'18; rec New College Chapel. CRD stereo digital CRD 1139 (lp), CRD 4139 (mc), CRD 3439 (cd 1986).

Domine, secundum actum meum
1.  Cantores in Ecclesia/Michael Howard [6'39]. L'Oiseau-Lyre stereo SOL313 (lp 1969).

Domine, secundum multitudinem dolorum meorum
1.   New College Oxford Choir//Edward Higginbottom 2'52. CRD stereo digital CRDD 1120 (lp), CRDCD 4120 (mc), CRD 3408 (cd 1984).

Domine, tu iurasti
1.   New College Oxford Choir/Edward Higginbottom 3'45; CRD stereo digital CRDD 1120 (lp), CRDCD 4120 (mc), CRD 3408 (cd 1984).

Ego sum panis vivus
1.   Ambrosian Singers/John McCarthy [1'33]; ed Grayson. Decca mono ADD 196, stereo SDD 196 (lp 1969).
2.   Deller Consort/Alfred Deller (ct) 2'20; rec All Saints Church Boughton Aluph 1970. Harmonia Mundi France stereo HM 40211 (mc 1977); HM 211–13 (3 lps 1979).
3.   Boston Church of the Advent Choir/Edith Ho 2'42; rec Boston Church of the Advent 1982. [Wilmington Mass.:] Afka stereo S 4676 (lp 1982).

Emendemus in melius
1.   Cantores in Ecclesia/Michael Howard [3'55]. L'Oiseau-Lyre stereo SOL 311 (lp 1969).
2.   London Early Music Group/James Tyler [3'34]; ed Tyler. RCA stereo RL 25110 (2 lps 1977).
3.   Deller Consort/Mark Deller (ct) 3'59; rec 4/1980. Harmonia Mundi France stereo HM 1053 (lp 1981).
4.   Boston Church of the Advent Choir/Fred Backhaus 3'12; rec Boston Church of the Advent 1982. [Wilmington Mass.:] Afka stereo S 4676 (lp 1982).

Exsurge, quare obdormis, Domine?
1.   English Singers [4'06]; ed Fellowes. His Master's Voice mono D 710 [sp 1923].
2.   Westminster Abbey Special Choir/Ernest Bullock [4'06]. His Master's Voice mono C 1678 [sp 1929].
3.   Westminster Abbey Choir/William McKie [3'45]; ed Fellowes, rec Westminster Abbey. Columbia mono LX 1605 [sp 1954].
4.   Worcester Cathedral Choir/Christopher Robinson [nt]; [rec Worcester Cathedral]. Abbey stereo 611 [lp 1967].
5.   St George's Chapel Windsor Choir/Sidney Campbell [3'41]; rec St George's Chapel [3/1974]. Argo stereo ZRG 789 (lp 1975).
6.   Lincoln Cathedral Choir/Philip Marshall [3'49]; [rec Lincoln Cathedral]. Alpha stereo APS 331 (lp), CAPS 331 (mc 1982).
7.   Guildford Cathedral Choir/Andrew Millington [3'45]; rec Guildford Cathedral 10/1983. Priory stereo PR 143 (lp 1983).
8.   New College Oxford Choir/Edward Higginbottom 3'40; rec New College Chapel. CRD stereo digital CRD 1139 (lp), CRD 4139 (mc), CRD 3439 (cd 1986).

Fac cum servo tuo
1.  New College Oxford Choir/Edward Higginbottom 3'23; rec New College Chapel. CRD stereo digital CRD 1139 (lp), CRD 4139 (mc), CRD 3439 (cd 1986).

Factus est repente de coelo sonus
1.  Scholars 1'27; rec Christ Church Chelsea 29/12/1971. Unicorn stereo UNS 254 (lp 1972).

Felix es, sacra virgo
1.  ⸱ Elizabethan Singers/Louis Halsey 1'45. Pan mono PAN 6204, stereo SPAN 6204 (lp 1967).

Gaudeamus omnes . . . beatae Mariae
1.  Chanticleer/Joseph Jennings (ct) [6'10]; rec St Ignatius Church San Francisco 6/1986. Harmonia Mundi USA stereo digital HMC 5182 (lp), HMC 405182 (mc), HMC 905182 (cd 1987).

Gaudeamus omnes . . . Sanctum omnium
1.  William Byrd Choir/Gavin Turner 5'17. Philips stereo 9502030 (lp 1981).
2.  King's Singers [2'30]; rec EMI studios Abbey Road London 1976. His Master's Voice stereo/quad CSD 3779 (lp), TC–CSD 3779 (mc 1977).

Haec dicit Dominus
1.  London Early Music Group/James Tyler, Antony Saunders (org) [5'54]; ed Tyler. RCA stereo RL 25110 (2 lps 1977).
2.  New College Oxford Choir/Edward Higginbottom 7'32; rec New College Chapel. CRD stereo digital CRD 1139 (lp), CRD 4139 (mc), CRD 3439 (cd 1986).
3.  Pro Cantione Antiqua/Bruno Turner [6'57]; rec St John-at-Hackney Church 5/1979. Libra stereo LRS 143 (mc 1986).

Haec dies, 5vv
1.  Chanticleer/Joseph Jennings (ct) [2'01]; rec St Ignatius Church San Francisco 6/1986. Harmonia Mundi USA stereo digital HMC 5182 (lp), HMC 405182 (mc), HMC 905182 (cd 1987).

Haec dies, 6vv
1.  St Paul's Cathedral Choir/John Dykes Bower [2'05]; rec St Paul's Cathedral. His Master's Voice mono HMS 37 [sp 1954]; HLP 9 [lp 1957].
2.  King's College Cambridge Choir/Boris Ord [2'47]; rec King's College Chapel. Argo mono RG 120 [lp 1958]; electronic stereo ECS 680 [lp 1973].
3.  St John's College Cambridge Choir/George Guest [2'27]; rec St John's College Chapel 7/1962. Musica Sacra mono AMS 37, stereo AMS 37STE (lp 1964).

4.  King's College Cambridge Choir/David Willcocks 2'35; rec King's College Chapel. His Master's Voice mono ALP 2094, stereo ASD 641 (lp 1965); SLS 5047 (3 lps 1976); CFP 4144811 [lp], CFP 4144814 [mc 1985].
5.  St Mary's Scottish Episcopal Cathedral Edinburgh Choir/Dennis Townhill [2'46]; rec St Mary's Scottish Episcopal Cathedral. His Master's Voice stereo CSD 3525 (lp 1966).
6.  Ambrosian Singers/John McCarthy [2'09]. Delyse mono ECB 3200, stereo DS 3200 [lp 1968]; L'Oiseau-Lyre OLSR 145 [lp 1972].
7.  Glasgow Cathedral Choir/John Turner [2'49]; [rec Glasgow Cathedral]. Vista stereo VPS 1023 [lp 1976].
8.  Deller Consort/Alfred Deller (ct) 2'00. Harmonia Mundi stereo HM 225 (lp), HM 40225 (mc 1977).
9.  King's Singers [2'01]; rec EMI studios Abbey Road London 1976. His Master's Voice stereo/quad CSD 3779 (lp), TC–CSD 3779 (mc 1977).
10. Christ Church Cathedral Oxford Choir/Simon Preston [2'57]; ed le Huray & Willcocks; rec Christ Church Cathedral. Oxford University Press stereo OUP 153 (lp 1979).
11. Cambridge Singers/John Rutter 2'23; rec Lady Chapel Ely Cathedral 10/1982. Word UK stereo WST 9636 (lp), WC 9636 (mc 1983); Collegium stereo digital COLC 107 (mc), COLCD 107 (cd 1988).
12. New College Oxford Choir/Edward Higginbottom 2'32; rec New College Chapel. CRD stereo digital CRD 1139 (lp), CRD 4139 (mc), CRD 3439 (cd 1986).
13. Llandaff Cathedral Choir/Michael Smith [nt]; [rec Llandaff Cathedral 1988]. Alpha stereo CACA 591 (mc 1988).
14. Uppingham School Chapel Choir/David Dunnett [nt]. Alpha stereo CAPS 381 (mc 1988).

Hodie Beata Virgo Maria
1.  Magdalen College Oxford Choir/Bernard Rose [3'09]; rec Magdalen College Chapel. Alpha mono AVM 009 (lp 1964); Saga mono XID 5387, stereo STXID 5287 [lp 1973].
2.  King's College Cambridge Choir/David Willcocks [3'33]; rec King's College Chapel. His Master's Voice mono ALP 2111, stereo ASD 653 (lp 1965); stereo ESD 7050 [lp], TC–ESD 7050 [mc 1977].

Hodie Christus natus est
1.  King's Singers [1'59]. His Master's Voice stereo HQS 1308 (lp 1973).
2.  Clare College Cambridge Choir/Timothy Brown [2'04]; rec Clare College Chapel. Meridian stereo E 77109 (lp), KE 77109 (mc 1985).

Infelix ego
1.  Tallis Scholars/Peter Phillips 12'02; rec Merton College Chapel Oxford. Gimell stereo digital BYRD 345 (2 lps), ZCBYRD 345 (mc 1984).

In resurrectione tua

1. New College Oxford Choir/David Lumsden [1'41]. Abbey stereo 629 (lp 1967).
2. New College Oxford Choir/Edward Higginbottom 1'40. CRD stereo digital CRDD 1120 (lp), CRDCD 4120 (mc), CRD 3408 (cd 1984).

Iustorum animae

1. St George's Singers [2'14]; ed Fellowes. Columbia mono 5547 [ssp 1929].
2. King's College Cambridge Choir/Boris Ord [2'55]; ed Fellowes; rec King's College Chapel. Columbia mono LX 1605 [sp 1954].
3. Renaissance Singers/Michael Howard [2'40]. Argo mono RG 42 [lp 1957].
4. St John's College Cambridge Choir/George Guest [2'35]; rec St John's College Chapel 7/1962. Musica Sacra mono AMS 37, stereo AMS 37STE (lp 1964).
5. King's College Cambridge Choir/David Willcocks 2'52; rec King's College Chapel. His Master's Voice mono ALP 2094, stereo ASD 641 (lp 1965); CFP 4144811 [lp], CFP 4144814 [mc 1985].
6. St Matthew's Church Northampton Choir/Michael Nicholas [3'24]. Abbey stereo LPB 655 (lp 1970).
7. St Bartholomew-the-Great Smithfield Priory Church Choir/Andrew Morris [2'37]; rec St Bartholomew-the-Great Church. Abbey stereo LPB 750 (lp 1975).
8. Deller Consort/Alfred Deller (ct) 3'58; rec All Saints Church Boughton Aluph. Harmonia France stereo HM 40212 (mc 1968); HM 211–13 (3 lps 1979).
9. Llandaff Cathedral Choir/Michael Smith [2'21]; [rec Llandaff Cathedral]. Alpha stereo APS 307 (lp 1980).
10. William Byrd Choir/Gavin Turner 3'05. Philips stereo 9502030 (lp 1981).
11. Boston Church of the Advent Choir/Fred Backhaus 2'39; rec Boston Church of the Advent 1982. [Wilmington Mass.:] Afka stereo S 4676 (lp 1982).
12. Quink 2'22. Etcetera stereo digital ETC 1031 (lp), XTC 1031 (mc 1985).

Laetentur coeli

1. Schola Cantorum Oxford/John Byrt [3'34]. Audiovision mono APR 266 (lp 1966).
2. New College Oxford Choir/David Lumsden [3'40]. Abbey stereo 629 (lp 1967).
3. Deller Consort/Alfred Deller (ct) 3'15; rec All Saints Church Boughton Aluph 1970. Harmonia Mundi France stereo HM 213 (lp 1978); HM 211–13 (3 lps 1979).
4. Corydon Singers/Matthew Best [nt]; rec St Augustine Chapel Tonbridge School. Cabaletta stereo CDN 5001 (lp 1981).
5. Hilliard Ensemble/Paul Hillier (bar) 3'41; rec St James Church Clerkenwell

10/1983. EMI stereo digital EX 2700963 (2 lps), TC–EX 2700969 (2 mcs 1984); CDS 7492058 (2 cds 1987).

6.   Psallite/Grahame O'Reilly [3'02]; rec St Michael's Church Highgate 6/1983. Libra stereo digital LRS 127 (mc 1984).

Laudate, pueri, Dominum
1.   Cantores in Ecclesia/Michael Howard [3'40]. L'Oiseau-Lyre stereo SOL 312 (lp 1969).
2.   Deller Consort/Mark Deller (ct), 4'00; rec 4/1980. Harmonia Mundi France stereo HM 1053 (lp 1981).

Laudibus in sanctis
1.   New College Oxford Choir/Herbert Andrews [6'17]; ed Fellowes; rec New College Chapel. Columbia mono LB 132 [ssp 1953].
2.   St John's College Cambridge Choir/George Guest [6'34]; rec St John's College Chapel 7/1962. Musica Sacra mono AMS 37, stereo AMS 37STE (lp 1964).
3.   New College Oxford Choir/David Lumsden [5'40]. Abbey stereo 629 (lp 1967).
4.   Deller Consort/Alfred Deller (ct) 5'22; rec All Saints Church Boughton Aluph. Harmonia Mundi France stereo HM 40212 (mc 1968); HM 211–13 (3 lps 1979).
5.   St Michael's College Tenbury Choir/Roger Judd [6'25]; ed Fellowes. Abbey stereo APR 303 (lp 1979).
6.   Canterbury Cathedral Choir/Allan Wicks [6'28]; rec Canterbury Cathedral. Abbey stereo ABY 817 (lp 1980).
7.   Winchester Cathedral Choir/Martin Neary [5'18]; rec Winchester Cathedral. ASV stereo ALH 943 [lp], ZCALH 943 (mc 1983).
8.   Psallite/Grahame O'Reilly [5'37]; rec St Michael's Church Highgate 6/1983. Libra stereo digital LRS 127 (mc 1984).
9.   New College Oxford Choir/Edward Higginbottom 5'47; rec New College Chapel. CRD stereo digital CRD 1139 (lp), CRD 4139 (mc), CRD 3439 (cd 1986).

*Laudibus in sanctis: Laudibus in sanctis [1st section]
*1.   Boston Camerata/Joel Cohen 1'07; rec Wellesley College Wellesley Mass. 5/1981. Erato stereo STU 71545 (lp 1984).

Libera me, Domine, de morte aeterna
1.   Cantores in Ecclesia/Michael Howard [5'24]. L'Oiseau-Lyre stereo SOL 313 (lp 1969).

Libera me, Domine, et pone me iuxta te
1.   Cantores in Ecclesia/Michael Howard [6'36]. L'Oiseau-Lyre stereo SOL 311 (lp 1969).

2. London Early Music Group/James Tyler [6'14]; ed Tyler. RCA stereo RL 25110 (2 lps 1977).
3. Deller Consort/Mark Deller (ct) 8'23; rec 4/1980. Harmonia Mundi France stereo HM 1053 (lp 1981).

Memento, homo
1. Cantores in Ecclesia/Michael Howard [3'04]. L'Oiseau-Lyre stereo SOL 312 (lp 1969).
2. Deller Consort/Mark Deller (ct) 1'28; rec 4/1980. Harmonia Mundi France stereo HM 1053 (lp 1981).

Miserere mei, Deus
1. St John's College Cambridge Choir/George Guest [2'59]; rec St John's College Chapel 7/1962. Musica Sacra mono AMS 37, stereo AMS 37STE (lp 1964).
2. King's College Cambridge Choir/David Willcocks 3'34; rec King's College Chapel. His Master's Voice mono ALP 2094, stereo ASD 641 (lp 1965); CFP 4144811 [lp], CFP 4144814 [mc 1985].
3. Guildford Cathedral Choir/Barry Rose [3'13]; rec Guildford Cathedral 1967. Guild mono GRM 7001, stereo GRS 7001 [lp 1969].
4. York Minster Choir/Francis Jackson [3'45]; rec York Minster. Abbey stereo LPB 721 (lp 1975).
5. Deller Consort/Alfred Deller (ct) 3'43; rec All Saints Church Boughton Aluph 1970. Harmonia Mundi France stereo HM 213 (lp 1978); HM 211–13 (3 lps 1979).
6. New College Oxford Choir/Edward Higginbottom 3'43; rec New College Chapel. CRD stereo digital CRD 1139 (lp). CRD 4139 (mc), CRD 3439 (cd 1986).
7. Cambridge Singers/John Rutter 3'46; rec Lady Chapel Ely Cathedral 10/1982. Collegium stereo digital COLC 107 (mc), COLCD 107 (cd 1988).

Miserere mihi, Domine
1. Cantores in Ecclesia/Michael Howard [1'53]. L'Oiseau-Lyre stereo SOL 313 (lp 1969).

Ne irascaris [see also O Lord, turn Thy wrath]
1. King's Singers [8'24]; rec EMI studios Abbey Road London 1976. His Master's Voice stereo/quad CSD 3779 (lp), TC-CSD 3779 (mc 1977).
2. Deller Consort/Alfred Deller (ct) 7'25; rec All Saints Church Boughton Aluph 1970. Harmonia Mundi France stereo HM 213 (lp 1978); HM 211–13 (3 lps 1979).
3. New College Oxford Choir/Edward Higginbottom 7'58. CRD stereo digital CRDD 1120 (lp), CRDCD 4120 (mc), CRD 3408 (cd 1984).
4. Pro Cantione Antiqua/Bruno Turner [8'49]; rec St John-at-Hackney Church 5/1979. Libra stereo LRS 143 (mc 1986).

*Ne irascaris: Civitas sancti tui [2nd section: see also Bow Thine ear]
  *1.  Renaissance Singers/Michael Howard [6'01]. Argo mono RG 114 [lp
       1958].
  *2.  Saltire Singers [4'21]; rec London. [New York:] Lyrichord mono LL 156,
       stereo LLST 7156 [lp 1966].
  *3.  London Oratory Choir/John Hoban [5'12]; [rec London Oratory]. Abbey
       stereo LPB 804 (lp 1979).
  *4.  Cardiff Cathedral Choir/David Neville [4'42]; rec Cardiff Cathedral
       4/1983. Alpha stereo APS 349 (lp 1983).
  *5.  St James' Church Great Grimsby Choir/Patrick Larley [4'49]; rec St James'
       Church Great Grimsby 20/6/1986. Priory stereo PRS 198 (mc 1986).

Non vos relinquam orphanos
  1.   New College Oxford Choir/David Lumsden [1'41]. Abbey stereo 629 (lp
       1967).
  2.   Deller Consort/Alfred Deller (ct) 1'05; rec All Saints Church Boughton
       Aluph. Harmonia Mundi France stereo HM 40212 (mc 1968); HM
       211–13 (3 lps 1979).
  3.   Tewkesbury Abbey School Choir/Michael Peterson [1'34]; rec Tewkesbury
       Abbey 7/1980. Alpha stereo APS 314 (lp 1980).
  4.   William Byrd Choir/Gavin Turner 1'36. Philips stereo 9502030 (lp 1981).
  5.   Boston Church of the Advent Choir/Edith Ho 2'02; rec Boston Church of
       the Advent 1982. [Wilmington Mass:] Afka stereo S 4676 (lp 1982).

O admirabile commercium
  1.   Clare College Cambridge Choir/Timothy Brown [4'18]; rec Clare College
       Chapel. Meridian stereo E 77109 (lp), KE 77109 (mc 1985).

Oculi omnium
  1.   London Oratory Choir/John Hoban [4'27]; rec London Oratory. Abbey
       stereo ABY 818 (lp 1980).

O lux, beata Trinitas
  1.   Cantores in Ecclesia/Michael Howard [4'37]. L'Oiseau-Lyre stereo SOL
       312 (lp 1969).
  2.   Deller Consort/Mark Deller (ct) 4'00; rec 4/1980. Harmonia Mundi France
       stereo HM 1053 (lp 1981).

O magnum misterium
  1.   Renaissance Singers/Michael Howard [4'50]. Argo mono RG 42 [lp
       1957].
  2.   Canby Singers/Edward Canby 3'09. Nonesuch mono H 1026, stereo H
       71026 [lp 1965].
  3.   St Bartholomew's Church Penn Choir/Timothy Storey [nt]. ATR stereo
       DEROY 1229 (lp 1975).

4.   Deller Consort/Alfred Deller (ct) [6'31]; rec All Saints Church Boughton Aluph 1970. Harmonia Mundi France stereo HM 40211 (mc 1977); HM 211–13 (3 lps 1979).
5.   Clare College Cambridge Choir/Timothy Brown [2'48]; rec Clare College Chapel. Meridian stereo E 77109 (lp), KE 77109 (mc 1985).
6.   Blackburn Cathedral Choir/David Cooper [nt]; [rec Blackburn Cathedral 1987]. Alpha stereo ACA 574 [lp 1987].

Optimam partem elegit
1.   Chanticleer/Joseph Jennings (ct) [2'46]; rec St Ignatius Church San Francisco 6/1986. Harmonia Mundi USA stereo digital HMC 5182 (lp), HMC 405182 (mc), HMC 905182 (cd 1987).

O quam gloriosum est regnum
1.   King's College Cambridge Choir/David Willcocks 5'12; rec King's College Chapel. His Masters's Voice mono ALP 2094, stereo ASD 641 (lp 1965); CFP 4144811 [lp], CFP 4144814 [mc 1985].
2.   Deller Consort/Alfred Deller (ct) 4'58; rec All Saints Church Boughton Aluph. Harmonia Mundi France stereo HM 40212 (mc 1968); HM 211–13 (3 lps 1979).
3.   New College Oxford Choir/Edward Higginbottom 4'23. CRD stereo digital CRDD 1120 (lp), CRDCD 4120 (mc), CRD 3408 (cd 1984).

O quam suavis est
1.   London Oratory Choir/John Hoban [4'26]; rec London Oratory. Abbey stereo ABY 818 (lp 1980).

O sacrum convivium
1.   Renaissance Singers/Michael Howard [2'57]. Argo mono RG 75 [lp 1956].
2.   Deller Consort/Alfred Deller (ct) 2'55; rec All Saints Church Boughton Aluph 1970. Harmonia Mundi France stereo HM 40211 (mc 1977); HM 211–13 (3 lps 1979).

[Pange lingua … misterium.] Nobis datus
1.   [London] Carmelite Priory Choir/John McCarthy [5'26]. His Master's Voice mono CLP 3519, stereo CSD 3519 (lp 1966).

Pascha nostrum … veritatis
1.   St Mary's Scottish Episcopal Cathedral Edinburgh Choir/Dennis Townhill [1'33]; rec St Mary's Scottish Episcopal Cathedral. His Master's Voice stereo CSD 3525 (lp 1966).
2.   Chanticleer/Joseph Jennings (ct) [2'35]; rec St Ignatius Church San Francisco 6/1986. Harmonia Mundi USA stereo digital HMC 5182 (1p), HMC 405182 (mc), HMC 905182 (cd 1987).

Peccantem me quotidie
1. Cantores in Ecclesia/Michael Howard [4'58]. L'Oiseau-Lyre stereo SOL 311 (lp 1969).
2. Deller Consort/Mark Deller (ct) 5'17; rec 4/1980. Harmonia Mundi France stereo HM 1053 (lp 1981).

Psallite Domino
1. St John's College Cambridge Choir/George Guest [0'57]. Argo mono RG 511, stereo ZRG 511 (lp 1967).
2. Lichfield Cathedral Choir/Richard Greening [0'55]; rec Lichfield Cathedral. Abbey stereo LPB 690 (lp 1970).
3. Southwell Minster Choir/Kenneth Beard 0'53; rec Southwell Minster. ATR stereo ATR/ST/740/1 (lp 1976).

Puer natus est
1. Clare College Cambridge Choir/Timothy Brown [4'53]; rec Clare College Chapel. Meridian stereo E 77109 (lp), KE 77109 (mc 1985).

Regina coeli
1. Chanticleer/Joseph Jennings (ct) [6'41]; rec St Ignatius Church San Francisco 6/1986. Harmonia Mundi USA stereo digital HMC 5182 (lp), HMC 405182 (mc), HMC 905182 (cd 1987).

Resurrexi
1. Chanticleer/Joseph Jennings (ct) [5'36]; rec St Ignatius Church San Francisco 6/1986. Harmonia Mundi USA stereo digital HMC 5182 (lp), HMC 405182 (mc), HMC 905182 (cd 1987).

Rorate coeli
1. Renaissance Singers/Ronald Lee [4'43]; rec St Anne's Cathedral Belfast 10/1987. Priory stereo PR 233 (lp 1987).

Sacerdotes Domini
1. Renaissance Singers/Michael Howard [1'15]. Argo mono RG 42 [lp 1957].
2. St Michael's College Tenbury Choir/Lucian Nethsingha [1'49]. Argo mono RG 423, stereo ZRG 5423 (lp 1965).
3. Lincoln Cathedral Choir/Philip Marshall 1'55; rec Lincoln Cathedral 7/1976. Vista stereo VPS 1037 (lp 1976).
4. Chesterfield Parish Church Choir/Michael Baker [1'19]; rec Chesterfield Parish Church. Abbey stereo LPB 788 (lp 1977).
5. Deller Consort/Alfred Deller (ct) 1'20; rec All Saints Church Boughton Aluph 1970. Harmonia Mundi France stereo HM 40211 (mc 1977); HM 211–13 (3 lps 1979).
6. Boy Singers of Our Lady of Grace Chiswick/Denis Cochrane [1'28]. Alpha stereo APS 312 (lp 1980).

Salve regina, 4vv
1.    Renaissance Singers/Michael Howard [4'51]. Argo mono RG 42 [lp
      1957].
2.    Chanticleer/Joseph Jennings (ct) [5'00]; rec St Ignatius Church San Franci-
      sco 6/1986. Harmonia Mundi USA stereo digital HMC 5182 (lp), HMC
      405182 (mc), HMC 905182 (cd 1987).

Salve sancta parens
1.    Elizabethan Singers/Louis Halsey 4'35. Pan mono PAN 6204, stereo
      SPAN 6204 (lp 1967).
2.    William Byrd Choir/Gavin Turner 5'07. Philips stereo 9502030 (lp
      1981).

*Salve sancta parens: Salve sancta parens [1st section]
*1.   Renaissance Singers/Michael Howard [1'43]. Argo mono RG 42 [lp
      1957].

*Salve sancta parens: Eructavit cor meum [2nd section]
*2.   Chanticleer/Joseph Jennings (ct) [1'45]; rec St Ignatius Church San Franci-
      sco 6/1986. Harmonia Mundi USA stereo digital HMC 5182 (lp), HMC
      405182 (mc), HMC 905182 (cd 1987).

Senex puerum portabat . . . adoravit
1.    Trapp Family Singers/Franz Wasner [2'07]. Brunswick mono LAT 8038
      [lp 1954].
2.    Renaissance Singers/Michael Howard [1'45]. Argo mono RG 42 [lp
      1957].
3.    King's College Cambridge Choir/David Willcocks [2'51]; rec King's
      College Chapel. His Master's Voice mono ALP 2111, stereo ASD 653 (lp
      1965); stereo ESD 7050 [lp], TC-ESD 7050 [mc 1977].
4.    Lincoln Cathedral Choir/Philip Marshall 2'53; rec Lincoln Cathedral
      7/1976. Vista stereo VPS 1037 (lp 1976).
5.    Deller Consort/Alfred Deller (ct) 2'25; rec All Saints Church Boughton
      Aluph 1970. Harmonia Mundi France stereo HM 40211 (mc 1977); HM
      211–13 (3 lps 1979).
6.    William Byrd Choir/Gavin Turner 2'38. Philips stereo 9502030 (lp
      1979).
7.    Boston Church of the Advent Choir/Edith Ho 2'58; rec Boston Church of
      the Advent 1982. [Wilmington Mass:] Afka stereo S 4676 (lp 1982).
8.    Renaissance Singers/Ronald Lee [3'24]; rec St Anne's Cathedral Belfast
      10/1987. Priory stereo PR 233 (lp 1987).

Senex puerum portabat . . . regebat
1.    King's College Cambridge Choir/Boris Ord [1'13]; ed Fellowes; rec King's
      College Chapel. Columbia mono LX 1604 [sp 1954].

Siderum rector
1.   Cantores in Ecclesia/Michael Howard [2′59]. L'Oiseau-Lyre stereo SOL
     312 (lp 1969).
2.   Deller Consort/Alfred Deller (ct) 2′57; rec All Saints Church Boughton
     Aluph. Harmonia Mundi France stereo HM 40212 (mc 1968); HM
     211–13 (3 lps 1979).
3.   Deller Consort/Mark Deller (ct) 2′45; rec 4/1980. Harmonia Mundi France
     stereo HM 1053 (lp 1981).

Surge illuminare, Ierusalem
1.   Boston Church of the Advent Choir/Edith Ho 1′50; rec Boston Church of
     the Advent 1982. [Wilmington Mass:] Afka stereo S 4676 (lp 1982).

Terra tremuit
1.   Ely Cathedral Choir/Arthur Wills [1′15]; rec Ely Cathedral. Alpha mono
     AVM 015 (lp 1964).
2.   Chanticleer/Joseph Jennings (ct) [1′08]; rec St Ignatius Church San Franci-
     sco 6/1986. Harmonia Mundi USA stereo digital HMC 5182 (lp), HMC
     405182 (mc), HMC 905182 (cd 1987).

Tollite portas
1.   Ambrosian Singers/John McCarthy [1′32]. Delyse mono ECB 3204, stereo
     DS 3204 (lp 1968); L'Oiseau-Lyre OLS 153 [lp 1973].

Tribue, Domine
1.   Cantores in Ecclesia/Michael Howard [10′13]. L'Oiseau-Lyre stereo SOL
     313 (lp 1969).
2.   Psallite/Graham O'Reilly [9′40]; rec St Michael's Church Highgate 6/1983.
     Libra stereo digital LRS 127 (mc 1984).

Tribulationes civitatum
1.   William Byrd Choir/Gavin Turner 10′33. Philips stereo 9502030 (lp
     1981).

Tribulatio proxima est
1.   New College Oxford Choir/Edward Higginbottom 4′22; rec New College
     Chapel. CRD stereo digital CRD 1139 (lp), CRD 4139 (mc), CRD 3439
     (cd 1986).

Tristitia et anxietas
1.   New College Oxford Choir/Edward Higginbottom 9′34. CRD stereo
     digital CRDD 1120 (lp), CRDCD 4120 (mc), CRD 3408 (cd 1984).
2.   Psallite/Grahame O'Reilly [8′23]; rec St Michael's Church Highgate
     6/1983. Libra stereo digital LRS 127 (mc 1984).

Tu es Petrus
1.  King's College Cambridge Choir/David Willcocks 2'15; rec King's College
    Chapel. His Master's Voice mono ALP 2094, stereo ASD 641 (lp 1965);
    CFP 4144811 [lp], CFP 4144814 [mc 1985].
2.  Liverpool Metropolitan Cathedral Choir/Philip Duffy [2'10]; rec celebra-
    tion of Solemn Mass of Pentecost by Pope John Paul II Liverpool Metro-
    politan Cathedral 30/5/1982. Alpha stereo LPM 30582 (lp), CLMP 30582
    (mc 1982).

Tui sunt coeli
1.  Clare College Cambridge Choir/Timothy Brown [1'15]; rec Clare College
    Chapel. Meridian stereo E 77109 (lp), KE 77109 (mc 1985).

Veni Sancte Spiritus, reple
1.  Lincoln Cathedral Choir/Philip Marshall 1'41; rec Lincoln Cathedral
    7/1976. Vista stereo VPS 1037 (lp 1976).

Victimae paschali laudes
1.  Exeter Cathedral Choir/Lucian Nethsingha [5'50]; rec Exeter Cathedral
    2/1984. Alpha stereo ACA 530 (lp), CACA 530 (mc 1984).
2.  Chanticleer/Joseph Jennings (ct) [6'55]; rec St Ignatius Church San Franci-
    sco 6/1986. Harmonia Mundi USA stereo digital HMC 5182 (lp), HMC
    405182 (mc), HMC 905182 (cd 1987).

*Victimae paschali laudes: Victimae paschali [1st section]
*1.  Boys of All Saints' Margaret Street London Choir, New English Singers/
     Simon Preston [3'21]; ed Terry. His Master's Voice stereo HQS 1147 (lp
     1968).
*2.  Hereford Cathedral Choir/Richard Lloyd [3'00]; rec Hereford Cathedral.
     Abbey stereo LPB 696 (lp 1973).

Vide, Domine, afflictionem nostram
1.  New College Oxford Choir/Edward Higginbottom 9'00. CRD stereo
    digital CRDD 1120 (lp), CRDCD 4120 (mc), CRD 3408 (cd 1984).

Viderunt . . . Dei nostri
1.  Clare College Cambridge Choir/Timothy Brown [1'13]; rec Clare College
    Chapel. Meridian stereo E 77109 (lp), KE 77109 (mc 1985).

Viderunt . . . omnis terra
1.  Clare College Cambridge Choir/Timothy Brown [1'53]; rec Clare College
    Chapel. Meridian stereo E 77109 (lp), KE 77109 (mc 1985).

Vidimus stellam
1.  Canterbury Cathedral Choir/Allan Wicks [2'26]; rec Canterbury Cathedral.
    Canterbury Cathedral Record Studios stereo CAN 1001 (lp 1978).

Vigilate
1. New College Oxford Choir/Edward Higginbottom 5'16. CRD stereo digital CRDD 1120 (lp), CRDCD 4120 (mc), CRD 3408 (cd 1984).

Virgo Dei genetrix
1. Elizabethan Singers/Louis Halsey [1'23]. Pan mono PAN 6204, stereo SPAN 6204 (lp 1967).

Viri Galilei
1. Scholars 3'58; rec Christ Church Chelsea 29/12/1971. Unicorn stereo UNS 254 (lp 1972).

Visita quaesumus, Domine
1. William Byrd Choir/Gavin Turner 3'50. Philips stereo 9502030 (lp 1981).

### English liturgical music

*First Preces & Psalms 47, 54: First Preces & Psalm 47
*1. King's College Cambridge Choir/Stephen Cleobury, Robert Graham-Campbell (cnr), Richard Farnes (org) 4'29; ed Wrightson; rec King's College Chapel 13–14/12/1985. EMI stereo digital EL 2705641 (lp), EL 2705644 (mc), CDC 7477712 (cd 1987).

*First Preces & Psalms 47, 54: Psalms 47 & 54
*2. New College Oxford Choir/David Lumsden [6'03]. Abbey stereo LPB 751 (lp 1976).

Great Service
1. St Thomas Church New York Choir/Gerre Hancock 42'34; ed Fellowes; [New York:] St Thomas Church stereo STC 1981 (lp 1981).
2. King's College Cambridge Choir/Stephen Cleobury, Robert Graham-Campbell (cnr), Richard Farnes (org) 44'17; ed Wrightson; rec King's College Chapel 13–14/12/1985. EMI stereo digital EL 2705641 (lp), EL 2705644 (mc), CDC 7477712 (cd 1987).

*Great Service: Venite, Te Deum, Benedictus, Creed, Magnificat & Nunc Dimittis
*1. Tallis Scholars/Peter Phillips 44'01; ed Phillips; rec St John-at-Hackney Church, Gimell stereo digital 158511 (lp), 1585T11 (mc), CDGIM 011 (cd 1987).

*Great Service: Magnificat & Nunc Dimittis
*2 King's College Cambridge Choir/David Willcocks 16'30; ed Fellowes; rec King's College Chapel. Argo mono RG 226, stereo ZRG 5226 (lp 1960); ZK 53–4 (2 lps 1979); 4143661 (lp), 4143664 (mc 1985).
*3. New College Oxford Choir/David Lumsden [14'40]. Abbey stereo LPB 751 (lp 1976).

*4.   Jesus College Cambridge Choir/Geraint Bowen [14'00]; rec Jesus College Chapel 3/1985. Alpha ACA 546 (lp 1985).

*Great Service: Nunc Dimittis
*5.   New College Oxford Choir/Herbert Andrews [4'45]; ed Fellowes; rec New College Chapel. Columbia mono LX 1381 [sp 1951].

*Great Service: Nunc Dimittis: Gloria
*6.   English Singers [2'27]; ed Fellowes. His Master's Voice mono E 291 [ssp 1923].

*Second Preces and Psalms 114, 55, 119, 24: Psalms 114, 55 & 119.
*1.   New College Oxford Choir/David Lumsden [9'51]. Abbey stereo LPB 751 (lp 1976).

*Second Preces and Psalms 114, 55, 119, 24: Second Preces & Psalm 119
*2.   St Andrew's Scottish Episcopal Cathedral Aberdeen Choir/Andrew Morrisson, Mark Duthie (org) [5'07]; rec Divine Service St Andrew's Scottish Episcopal Cathedral 1/5/1988. Donselco stereo KB 1 (mc 1988).

*Second Preces and Psalms 114, 55, 119, 24: Psalm 119
*3.   Birmingham Blue Coat School Chapel Choir/Hugh Shelton, Michael Peterson (org) [3'32]; rec Tewkesbury Abbey. Abbey stereo LPB 766 (lp 1976).
*4.   Guildford Cathedral Choir/Philip Moore [3'55]; rec Guildford Cathedral 7/1976. Abbey stereo LPB 771 (lp 1976).
*5.   John Bobby (tr), Magdalen College Oxford Choir/John Harper, Paul Brough (cha org) [3'34]; rec Magdalen College Chapel 4/1985. Alpha stereo ACA 543 (lp), CACA 543 (mc 1985).
*6.   St Columba's Church Sutton Coldfield Choir/Richard Mason, Anthony Pinel (org) [nt]; rec St Columba's Church 10/1986. Alpha stereo APS 373 (lp 1986).

*Second Preces and Psalms 114, 55, 119, 24: Psalm 24 [see Lift up your heads]

Second Service
1.   Westminster Abbey Choir/William McKie, Simon Preston (org) [7'04]. Argo mono RG 371, stereo ZRG 5371 (lp 1963).
2.   Winchester Cathedral Choir/Martin Neary, James Lancelot (org) [6'35]; rec Winchester Cathedral. ASV stereo ALH 915 (lp), ZCALH 915 (mc 1982).
3.   St Andrew's Scottish Episcopal Cathedral Aberdeen Choir/Andrew Morrisson, Mark Duthie (org) [6'38]; rec Divine Service St Andrew's Scottish Episcopal Cathedral 1/5/1988. Donselco stereo KB 1 (mc 1988).

*Second Service: Magnificat
  *1.  Liverpool Cathedral Choir/Ian Tracey, Ian Wells (org) [3'42]; rec
       Liverpool Cathedral 10/1987. Solitaire stereo digital SOLI 107 [lp 1988].

*Short Service: Creed
  *1.  Coronation Choir [4'28]; ed Fellowes; rec King George VI coronation
       Westminster Abbey 12/5/1937. His Master's Voice mono RG 1–15 [15 sps
       1937].

*Short Service: Magnificat
  *2.  English Singers [2'59]; ed Fellowes. His Master's Voice mono E 291 [ssp
       1923].
  *3.  Coventry Cathedral Chapter House Choir/Geoffrey Holroyde [3'26]; ed
       Fellowes; rec Coventry Cathedral 9/1986. Alpha stereo APS 372 (lp
       1986).

*Short Service: Venite
  *4.  Worcester Cathedral Choir/Donald Hunt [3'59]; rec Worcester Cathedral
       9/1982. Capriole stereo digital CAP 1002 (lp), CAPT 1002 (mc 1984).

Third Preces and Responses
  1.   King's College Cambridge Choir/David Willcocks, Peter Cameron (cnr)
       [3'42]; rec King's College Chapel. Argo mono RG 365, stereo ZRG 5365
       (lp 1964).
  2.   Winchester Cathedral Choir/Martin Neary [3'43]; rec Winchester Cathe-
       dral. ASV stereo ALH 915 (lp), ZCALH 915 (mc 1982).

*Third Preces and Responses: Responses
  *1.  St Andrew's Scottish Episcopal Cathedral Aberdeen Choir/Andrew Mor-
       risson, Mark Duthie (org) [5'42]; rec Divine Service St Andrew's Scottish
       Episcopal Cathedral 1/5/1988. Donselco stereo KB 1 (mc 1988).

### Other English music

Ah silly soul
  1.   Ulrike Taube (s), Capella Fidicinia/Hans Gruss [3'22]. Archiv stereo
       199014 (lp 1969).
  2.   James Bowman (ct), English Consort of Viols 3'15; rec 11/1976. Turn-
       about stereo TVS 34709 (lp), KTVC 34709 (mc 1980).

All as a sea
  1.   James Bowman (ct), English Consort of Viols 3'12; rec 11/1976. Turna-
       bout stereo TVS 34709 (lp), KTVC 34709 (mc 1980).
  2.   Mary Nichols (a), Consort of Musicke/Anthony Rooley 3'09. L'Oiseau-
       Lyre stereo DSLO 596 (lp), KCSP 596 (mc 1982).

An earthly tree
1.  Saltire Singers, Roy Jesson (org) [5'50]; rec London. [New York:] Lyri-
    chord mono LL 156, stereo LLST 7156 [lp 1966].
2.  Birmingham Cathedral Choir/Hubert Best, Timothy Storey (org) [8'20];
    rec Festival of Nine Lessons & Carols 24 December 1979: stereo [un-
    numbered] (mc 1980).

*An earthly tree: An earthly tree [verse]
*1.  Ely Cathedral Choristers/Michael Howard, Arthur Wills (org) [5'01]. Argo
     mono RG 148, stereo ZRG 5148 (lp 1958); mono EAF 8, stereo ZFA 8
     (ep 1960); ECS 660 [lp 1973].
*2.  St Michael's College Tenbury Choir/Roger Judd, Roy Massey (org) [5'38];
     rec St Michael's College Chapel 7/1981. Alpha stereo APS 324 (lp), CAPS
     324 (mc 1981).

Arise, Lord, into thy rest
1.  Oriana Madrigal Society/Chas. Kennedy Scott [3'52]. [London W14:]
    Olympia Sound mono [un-numbered] (slp 1958).

As Caesar wept
1.  Anne Verkinderen (s), Liege Musica Aurea 1'57. [Brussels:] Alpha stereo
    DB 267 (lp 1978).

Blame I confess
1.  Anne Verkinderen (s), Liege Musica Aurea 2'27. [Brussels:] Alpha stereo
    DB 267 (lp 1978).

Blessed is he that fears the Lord
1.  †Russell Oberlin (ct), In Nomine Players/Denis Stevens [1'42]; ed Stevens;
    rec London. [New York:] Experiences Anonymes stereo EA 37 (lp 1960).

Bow thine ear [contrafact]
1.  Christ Church Cathedral Oxford Choir/Sydney Watson [nt]; rec Christ
    Church Cathedral 11/3/1961. Delyse mono ECB 3159, stereo DS 6059 [lp
    1961].
2.  St Paul's Cathedral Choristers, Purcell Chorus of Voices, Elizabethan
    Consort of Viols/Grayston Burgess, Andrew Davis (org) [5'03]. Argo
    stereo ZRG 659 (lp 1970).
3.  New College Oxford Choir/David Lumsden [5'40]. Abbey stereo LPB 751
    (lp 1976).
4.  Cambridge Singers/John Rutter 4'08; rec Lady Chapel Ely Cathedral
    10/1982. Word UK stereo WST 9636 (lp), WC 9636 (mc 1983); Colle-
    gium stereo digital COLC 107 (mc), COLCD 107 (cd 1988).
5.  Liverpool Cathedral Choir/Ian Tracey [3'44]; rec Liverpool Cathedral
    10/1987. Solitaire stereo digital SOLI 107 [lp 1988].

Care for thy soul
1.    †Evelyn Tubb (ms), Consort of Musicke/Anthony Rooley 6'38. L'Oiseau-Lyre stereo DSLO 596 (lp), KCSP 596 (mc 1982).

Christ rising again
1.    Hilliard Ensemble, London Baroque/Paul Hillier (bar) 6'01; ed Dunkley; rec Abbey Road Studio 1 London 3/1986. EMI stereo digital EL 7479611 (lp), EL 7479614 (mc), CDC 7479612 (cd 1987).

*Christ rising again: Christ rising again [1st section]
*1.   James Bowman, Mark Deller (cts), St Paul's Cathedral Choristers, Purcell Chorus of Voices, Elizabethan Consort of Viols/Grayston Burgess, Andrew Davis (org) [3'08]. Argo stereo ZRG 659 (lp 1970).

Come help, O God
1.    Scholars 3'53; rec Christ Church Chelsea 29/12/1971. Unicorn stereo UNS 254 (lp 1972).
2.    Quink 3'06. Etcetera stereo digital ETC 1031 (lp), XTC 1031 (mc 1985).

Come, pretty babe
1.    Alfred Deller (ct), Wenzinger Consort of Viols of the Schola Cantorum Basiliensis/August Wenzinger [1'26]; ed le Huray & Dart. Vanguard mono PVL 7035 [lp 1958].

Come to me, grief, for ever
1.    English Singers [1'20]; ed Fellowes. His Master's Voice mono D 711 [sp 1923].
2.    †Martyn Hill (t), English Consort of Viols [3'48]. Turnabout stereo TV 34443S (lp 1971).
3.    †Glenda Simpson (ms), Camerata of London 2'41; rec St Michael's Church Highgate. CRD stereo CRD 1055 (lp), CRDC 4055 (mc 1978).
4.    Consort of Musicke/Anthony Rooley 4'56. L'Oiseau-Lyre stereo DSLO 596 (lp), KCSP 596 (mc 1982).
5.    Quink 1'55. Etcetera stereo digital ETC 1031 (lp), XTC 1031 (mc 1985).
6.    †John Potter (t), London Baroque/Paul Hillier 4'04; ed Dunkley; rec Abbey Road Studio 1 London 3/1986. EMI stereo digital EL 7479611 (lp), EL 7479614 (mc), CDC 7479612 (cd 1987).
7.    †Emily Van Evera (s), Musicians of Swanne Alley 6'13; rec Bethel United Church of Christ Michigan 3/1986. Harmonia Mundi USA stereo digital HMC 5192 (lp), HMC 405192 (mc), HMC 905192 (cd 1987).
8.    †Michael Chance (ct), Fretwork 6'00; rec Forde Abbey 1/1988. Virgin stereo digital VC 7907221 (lp), VC 7907224 (mc), VC 7907222 (cd 1988).

Come, woeful Orpheus
1.    London Early Music Group/James Tyler [4'33]; ed Tyler. RCA stereo RL 25110 (2 lps 1977).

2.    Hilliard Ensemble/Paul Hillier (bar) 4'02; ed Dunkley; rec Abbey Road
      Studio 1 London 3/1986. EMI stereo digital EL 7479611 (lp), EL
      7479614 (mc), CDC 7479612 (cd 1987).

Constant Penelope
1.    Scholars 3'50; [rec St George the Martyr Church Queen Square London
      4/1976]. Prelude stereo PRS 2501 (lp 1976).

Content is rich
1.    Paul Elliott (t), London Early Music Group/James Tyler [4'25]; ed Tyler.
      RCA stereo RL 25110 (2 lps 1977).

Exalt thyself, O God
1.    Lichfield Cathedral Choir/Jonathan Rees-Williams [4'28]; ed James; rec
      Lichfield Cathedral 7/1980. Alpha stereo APS 311 (lp 1980).
2.    Magdalen College Oxford Choir/John Harper [4'36]; rec Magdalen
      College Chapel 4/1985. Alpha stereo ACA 543 (lp), CACA 543 (mc 1985).

Farewell, false love
1.    †Glenda Simpson (ms), Camerata of London 3'36; rec St Michael's Church
      Highgate. CRD stereo CRD 1055 (lp), CRDC 4055 (mc 1978).

From Virgin's womb
1.    James Bowman (ct), St Paul's Cathedral Choristers, Purcell Chorus of
      Voices, Elizabethan Consort of Viols/Grayston Burgess [4'18]. Argo stereo
      ZRG 659 (lp 1970).
2.    Lichfield Cathedral Choristers, Duggan Consort/Richard Greening
      [3'25];rec Great Hall Bishop's Palace Lichfield. Abbey stereo XMS 698
      (lp 1972).
3.    St Michael's College Tenbury Choir/Roger Judd, Andrew Millington (org)
      [3'18]; ed Judd. Abbey stereo APR 303 (lp 1979).
4.    Hilliard Ensemble, London Baroque/Paul Hillier (bar) 8'58; ed Dunkley;
      rec Abbey Road Studio 1 London 3/1986. EMI stereo digital EL 7479611
      (lp), EL 7479614 (mc), CDC 7479612 (cd 1987).

*From virgin's womb: Rejoice, rejoice
*1.   Trinity College Cambridge Choir/Richard Marlow [nt]. Cambridge stereo
      CCRS 1006 [lp 1985].

Have mercy upon me, O God
1.    St John's College Cambridge Choir, string quartet [6'12]. His Master's
      Voice mono B 2448 [ssp 1926].
2.    Prague Madrigal Singers, Vienna Musica Antiqua/Miroslav Venhoda [nt].
      Supraphon stereo SUAST 50714 [lp 1967].
3.    Hilliard Ensemble, London Baroque/Paul Hillier (bar) 4'28; ed Dunkley;

rec Abbey Road Studio 1 London 3/1986. EMI stereo digital EL 7479611 (lp), EL 7479614 (mc), CDC 7479612 (cd 1987).

\*Have mercy upon me, O God: [instrumental introduction shortened from 5 bars to 1]
  \*1.  Saltire Singers, Roy Jesson (org) [3'57]; rec London. [New York:] Lyrichord mono LL 156, stereo LLST 7156 [lp 1966].

If women could be fair
  1.  Consort of Musicke/Anthony Rooley 3'51. L'Oiseau-Lyre stereo DSLO 596 (lp), KCSP 596 (mc 1982).

I joy not in no earthly bliss
  1.  [Judith Nelson] (s), Academy of Ancient Music/Christopher Hogwood 1'55; rec Christ Church Sutton Surrey 4/1978. Folio Society stereo FS 1003–4 (2 lps 1978); L'Oiseau-Lyre DSLO 606 (lp 1983).

In angel's weed
  1.  Lorna Anderson (s), Scottish Early Music Consort/Warwick Edwards (b vl) 3'40; rec SNO Centre Glasgow 9/1983. Chandos stereo digital ABRD 1103 (lp), ABTD 1103 (mc), CHAN 8332 (cd 1984).
  2.  Michael Chance (ct), Fretwork 3'23; rec Forde Abbey 1/1988. Virgin stereo digital VC 7907221 (lp), VC 7907224 (mc), VC 7907222 (cd 1988).

In fields abroad
  1.  †Andrew Brunt (tr), Jaye Consort of Viols 4'40. Pye stereo GSGC 14139 (lp 1972).
  2.  †Emma Kirkby (s), Consort of Musicke/Anthony Rooley 4'05. L'Oiseau-Lyre stereo DSLO 596 (lp), KCSP 596 (mc 1982).

Is love a boy?
  1.  Saltire Singers [5'18]; rec London. [New York:] Lyrichord mono LL 156, stereo LLST 7156 [lp 1966].
  2.  King's Singers 3'44. HMV stereo digital ASD 4092 (lp), TCC-ASD 4092 (mc 1982); CDC 7492652 (cd 1987).

I thought that love had been a boy
  1.  Saltire Singers [1'02]; rec London. [New York:] Lyrichord mono LL 156, stereo LLST 7156 [lp 1966].

La virginella
  1.  †Russell Oberlin (ct), In Nomine Players/Denis Stevens [2'15]; ed Stevens; rec London. [New York:] Experiences Anonymes stereo EA 37 (lp 1960).

Lift up your heads [contrafact]
1.   King's College Cambridge Choir/Stephen Cleobury 5′07; ed Wrightson;
     rec King's College Chapel 13–14/12/1985. EMI stereo digital EL 2705641
     (lp), EL 2705644 (mc), CDC 7477712 (cd 1987).

Lord, hear my prayer
1.   Saltire Singers [1′58]; rec London. [New York:] Lyrichord mono LL 156,
     stereo LLST 7156 [lp 1966].
2.   Guildford Cathedral Choir/Barry Rose [2′11]; rec Guildford Cathedral
     1967. Guild mono GRM 7001, stereo GRS 7001 [lp 1969].

Lullaby, my sweet little baby
1.   St George's Singers [5′27]; ed Fellowes. Columbia mono 5546 [ssp 1929].
2.   †Alfred Deller (ct), Wenzinger Consort of Viols of the Schola Cantorum
     Basiliensis/August Wenzinger [6′50]; ed Fellowes. Vanguard mono PVL
     7035 [lp 1958].
3.   †James Bowman (ct), New College Oxford Choir, English Consort of
     Viols/David Lumsden [7′00]. Abbey stereo 652 [lp 1967].
4.   †Michael Criswell (tr), Dolmetsch Consort, David Lumsden (hpsc) [nt];
     rec New College Chapel Oxford 1976. Abbey stereo LPB 762 [lp 1978].
5.   †Richard Hill (ct), Landini Consort/Peter Syrus [3′52]; rec College of
     Ripon & York St John Chapel York 8/1978. Hill & Dale stereo HD 001 (lp
     1978).
6.   Rosemary Hardy, Elizabeth Lane, Mary Thomas (ss), Pro Cantione
     Antiqua/Philip Ledger [4′27]; ed Ledger & Parker; rec St Mark's Church
     Hamilton Terrace London. Oxford University Press stereo OUP 151–2 (2
     lps 1979).
7.   †Jacqueline Fox (ms), Consort of Musicke/Anthony Rooley 8′54.
     L'Oiseau-Lyre stereo DSLO 596 (lp), KCSP 596 (mc 1982).
8.   Magdalen College Oxford Choir/John Harper [4′28]; rec Magdalen
     College Chapel 12/1983. Alpha stereo ACA 527 (lp), CACA 527 (mc
     1984).
9.   Tallis Scholars/Peter Phillips 6′27; rec St Peter & St Paul Church Salle.
     Gimell stereo digital 158510 (lp), 1585T10 (mc), CDGIM 010 (cd 1986).
10.  †[David James] (ct), Hilliard Ensemble, London Baroque/Paul Hillier
     (bar) 7′34; ed Dunkley; rec Abbey Road Studio 1 London 3/1986. EMI
     stereo digital EL 7479611 (lp), EL 7479614 (mc), CDC 7479612 (cd
     1987).

* Lullaby, my sweet little baby: [chorus]
*1.  Abbey Singers [1′48]. Brunswick mono AXA 4518, stereo SXA 4518 (lp
     1964).
*2.  April Cantelo (s), Helen Watts, Sybil Michelow (cs), Gerald English (t),
     Christopher Keyte (b)/Raymond Leppard [2′18]; ed Fellowes. His
     Master's Voice stereo HQS 1147 (lp 1968).

*3.  Purcell Consort of Voices/Grayston Burgess (ct) [2'03]; rec Decca Studios London 7/1967. Turnabout stereo TV 34202 (lp), KTVC 34202 (mc 1969).

*4.  Corydon Singers/Matthew Best [nt]; rec St Augustine Chapel Tonbridge School. Cabaletta stereo CDN 5001 (lp 1981).

*5.  Cambridge Singers/John Rutter 2'05; rec Henry Wood Hall London. Collegium stereo digital COL 105 (lp), COLC 105 (mc 1987).

Make ye joy to God
1.  St Paul's Cathedral Choristers, Purcell Chorus of Voices, London Cornet & Sackbut Ensemble/Grayston Burgess, Andrew Davis (org) [2'32]. Argo stereo ZRG 659 (lp 1970).

2.  Scholars 2'06; rec Christ Church Chelsea 29/12/1971. Unicorn stereo UNS 254 (lp 1972).

3.  St Bartholomew-the-Great Smithfield Priory Church Choir/Andrew Morris [2'11]; rec St Bartholomew-the-Great Church. Abbey stereo LPB 750 (lp 1976).

4.  Hilliard Ensemble/Paul Hillier (bar) 2'16; ed Dunkley; rec Abbey Road Studio 1 London 3/1986. EMI stereo digital EL 7479611 (lp), EL 7479614 (mc), CDC 7479612 (cd 1987).

My mistress had a little dog
1.  Anne Verkinderen (s), Liege Musica Aurea 4'32. [Brussels:] Alpha stereo DB 267 (lp 1978).

O dear life
1.  James Bowman (ct), English Consort of Viols 3'05; rec 11/1976. Turnabout stereo TVS 34709 (lp), KTVC 34709 (mc 1980).

2.  Emily Van Evera (s), Musicians of Swanne Alley 3'10; rec Bethel United Church of Christ Michigan 3/1986. Harmonia Mundi USA stereo digital HMC 5192 (lp), HMC 405192 (mc), HMC 905192 (cd 1987).

O God, give ear
1.  Consort of Musicke/Anthony Rooley 4'41. L'Oiseau-Lyre stereo DSLO 596 (lp), KCSP 596 (mc 1982).

O God, the proud are risen against me
1.  Tallis Scholars/Peter Phillips 3'00; ed Phillips; rec St John-at-Hackney Church. Gimell stereo digital 158511 (lp), 1585T11 (mc), CDGIM 011 (cd 1987).

O God, whom our offences have justly displeased
1.  New College Oxford Choir/Herbert Andrews [4'10]; ed Fellowes; rec New College Chapel. Columbia mono LX 1381 [sp 1951].

2.  New College Oxford Choir/David Lumsden [4'36]. Abbey stereo 629 (lp 1967).

O Lord, how long wilt thou forget?
1.   † Russell Oberlin (ct), In Nomine Players/Denis Stevens [1′43]; ed Stevens;
     rec London. [New York:] Experiences Anonymes stereo EA 37 (lp 1960).
2.   † Joseph Cornwell (t), Consort of Musicke/Anthony Rooley 5′59.
     L'Oiseau-Lyre stereo DSLO 596 (lp), KCSP 596 (mc 1982).

O Lord, how vain
1.   Barbara Elsy (s), Jaye Consort of Viols/Grayston Burgess 4′57. Turnabout
     mono TV 4017, stereo TV 34017S (lp 1966).
2.   Anne Verkinderen (s), Liege Musica Aurea 4′56. [Brussels:] Alpha stereo
     DB 267 (lp 1978).
3.   Glenda Simpson (ms), Camerata of London 7′18; rec St Michael's Church
     Highgate. CRD stereo CRD 1055 (lp), CRDC 4055 (mc 1978).
4.   Emily Van Evera (s), Musicians of Swanne Alley 6′18; rec Bethel United
     Church of Christ Michigan 3/1986. Harmonia Mundi USA stereo digital
     HMC 5192 (lp), HMC 405192 (mc), HMC 905192 (cd 1987).

O Lord, make thy servant
1.   St Peter ad Vincula Tower of London Chapel Royal Choir/John Williams
     [3′35]. RCA stereo INTS 1115 (lp 1972); Chandos CBR 1006 (lp), CBT
     1006 (mc 1982).
2.   Tallis Scholars/Peter Phillips [2′41]; ed Ashfield; rec All Hallows Church
     Hampstead. Fanfare stereo FR 2197 (lp 1977); United Artists UACL
     10005 [lp 1978].
3.   St Paul's Cathedral Choir/Christopher Dearnley & Barry Rose [3′27]; rec
     St Paul's Cathedral 2/1977. Guild stereo GRSP 7010 (lp 1977).
4.   King's College Cambridge Choir/Stephen Cleobury 2′43; ed Wrightson;
     rec King's College Chapel 13–14/12/1985. EMI stereo digital EL 2705641
     (lp), EL 2705644 (mc), CDC 7477712 (cd 1987).
5.   Tallis Scholars/Peter Phillips 2′52; ed Phillips; rec St John-at-Hackney
     Church. Gimell stereo digital 158511 (lp), 1585T11 (mc), CDGIM 011
     (cd 1987).
6.   Peterborough Cathedral Choir/Christopher Gower [nt]; rec Peterborough
     Cathedral 11/1987. Alpha stereo ACA 575 (lp), CACA 575 (mc 1988).

O Lord, rebuke me not
1.   Michael Deason-Barrow (tr), Salisbury Cathedral Choir/Christopher
     Dearnley, Richard Lloyd (org) [5′43]; ed Fellowes; rec Salisbury Cathedral
     3/1965. Oryx mono 706, stereo 1806 (lp 1966).
2.   Daniel Norman (tr), Lichfield Cathedral Choir/Jonathan Rees-Williams,
     Peter King (org) [6′12]; ed James; rec Lichfield Cathedral 5/1983. Alpha
     stereo ACA 516 (lp), CACA 516 (mc 1983).

O Lord, turn thy wrath [contrafact]
1.   Magdalen College Oxford Choir/John Harper [8′03]; rec Magdalen

College Chapel 4/1985. Alpha stereo ACA 543 (lp), CACA 543 (mc 1985).

**O that most rare breast**
1.   † John York Skinner (ct), Consort of Musicke/Anthony Rooley 8'00. L'Oiseau-Lyre stereo DSLO (596) (lp), KCSP 596 (mc 1982).

**Out of the orient crystal skies**
1.   Leeds Parish Church Choir/Donald Hunt [nt]; ed Dart. Abbey stereo XMS 697 (lp 1970).

**Praise our Lord, all ye Gentiles**
1.   English Singers [3'28]; ed Fellowes. His Master's Voice mono D 710 [sp 1923].
2.   St Paul's Cathedral Choristers, Purcell Chorus of Voices, London Cornet & Sackbut Ensemble, Elizabethan Consort of Viols/Grayston Burgess, Andrew Davis (org) [2'50]. Argo stereo ZRG 659 (lp 1970).
3.   New College Oxford Choir/David Lumsden [3'08]. Abbey stereo LPB 751 (lp 1976).
4.   Chichester Cathedral Choir/John Birch [3'20]; rec Chichester Cathedral 1976. Abbey stereo LPB 770 (lp 1976).
5.   London Early Music Group/James Tyler [3'06]; ed Tyler. RCA stereo RL 25110 (2 lps 1977).
6.   Magdalen College Oxford Choir/John Harper [3'12]; rec Magdalen College Chapel 3/1984. Alpha stereo ACA 537 (lp), CACA 537 (mc 1984).
7.   Hilliard Ensemble/Paul Hillier (bar) 2'58; ed Dunkley; rec Abbey Road Studio 1 London 3/1986. EMI stereo digital EL 7479611 (lp), EL 7479614 (mc), CDC 7479612 (cd 1987).

**Prevent us, O Lord**
1.   Christ Church Cathedral Oxford Choir/Sydney Watson [2'27]; rec Christ Church Cathedral 11/3/1961. Delyse mono ECB 3159, stereo DS 6059 [lp 1961].
2.   St Alban's Abbey Choir/Peter Hurford [3'06]; rec St Alban's Abbey. Abbey stereo 605 (lp 1966).
3.   Scholars 2'48; rec Christ Church Chelsea 29/12/1971. Unicorn stereo UNS 254 (lp 1972).
4.   New College Oxford Choir/David Lumsden [2'29]. Abbey stereo LPB 751 (lp 1976).
5.   Quink 2'30. Etcetera stereo digital ETC 1031 (lp), XTC 1031 (mc 1985).

**Rejoice unto the Lord**
1.   Michael Chance (ct), Fretwork 5'15; rec Forde Abbey 1/1988. Virgin stereo digital VC 7907221 (lp), VC 7907224 (mc), VC 7907222 (cd 1988).

Retire, my soul
1. Quink [4'05]. Etcetera stereo digital ETC 1031 (lp), XTC 1031 (mc 1985).

Sing joyfully unto God our strength
1. Christ Church Cathedral Oxford Choir/Sydney Watson [2'26]; rec Christ Church Cathedral 11/3/1961. Delyse mono ECB 3159, stereo DS 6059 [lp 1961].
2. St Michael's College Tenbury Choir/Lucian Nethsingha [2'36]. Argo mono RG 423, stereo ZRG 5423 (lp 1965).
3. Westminster Abbey Choir/Douglas Guest [2'34]; ed le Huray. His Master's Voice mono CLP 3536, stereo ÇSD 3536 (lp 1966).
4. New College Oxford Choir/David Lumsden [2'32]. Abbey stereo 629 (lp 1967).
5. St James' Church Great Grimsby Choir/Robert Walker [2'29]. Abbey stereo LPB 669 (lp 1970).
6. St Paul's Cathedral Choristers, Purcell Chorus of Voices, London Cornet & Sackbut Ensemble, Elizabethan Consort of Viols/Grayston Burgess, Andrew Davis (org) [2'32]. Argo stereo ZRG 659 (lp 1970); Decca SPA 335 (lp 1974).
7. New College Oxford Choir/David Lumsden [2'41]. Abbey stereo LPB 751 (lp 1976).
8. Norwich Cathedral Choir/Michael Nicholas [2'35]; rec Norwich Cathedral 1/1978. Vista stereo VPS 1066 (lp 1978).
9. Belfast Cathedral Choir/Jonathan Gregory [2'42]. Abbey stereo LPB 802 (lp 1979).
10. St Peter ad Vincula Tower of London Choir/John Williams [2'25]. Abbey stereo ABY 814 (lp 1980).
11. Boston Church of the Advent Choir/Fred Backhaus 2'32; rec Boston Church of the Advent 1982. [Wilmington Mass.:] Afka stereo S 4676 (lp 1982).
12. Magdalen College Oxford Choir/John Harper [2'58]; rec Magdalen College Chapel 3/1984. Alpha stereo ACA stereo ACA 537 (lp), CACA 537 (mc 1984).
13. Ripon Cathedral Choir/Ronald Perrin [2'33]; rec Ripon Cathedral 3/1987. Alpha stereo ACA 564 (lp 1987).
14. Jesus College Cambridge Mixed Choir/David Swinson [2'38]; rec Jesus College Chapel 6/1987. Alpha stereo ACA 568 (lp 1987).
15. King's College Cambridge Choir/Stephen Cleobury 2'47; ed Wrightson; rec King's College Chapel 13–14/12/1985. EMI stereo digital EL 2705641 (lp), EL 2705644 (mc), CDC 7477712 (cd 1987).
16. Tallis Scholars/Peter Phillips 2'50; ed Phillips; rec St John-at-Hackney Church. Gimell stereo digital 158511 (lp), 1585T11 (mc), CDGIM 011 (cd 1987).
17. Liverpool Cathedral Choir/Ian Tracey [nt]; rec Liverpool Cathedral. Solitaire stereo digital SOLI 102 [lp 1988].

Sing ye to our Lord
1.    Northern Convent School [1'42]. His Master's Voice mono C 3523 [sp 1947].

Susanna fair
1.    † New York Pro Musica/Noah Greenberg [2'38]. Brunswick mono AXA 4524, stereo SXA 4524 (lp 1964).
2.    April Cantelo (s), Helen Watts, Sybil Michelow (cs), Gerald English (t), Christopher Keyte (b)/Raymond Leppard [3'04]; ed Poulton. His Master's Voice stereo HQS 1147 (lp 1968).
3.    † Sheila Armstrong (s), English Consort of Viols [4'19]. Pan mono PAN 6208, stereo SPAN 6208 (lp 1967); Saga 5338 (lp 1974).
4.    † Emma Kirkby (s), Consort of Musicke/Anthony Rooley 4'00. L'Oiseau-Lyre stereo DSLO 596 (lp), KCSP 596 (mc 1982).

The man is blest
1.    Russell Oberlin (ct), In Nomine Players/Denis Stevens [1'56]; ed Stevens; rec London. [New York:] Experiences Anonymes stereo EA 37 (lp 1960).

The match that's made
1.    Poppy Holden (s), Consort of Musicke/Anthony Rooley 5'07. L'Oiseau-Lyre stereo DSLO 596 (lp), KCSP 596 (mc 1982).

The nightingale
1.    Saltire Singers [2'04]; rec London. [New York:] Lyrichord mono LL 156, stereo LLST 7156 [lp 1966].
2.    April Cantelo (s), Helen Watts (c), Gerald English (t)/Raymond Leppard [2'58]; ed Fellowes. His Master's Voice stereo HQS 1147 (lp 1968).

The noble famous queen
1.    James Bowman (ct), Dennis Nesbitt (tr vl), Oliver Brookes (b vl), Robert Spencer (lt) [2'07]. His Master's Voice stereo HQS 1281 (lp 1972); EMI EMX 2101 [lp], TC–EMX 2101 [mc 1987].
2.    Lorna Anderson (s), Scottish Early Music Consort/Warwick Edwards (b vl) 2'15; rec SNO Centre Glasgow 9/1983. Chandos stereo digital ABRD 1103 (lp), ABTD 1103 (mc), CHAN 8332 (cd 1984).

This day Christ was born
1.    English Singers [2'54]; ed Fellowes. His Master's Voice mono E 305 [sp 1925].
2.    York Minster Choir [3'34]. His Master's Voice mono C 1334 [sp 1927].
3.    April Cantelo, Eileen Poulter (ss), Helen Watts, Sybil Michelow (cs), Gerald English (t), Christopher Keyte (b)/Raymond Leppard [3'00]; ed Fellowes. His Master's Voice stereo HQS 1147 (lp 1968).

4.  St Paul's Cathedral Choristers, Purcell Chorus of Voices, Elizabethan Consort of Viols/Grayston Burgess, Andrew Davis (org) [2'43]. Argo stereo ZRG 659 (lp 1970).
5.  Christ Church Cathedral Oxford Choir/Simon Preston [2'53]; rec Christ Church Cathedral. Oxford University Press OUP 153 (lp 1979).
6.  Magdalen College Oxford Choir/John Harper [2'47]; rec Magdalen College Chapel 12/1983. Alpha stereo ACA 527 (lp), CACA 527 (mc 1984).

This sweet and merry month of May, 4vv
1.  Ambrosian Consort/Dennis Stevens [3'15]; ed Stevens. His Master's Voice mono HQM 1080, stereo HQS 1080 (lp 1967).
2.  Ambrosian Singers/Denis Stevens [3'24]; ed Stevens; rec London. Oryx stereo EXP 31 [lp 1970].

This sweet and merry month of May, 6vv
1.  English Singers [2'49]; ed Fellowes. His Master's Voice mono E 292 (ssp 1923].
2.  Cambridge University Madrigal Society/Boris Ord [2'23]; ed Fellowes. His Master's Voice mono C 3739 [sp 1948].
3.  English Singers [2'38]. Columbia mono 33SX 1078 [lp 1958].
4.  New York Pro Musica/Noah Greenberg [1'48]. Brunswick mono AXA 4515, stereo SXA 4515 (lp 1959).
5.  Purcell Consort of Voices/Grayston Burgess (ct) [2'27]; rec Decca Studios London 7/1967. Turnabout TV 34202 (lp), KTVC 34202 (mc 1969).
6.  Ambrosian Singers/Denis Stevens [2'23]; ed Stevens; rec London. Oryx stereo EXP 31 [lp 1970].
7.  King's Singers [1'54]; rec concert Royal Festival Hall London 1/5/1978. EMI stereo KS 1001 (lp), TC–KS 1001 (mc 1978); EX 2909593 [lp], EX 2909595 [mc 1987].
8.  King's Singers 2'01. His Master's Voice stereo digital ASD 4092 (lp), TCC–ASD 4092 (mc 1982); CDC 7492652 (cd 1987).
9.  Cambridge Singers/John Rutter 2'38; rec Henry Wood Hall London. Collegium stereo digital COL 105 (lp), COLC 105 (mc 1987).

Though Amaryllis dance in green
1.  English Singers [2'45]; ed Fellowes. His Master's Voice E 292 [ssp 1923].
2.  Cambridge University Madrigal Society/Boris Ord [2'12]; ed Fellowes. His Master's Voice mono C 3739 [sp 1948].
3.  † Russell Oberlin (ct), In Nomine Players/Denis Stevens [2'22]; ed Stevens; rec London. [New York:] Experiences Anonymes stereo EA 37 (lp 1960).
4.  Madrigal Singers/Richard White [2'13]; ed Fellowes. His Master's Voice mono 7EP 7169, stereo PES 5286 (ep 1964).
5.  Purcell Consort of Voices/Grayson Burgess (ct) [2'09]; rec Decca Studios

London 7/1967. Turnabout stereo TV 34202 (lp), KTVC 34202 (mc 1969).

6.  † [Judith Nelson] (s), Academy of Ancient Music/Christopher Hogwood 2'12; rec Christ Church Sutton Surrey 4/1978. Folio Society stereo FS 1003–4 (2 lps 1978); L'Oiseau-Lyre DSLO 606 (lp 1983).

7.  Rosemary Hardy, Elizabeth Lane, Mary Thomas (ss), Pro Cantione Antiqua/Philip Ledger [2'07]; ed Ledger & Parker; rec St Mark's Church Hamilton Terrace London. Oxford University Press stereo OUP 151–2 (2 lps 1979).

8.  Clare College Cambridge Chapel Choir/Timothy Brown [2'22]; ed Ledger & Parker; rec Concert Hall University Music School Cambridge. Cambridge Classical Records stereo CCRS 1004 (lp 1982).

9.  Tallis Scholars/Peter Phillips 4'45; rec The Great Hall Deene Park Northamptonshire 4/1982. Music for Pleasure stereo digital CFP 4391 (lp), TC–CFP 4391 (mc 1982).

10. Mosaic [nt]. Whitetower ENS 148 (mc 1986).

11. I Fagiolini [nt]. Whitetower ENS 156 (mc 1987).

12. Cambridge Singers/John Rutter 2'10; rec Henry Wood Hall London. Collegium stereo digital COL 105 (lp), COLC 105 (mc), COLCD 105 (cd 1987).

13. † [Lynne Dawson (s), John Potter (t),] Hilliard Ensemble, London Baroque/Paul Hillier (bar) 5'10; ed Dunkley; rec Abbey Road Studio 1 London 3/1986. EMI stereo digital EL 7479611 (lp), EL 7479614 (mc), CDC 7479612 (cd 1987).

14. Amaryllis Consort/Charles Brett (ct) [2'23]. Pickwick stereo digital CIMPC 873 (mc), PCD 873 (cd 1988).


Turn our captivity, O Lord

1.  English Singers [4'14]; ed Fellowes. His Master's Voice mono D 711 [sp 1923].

2.  St Paul's Cathedral Choristers, Purcell Chorus of Voices, London Cornet & Sackbut Ensemble, Elizabethan Consort of Viols/Grayston Burgess, Andrew Davis (org) [4'45]. Argo stereo ZRG 659 (lp 1970).

3.  Boston Camerata, Boston Shawm & Sackbut Ensemble/Joel Cohen 4'31; rec Trinity Church Boston 10/1984. Erato stereo digital NUM 75252 (lp), MCE 75252 (mc), ECD 88168 (cd 1986).

4.  Hilliard Ensemble/Paul Hillier (bar) 3'51; ed Dunkley; rec Abbey Road Studio 1 London 3/1986. EMI stereo digital EL 7479611 (lp), EL 7479614 (mc), CDC 7479612 (cd 1987).


Wedded to will is witless

1.  London Early Music Group/James Tyler [2'25]; ed Tyler. RCA stereo RL 25110 (2 lps 1977).

What pleasure have great princes?
1. †Russell Oberlin (ct), In Nomine Players/Denis Stevens [3'29]; ed Stevens; rec London. [New York:] Experiences Anonymes stereo EA 37 (lp 1960).
2. Scholars 1'15; [rec St George the Martyr Church Queen Square London 4/1976]. Prelude stereo PRS 2501 (lp 1976).
3. †Paul Elliott (t), London Early Music Group/James Tyler [5'58]; ed Tyler. RCA stereo RL 25110 (2 lps 1977).
4. †John York Skinner (ct), Consort of Musicke/Anthony Rooley 5'19. L'Oiseau-Lyre stereo DSLO 596 (lp), KCSP 596 (mc 1982).

When I was otherwise
1. †James Bowman (ct), English Consort of Viols 3'00; rec 11/1976. Turnabout stereo TVS 34709 (lp), KTVC 34709 (mc 1980).

Who made thee, Hob, forsake the plough?
1. Ulrike Taube (s), Wolf Reinhold (t), Capella Fidicinia/Hans Gruss (b vl) [1'16]. Archiv 199014 [lp 1969].
2. Gerald English (t), Christopher Keyte (b), English Consort of Viols [nt]. Saga stereo 5348 (lp 1974).
3. Anthony Holt, Simon Carrington (bars), Consort of Musicke/Anthony Rooley 1'19. EMI stereo SLS 1078393 (2 lps), TC-SLS 1078395 (2 mcs 1984).
4. David James, Ashley Stafford (cts), London Baroque/Paul Hillier 1'46; ed Dunkley; rec Abbey Road Studio 1 London 3/1986. EMI stereo digital EL 7479611 (lp), EL 7479614 (mc), CDC 7479612 (cd 1987).

Why do I use my paper, ink and pen?
1. English Singers [2'11]; ed Fellowes. His Master's Voice mono D 711 [sp 1923].
2. †Russell Oberlin (ct), In Nomine Players/Denis Stevens [3'15]; ed Stevens; rec London. [New York:] Experiences Anonymes stereo EA 37 (lp 1960).

Wounded I am
1. Saltire Singers [4'00]; rec London. [New York:] Lyrichord mono LL 156, stereo LLST 7156 [lp 1966].

Ye sacred muses
1. Alfred Deller (ct), Wenzinger Consort of Viols of the Schola Cantorum Basiliensis/August Wenzinger [3'42]; ed Fellowes. Vanguard mono PVL 7035 [lp 1958].
2. John Whitworth (ct), Diana Poulton (lt), Michael Thomas (clvc) [3'27]; ed Whitworth. Saga mono XID 5222 (lp 1964).
3. Ian Partridge (t), Jaye Consort of Viols/Grayston Burgess 3'18. Turnabout mono TV 4017, stereo TV 34017S (lp 1966).

4.   Gerald English (t), Jaye Consort/Francis Baines [3'02]; ed Fellowes. His
     Master's Voice stereo HQS 1141 (lp 1968).
5.   Anne Verkinderen (s), Liege Musica Aurea 3'17. [Brussels:] Alpha stereo
     DB 267 (lp 1978).
6.   David James (ct), London Baroque/Paul Hillier 3'35; ed Dunkley; rec
     Abbey Road Studio 1 3/1986. EMI stereo digital EL 7479611 (lp), EL
     7479614 (mc), CDC 7479612 (cd 1987).
7.   A. Zaepffel (s), Les Elements Viol Ensemble [nt]. Adda stereo digital
     581033 [cd 1988].

*Consort music*

*Fantasias, grounds and dances*
Browning a 5
1.   New York Pro Musica/Noah Greenberg [4'26]. Brunswick mono AXA
     4524, stereo SXA 4524 (lp 1964).
2.   Barbara Elsy, Susan Longfield (ss), Noreen Willett (c), Gerald English (t),
     Geoffrey Shaw (b), Jaye Consort of Viols/Christopher Bishop [5'54]; ed
     Fellowes. His Master's Voice stereo HQS 1147 (lp 1968).
3.   Bruggen Consort/Frans Bruggen [4'18]; rec Bennebroek 3/1967. Tele-
     funken mono AWT 9511, stereo SAWT 9511 (lp 1968).
4.   English Consort of Viols [4'15]. Turnabout stereo TV 34443S (lp 1971).
5.   Linde Consort/Hans-Martin Linde (rec) [4'29]. [Cologne:] EMI stereo lC
     06330105 (lp 1972).
6.   David Munrow Recorder Consort [4'38]. His Master's Voice stereo SLS
     5022 (2 lps 1975).
7.   Musica Dolce/Clars Pehrsson (rec) 4'16; rec Castle Wik Sweden 1976. Bis
     stereo LP 57 (lp 1977).
8.   Consort of Musicke/Trevor Jones 4'49. L'Oiseau-Lyre stereo DSLO 599
     (lp 1983).

Fantasia a 3 in C, no. 2
1.   London Early Music Group/James Tyler [1'51]; ed Tyler. RCA stereo RL
     25110 (2 lps 1977).
2.   Consort of Musicke/Trevor Jones 2'15. L'Oiseau-Lyre stereo DSLO 599
     (lp 1983).
3.   Julian Bream Consort 2'32; rec Wigmore Hall London 9/1987. RCA
     stereo digital RL 87801 (lp), RK 87801 (mc), RD 87801 (cd 1988).

Fantasia a 3 in C, no. 3
1.   Fretwork 1'14; rec The Meeting House Frenchay Nr Bristol 2/1987. Amon
     Ra stereo digital CSAR 29 (mc), CD-SAR 29 (cd 1987).

Fantasia a 4 in A minor
1.   Consort of Musicke/Trevor Jones 2'25. L'Oiseau-Lyre stereo DSLO 599
     (lp 1983).

Fantasia a 4 in G minor
1.  Wenzinger Consort of Viols of the Schola Cantorum Basiliensis/August Wenzinger [3'08]. Vanguard mono PVL 7035 [lp 1958].
2.  London Early Music Group/James Tyler [2'45]; ed Tyler. RCA stereo RL 25110 (2 lps 1977).
3.  Liege Musica Aurea 2'44. [Brussels:] Alpha stereo DB 267 (lp 1978).
4.  Consort of Musicke/Trevor Jones 2'44. L'Oiseau-Lyre stereo DSLO 599 (lp 1983).

Fantasia a 5 in C
1.  Consort of Musicke/Trevor Jones 5'48. L'Oiseau-Lyre stereo DSLO 599 (lp 1983).
2.  Musica Dolce/Clars Pehrsson 5'35. Bis CD 305 [cd 1988].
3.  Fretwork 6'00; rec Boxgrove Priory Chichester 6/1986. Virgin stereo digital VC 7907061 (lp), VC 7907064 (mc), VC 7907062 (cd 1988).

Fantasia a 6 in G minor, no. 1
1.  In Nomine Players/Denis Stevens (vdb) [6'12]; ed Ward; rec London. [New York:] Experiences Anonymes stereo EA 37 (lp 1960).
2.  Leonhardt Consort/Gustav Leonhardt [5'19]; rec Hervormde Kerk Bennebroek 10/1965. Telefunken mono AWT 9481, stereo SAWT 9481 [lp 1966]; 6DX 35286 [2 lps 1976].
3.  Scottish Baroque Ensemble/Leonard Friedman 6'15; ed Elliott; rec St Mary's Church Haddington. CRD stereo CRD 1043 (lp), CRDC 4043 (mc 1978).
4.  Consort of Musicke/Trevor Jones 5'53. L'Oiseau-Lyre stereo DSLO 599 (lp 1983).
5.  Musica Dolce/Clars Pehrsson [nt]. Bis CD 305 [cd 1988].

Fantasia a 6 in G minor, no. 2
1.  Byrd String Sextet [5'22]; ed Fellowes. His Master's Voice mono E 293 [ssp 1923].
2.  Boyd Neel String Orchestra/Boyd Neel [4'09]; ed Fellowes. Decca mono K 1832–3 (2 sps 1948).
3.  Consort of Musicke/Trevor Jones 4'19. L'Oiseau-Lyre stereo DSLO 599 (lp 1983).
4.  Musica Dolce/Clars Pehrsson 5'08. Bis CD 305 [cd 1988].

Pavan a 5 in C minor
1.  Liege Musica Aurea 3'59. [Brussels:] Alpha stereo DB 267 (lp 1978).

Pavan and Galliard a 6 in C
1.  Leonhardt Consort/Gustav Leonhardt [4'04]; rec Hervormde Kerk Bennebroek 10/1965. Telefunken mono AWT 9481, stereo SAWT 9481 [lp 1966]; 6DX 35286 [2 lps 1976].

2.   English Consort of Viols/Dennis Nesbitt [5'01]. Saga stereo 5347 (lp 1974).

3.   Consort of Musicke/Trevor Jones 4'23. L'Oiseau-Lyre stereo DSLO 599 (lp 1983).

*Pavan and Galliard a 6 in C: Galliard
   *1.   Exempore String Ensemble [nt]. Meridian E77003 (lp 1978).

Prelude [and Ground]
   1.   In Nomine Players/Denis Stevens [6'03]; ed Ward; rec London. [New York:] Experiences Anonymes stereo EA 37 (lp 1960).
   2.   Consort of Musicke/Trevor Jones 5'50. L'Oiseau-Lyre stereo DSLO 599 (lp 1983).

*In Nomines*
In Nomine a 4, no. 1
   1.   English Consort of Viols [2'12]. National Trust stereo NT 003 (lp 1977).
   2.   Liege Musica Aurea 2'13. [Brussels:] Alpha stereo DB 267 (lp 1978).
   3.   Consort of Musicke/Trevor Jones 2'10. L'Oiseau-Lyre stereo DSLO 599 (lp 1983).

In Nomine a 4, no. 2
   1.   Liege Musica Aurea 2'05. [Brussels:] Alpha stereo DB 267 (lp 1978).
   2.   Consort of Musicke/Trevor Jones 2'13. L'Oiseau-Lyre stereo DSLO 599 (lp 1983).
   3.   Fretwork 2'56; rec The Meeting House Frenchay Nr Bristol 2/1987. Amon Ra stereo digital CSAR 29 (mc), CD-SAR 29 (cd 1987).

In Nomine a 5, no. 2, 'on the sharpe'
   1.   Jaye Consort of Viols/Grayston Burgess 2'57. Turnabout mono TV 4017, stereo TV 34017S (lp 1966).
   2.   Consort of Musicke/Trevor Jones 2'20. L'Oiseau-Lyre stereo DSLO 599 (lp 1983).

In Nomine a 5, no. 4
   1.   Consort of Musicke/Trevor Jones 3'16. L'Oiseau-Lyre stereo DSLO 599 (lp 1983).

In Nomine a 5, no. 5
   1.   In Nomine Players/Denis Stevens [2'41]; ed Ward; rec London. [New York:] Experiences Anonymes stereo EA 37 (lp 1960).
   2.   Bruggen Consort/Frans Bruggen [3'03]; rec Bennebroek 3/1967. Telefunken mono AWT 9511, stereo SAWT 9511 (lp 1968).

*Hymn and Miserere settings*
Christe qui lux es a 4, no. 1
1.   Landini Consort/Peter Syrus [2'44]; rec College of Ripon & York St John Chapel York 8/1978. Hill & Dale stereo HD 001 (lp 1978).

Christe qui lux es a 4, no. 3
1.   Liege Musica Aurea 0'51. [Brussels:] Alpha stereo DB 267 (lp 1978).

Christe Redemptor a 4
1.   Jaye Consort of Viols 4'05. Arion stereo ARN 38215 (lp 1974).
2.   Consort of Musicke/Trevor Jones 2'51. L'Oiseau-Lyre stereo DSLO 599 (lp 1983).

Sermone blando a 4, no. 2
1.   Amsterdam Loeki Stardust Quartet 3'05; rec Concertgebouw Small Hall Amsterdam 6/1984. L'Oiseau-Lyre stereo digital 4142771 [lp], 4142774 [mc], 4142772 [cd 1985].

## Keyboard music

*Fantasias, preludes, hymns and antiphons*
Christe qui lux
1.   Mark Duthie (org) [0'58]; rec St Andrew's Scottish Episcopal Cathedral Aberdeen 1/1988. Tape to Disc Service stereo TD 8801 (mc 1988).

Clarifica me, Pater, setting 1
1.   Mark Duthie (org) [1'45]; rec Divine Service St Andrew's Scottish Episcopal Cathedral Aberdeen 1/5/1988. Donselco stereo KB 1 (mc 1988).

Clarifica me, Pater, setting 2
1.   Andrew Davis (org) [2'51]. Argo stereo ZRG 659 (lp 1970).

Clarifica me, Pater, setting 3
1.   Roy Jesson (org) [2'19]; rec London. [New York:] Lyrichord mono LL 156, stereo LLST 7156 [lp 1966].
2.   Joseph Payne (org) 4'00; rec King's Chapel Boston. Vox mono VBX 72, stereo SVBX 572 (3 lps 1966).
3.   Gustav Leonhardt (cha org) [2'35]; rec Hervormde Kerk Bennebroek 10/1965. Telefunken mono AWT 9481, stereo SAWT 9481 [lp 1966]; 6DX 35286 [2 lps 1976].
4.   Lionel Rogg (hist hpsc) [2'34]. RCA stereo LSB 4038 (lp 1971).
5.   Antony Saunders (cha org) [2'52]; ed Tyler. RCA stereo RL 25110 (2 lps 1977).
6.   Hans Fagius (org) 2'39; rec Norra Asarp Church Sweden 7/5/1979. Bis stereo LP 141 [lp 1980].

Fantasia in A minor
1.  Colin Tilney (hpsc) [8'17]. Argo stereo ZRG 675 (lp 1973).
2.  John Beckett (hpsc) [7'11]. Saga stereo 5347 (lp 1974).
3.  Elisabeth Garnier (virg) 7'37; rec Grand'Combe-Chateleu Church. Arion stereo ARN 36572 (lp 1980).
4.  John Whitelaw (hpsc) 7'52; ed Brown. [New York:] Spectrum stereo SR 139 (lp 1981).
5.  Ton Koopman (hpsc) [7'50]. Philips stereo 9502121 (lp), 7313121 (mc 1983).

*Fantasia in A minor: [bars 1–185, 189–end]
*1.  Fritz Neumeyer (hpsc) [8'46]; rec Paulus Saal Freiburg 5/1954. Archiv mono AP 13026 [slp 1955].

*Fantasia in A minor: [section 1]
*2.  Jiri Rheinberger (hist org) 4'25; rec Krumlow Monastery. Supraphon mono SUA 10901, stereo SUAST 50901 (lp 1968).

Fantasia in C, no. 1
1.  Christopher Hogwood (cha org) 7'35; rec Finchcocks Kent. L'Oiseau-Lyre stereo D29D4 (4 lps 1977).

Fantasia in C, no. 2
1.  Thurston Dart (hist org) [5'37]; rec St Lawrence Church Appleby West-morland. His Master's Voice mono CLP 1212 (lp 1958).
2.  Paul Maynard (org) [4'28]; rec General Theological Seminary Chapel New York. [New York:] Decca mono DL 10040, stereo DL 711040 [lp 1962].
3.  Joseph Payne (org) 5'00; rec King's Chapel Boston. Vox mono VBX 72, stereo SVBX 572 (3 lps 1966).
4.  Christopher Hogwood (hpsc) 4'55; rec Finchcocks Kent. L'Oiseau-Lyre stereo D29D4 (4 lps 1977).
5.  Tom Pixton (hpsc) 4'30; rec 7/1977. [Cambridge Mass.:] Titanic stereo Ti-20 (lp 1978).
6.  Margaret Phillips (org) [5'14]; rec St Giles without Cripplegate London. Aerco AERL 30 (lp 1980).
7.  Hans Fagius (org) 5'49; rec Norra Asarp Church Sweden 7/5/1979. Bis stereo LP 141 [lp 1980].
8.  Frances Fitch (org) 5'46; rec Wellesley College Mass. [Cambridge Mass.:] Titanic stereo Ti-95 (lp 1982).
9.  Ton Koopman (hpsc) 6'11. Philips stereo 9502121 (lp), 7313121 (mc 1983).
10.  Simon Preston (hist cha org) 5'37; ed Ledger; rec Knole House Chapel Sevenoaks Kent 12/1984. Archiv stereo digital 4156751 (lp), 4156752 (cd 1986).
11.  Paul Nicholson (org) 5'22; rec Boxgrove Priory Chichester 6/1986. Virgin

stereo digital VC 7907061 (lp), VC 7907064 (mc), VC 7907062 (cd 1988).

Fantasia in C, no. 3
1. Tom Pixton (hpsc) 3'20; rec 7/1977. [Cambridge Mass.:] Titanic stereo Ti-20 (lp 1978).

*Fantasia in C, no. 3: [bar 46 to end]
*1. Thurston Dart (hist org) [2'27]; rec St Lawrence Church Appleby West-morland. His Master's Voice mono CLP 1212 (lp 1958).
*2. Paul Maynard (org) [2'29]; rec General Theological Seminary Chapel New York. [New York:] Decca mono DL 10040, stereo DL 711040 [lp 1962].
*3. Christopher Hogwood (cha org) 3'50; rec Finchcocks Kent. L'Oiseau-Lyre stereo D29D4 (4 lps 1977).

Fantasia in D minor
1. Paul Maynard (hpsc) [4'04]. [New York:] Decca mono DL 10040, stereo DL 711040 [lp 1962].
2. Igor Kipnis (hpsc) 4'38; rec Unitarian Church Westport Conn. [Holly-wood:] EMI stereo SB-3816 (2 lps 1974).
3. Colin Tilney (hist hpsc) [5'38]; [rec German National Museum Nurem-berg]. [Cologne:] EMI stereo lC 06330120 (lp 1974).
4. Christopher Hogwood (virg) 4'55; rec Finchcocks Kent. L'Oiseau-Lyre stereo D29D4 (4 lps 1977).

Fantasia in G, no. 2
1. Joseph Payne (org) 9'48; rec King's Chapel Boston. Vox mono VBX 72, stereo SVBX 572 (3 lps 1966).
2. Jorg Ewald Dahler (virg) 7'15; rec Aula Museum fur Volkerkunde Basel. Claves stereo D 511 (lp 1975); digitally remastered CD 50–511 (cd 1987).
3. Malcolm Proud (hpsc) [7'52]; ed Brown; rec Aula Maxima Maynooth College. Claddagh stereo CSM 59 (lp 1985).

Fantasia in G, no. 3
1. Wolfgang Walter (hist clvg) [5'39]; rec Salzburg [Cathedral]. [Cologne:] EMI stereo lC 06599818 (lp 1976).

Miserere, setting 1
1. Mark Duthie (org) [1'19]; rec St Andrew's Scottish Episcopal Cathedral Aberdeen 1/1988. Tape to Disc Service stereo TD 8801 (mc 1988).

Miserere, setting 2
1. Paul Maynard (org) [1'10]; rec General Theological Seminary Chapel New York. [New York:] Decca mono DL 10040, stereo DL 711040 [lp 1962].
2. Mark Duthie (org) [1'22]; rec St Andrew's Scottish Episcopal Cathedral Aberdeen 1/1988. Tape to Disc Service stereo TD 8801 (mc 1988).

Prelude in A minor
1. Fritz Neumeyer (hpsc) [0'43]; rec Paulus Saal Freiburg, 5/1954. Archiv mono AP 13026 [slp 1955].
2. John Beckett (hpsc) [0'34]. Saga stereo 5347 (lp 1974).
3. John Whitelaw (hpsc) 0'50; ed Brown. [New York:] Spectrum stereo SR 139 (lp 1981).
4. Ton Koopman (hpsc) [0'57]. Philips stereo 9502121 (lp), 7313121 (mc 1983).

Prelude in C
1. Geraint Jones (org) [1'16]; ed Donington. Decca mono X 549 [sp 1951]; LXT 2795–6 [2 lps 1953].
2. Roy Jesson (org) [1'02]; rec London. [New York:] Lyrichord mono LL 156, stereo LLST 7156 [lp 1966].
3. Colin Tilney (hist hpsc) [0'53]. Pye stereo GSGC 14129 (lp), ZCGC 7053 (mc 1968).
4. Colin Tilney (hist virg) [0'50]; [rec German National Museum Nuremberg]. [Cologne:] EMI stereo lC 06330120 (lp 1974).

Prelude in F
1. Davitt Moroney (hist hpsc) [0'59]; rec St Martin du Mejan Arles 5/1986. Harmonia Mundi France stereo digital HMC 1241–2 (2 lps), HMC 40241–2 (2 mcs), HMC 901241–2 (2 cds 1986).

Prelude in G
1. Mark Duthie (org) [1'17]; rec Divine Service St Andrew's Scottish Episcopal Cathedral Aberdeen 1/5/1988. Donselco stereo KB 1 (mc 1988).

Prelude in G minor
1. Colin Tilney (hist hpsc) [0'33]. Pye stereo GSGC 14129 (lp), ZCGC 7053 (mc 1968).
2. Colin Tilney (hist hpsc) 0'36; rec German National Museum Nuremberg, 3/1977. Archiv stereo 2533379 (lp 1978); 2547069 (lp), 3347069 (mc 1982).
3. John Whitelaw (hpsc) 0'40; ed Brown. [New York:] Spectrum stereo SR 139 (lp 1981).
4. Davitt Moroney (hist hpsc) [0'42]; rec St Martin du Mejan Arles 5/1986. Harmonia Mundi France stereo digital HMC 1241–2 (2 lps), HMC 401241–2 (2 mcs), HMC 901241–2 (2 cds 1986).

Salvator mundi, setting 1
1. Paul Maynard (org) [1'08]; rec General Theological Seminary Chapel New York. [New York:] Decca mono DL 10040, stereo DL 711040 [lp 1962].

Salvator mundi, setting 2
1.   Paul Maynard (org) [1'05]; rec General Theological Seminary Chapel New York. [New York:] Decca mono DL 10040, stereo DL 711040 [lp 1962].

Ut re mi fa sol la, in G
1.   Christopher Hogwood (cha org) 7'50; rec Finchcocks Kent. L'Oiseau-Lyre stereo D29D4 (4 lps 1977).
2.   John Whitelaw (hpsc) 6'43; ed Brown. [New York:] Spectrum stereo SR 139 (lp 1981).

Verse [Fantasia in C, no. 4]
1.   Andrew Davis (org) [1'41]. Argo stereo ZRG 659 (lp 1970).

Voluntary for my Lady Nevell [Fantasia in G, no. 1]
1.   Glenn Gould (pf) 3'30. CBS stereo 72988 (lp 1973); MP 39552 (lp), MPT 39552 (mc 1987).
2.   Christopher Hogwood (hpsc) 5'15; rec Finchcocks Kent. L'Oiseau-Lyre stereo D29D4 (4 lps 1977); DSLO 566 (lp 1980).

*Grounds and related pieces*
Hugh Aston's Ground
1.   Glenn Gould (pf) 9'52. CBS stereo 72988 (lp 1973); MP 39552 (lp), MPT 39552 (mc 1987).
2.   Colin Tilney (hist hpsc) [8'28]; [rec German National Museum Nuremberg]. [Cologne:] EMI stereo lC 06330120 (lp 1974).
3.   Christopher Hogwood (hpsc) 7'15; rec Finchcocks Kent. L'Oiseau-Lyre stereo D29D4 (4 lps 1977); DSLO 566 (lp 1980).

My Lady Nevell's Ground
1.   Christopher Hogwood (virg) 5'20; rec Finchcocks Kent. L'Oiseau-Lyre stereo D29D4 (4 lps 1977).
2.   Elisabeth Garnier (virg) 5'31; rec Grand'Combe-Chateleu Church. Arion Stereo ARN 36571 (lp 1980).
3.   John Whitelaw (hpsc) 5'05; ed Brown. [New York:] Spectrum stereo SR 139 (lp 1981).

Qui passe [Chi passa] for my Lady Nevell
1.   Christopher Hogwood (virg) 3'10; rec Finchcocks Kent. L'Oiseau-Lyre stereo D29D4 (4 lps 1977); DSLO 566 (lp 1980).
2.   Tom Pixton (hpsc) 4'10; rec 7/1977. [Cambridge Mass.:] Titanic stereo Ti–20 (lp 1978).

The Bells
1.   Fritz Neumeyer (hpsc) 7'05; rec Paulus Saal Freiburg 5/1954. Archiv mono AP 13026 [slp 1955]; EPA 37127 [ep 1959].

2.  Sylvia Marlowe (hpsc) [7'47]. Brunswick mono AXA 4531, stereo SXA 4531 (lp 1965).
3.  Sylvia Kind (hpsc) 5'32. Turnabout stereo TV 34200 (lp 1969).
4.  Trevor Pinnock (hist spt) [6'05]; rec Victoria & Albert Museum London. CRD stereo CRD 1007 (lp), CRDC 4007 (mc 1973).
5.  Tom Pixton (hpsc) 5'25; rec 7/1977. [Cambridge Mass.:] Titanic stereo Ti–20 (lp 1978).
6.  John Whitelaw (hpsc) 5'22; ed Brown. [New York:] Spectrum stereo SR 139 (lp 1981).
7.  Ton Koopman (hpsc) 5'20. Philips stereo 9502121 (lp), 7313121 (mc 1983).
8.  Robert Aldwinckle (hpsc) [5'52]. Pickwick stereo digital CIMPC 850 (mc), PCD 850 (cd 1987).

*The Bells: [sections 1–4, 8–9]
*1.  Pauline Aubert (hpsc) [3'42]. L'Anthologie Sonore mono AS 14 [sp 1936].

The Hunt's Up, or Pescodd Time
1.  Christopher Hogwood (hpsc) 6'20; rec Finchcocks Kent. L'Oiseau-Lyre stereo D29D4 (4 lps 1977).
2.  Colin Tilney (hist virg) 7'13; rec German National Museum Nuremberg 3/1977. Archiv stereo 2533379 (lp 1978); 2547069 (lp), 3347069 (mc 1982).
3.  Elisabeth Garnier (virg) 7'15; rec Grand'Combe-Chateleu Church. Arion stereo ARN 36571 (lp 1980).

The seconde grownde, in C
1.  Christopher Hogwood (hpsc) 8'00; rec Finchcocks Kent. L'Oiseau-Lyre stereo D29D4 (4 lps 1977); DSLO 566 (lp 1980).

Ut re mi fa sol la, in F
1.  Paul Wolfe (hpsc) [3'18]; rec Esoteric Sound Studios New York City. [New York:] Experience Anonymes mono EA 13 (lp 1956).
2.  Paul Maynard (org) [3'25]; rec General Theological Seminary Chapel New York. [New York:] Decca mono DL 10040, stereo DL 711040 [lp 1962].
3.  Thurston Dart, Igor Kipnis (hpscs) 3'25. CBS stereo 61300 (lp 1972).
4.  Peter Hurford (org) [3'39]; rec Our Lady of Sorrows Church Toronto. Argo stereo ZRG 806 (lp 1975).
5.  Murray Somerville, Hazel Somerville (org) [3'37]; rec New College Chapel Oxford. Abbey stereo LPB 752 (lp 1976).

*Variations*
All in a garden green
1.  Christopher Hogwood (hpsc) 5'40; rec Finchcocks Kent. L'Oiseau-Lyre stereo D29D4 (4 lps 1977).

Callino casturame
1.  Michael Thomas (hpsc) [1'59]. Pan mono PAN 6202, stereo SPAN 6202 (lp 1966).
2.  Lionel Rogg (hist cha org) [1'58]. RCA stereo LSB 4038 (lp 1971).
3.  Igor Kipnis (hpsc) 2'04; rec Unitarian Church Westport Conn. [Hollywood:] EMI stereo SB–3816 (2 lps 1974).
4.  Judith Lambden (spt) [2'07]. [Haslemere:] Chantry mono CRLP 19 [lp 1978].
5.  Harold Lester (hist hpsc) 2'25; rec Colt Collection Bethersden. Harmonia Mundi stereo HM 227 (lp 1980).
6.  Christopher Hogwood (hist hpsc) [2'10]; [rec Fitzwilliam Museum Cambridge]. L'Oiseau-Lyre stereo D261D2 (2 lps 1982).
7.  Christopher Kite (hist virg) 2'08; rec Bishopsgate Institute London 11/1981. Hyperion stereo A 66067 (lp 1983).
8.  Alexei Semenov (hpsc) 4'06; rec 1980. [Moscow:] Melodiya stereo C10 19015000 (lp 1983).

Fortune
1.  Fritz Neumeyer (hpsc) 4'41; rec Paulus Saal Freiburg 5/1954. Archiv mono AP 13026 [slp 1955]; EPA 37127 [ep 1959].
2.  Fritz Heitmann (org) [3'34]. Telefunken mono LGX 66037 [lp 1955].
3.  Nicholas McGegan (virg) [3'45]. National Trust stereo NT 003 (lp 1977).
4.  Tom Pixton (hpsc) 4'35; rec 7/1977. [Cambridge Mass.:] Titanic stereo Ti–20 (lp 1978).
5.  Elisabeth Garnier (msr) 3'30; rec Grand'Combe-Chateleu Church. Arion stereo ARN 36572 (lp 1980).

John come kiss me now
1.  Paul Maynard (hpsc) [5'03]. [New York:] Decca mono DL 10040, stereo DL 711040 [lp 1962].
2.  Lionel Rogg (hpsc) [5'35]. RCA stereo LSB 4038 (lp 1971).
3.  John Beckett (hpsc) [4'56]. Saga stereo 5347 (lp 1974).
4.  John Whitelaw (hpsc) 6'17; ed Brown. [New York:] Spectrum stereo SR 139 (lp 1981).
5.  Christopher Hogwood (hist virg) 6'12; [rec Victoria & Albert Museum London]. L'Oiseau-Lyre stereo D261D2 (2 lps 1982).
6.  Zsuzsa Pertis (hpsc) [4'51]. Hungaraton stereo HRC 079 (cd 1988).

O mistress mine, I must
1.  Michael Thomas (clvg) [5'44]. Pan mono PAN 6202, stereo SPAN 6202 (lp 1966).
2.  Tom Pixton (hpsc) 4'50; rec 7/1977. [Cambridge Mass.:] Titanic stereo Ti–20 (lp 1978).
3.  Ton Koopman (hpsc) 5'02. Philips stereo 9502121 (lp), 7313121 (mc 1983).

*O mistress mine, I must: [variations 1–3, 6]
*1.   George Dyson (pf) [3'08]. Columbia mono D 40137 [sp 1929].
*2.   Margaret Hodsdon (virg) [3'10]; ed Hodsdon. His Master's Voice mono
      CLP 1633–4, stereo CSD 1487–8 (2 lps 1963).

Rowland, or Lord Willoughby's Welcome home
1.    Violet Gordon Woodhouse (hpsc) [2'17]. His Master's Voice mono E 295
      [ssp 1923].
2.    Thurston Dart (hpsc) [2'18]. L'Oiseau-Lyre mono OL 50076 [lp 1955];
      electronic stereo OLS 114–18 (5 lps 1971).
3.    Paul Maynard (hpsc) [1'33]. Brunswick mono AXTL 1099, stereo SXA
      4007 (lp 1962).
4.    Susi Jeans (hist virg) [2'42]; rec 8/1961. Archiv mono APM 14301, stereo
      SAPM 198301 (lp 1964); 199001 [lp 1969].
5.    Michael Thomas (clvc) [3'07]. Pan mono PAN 6202, stereo SPAN 6202
      (lp 1966).
6.    Margaret Hodsdon (hist spt) [2'16]; [rec Victoria & Albert Museum
      London]. Musica Rara stereo MUS 70 (lp 1968).
7.    Igor Kipnis (hpsc) 2'24; rec Unitarian Church Westport Conn. [Holly-
      wood:] EMI stereo SB–3816 (2 lps 1974).
8.    Christopher Hogwood (virg) 2'25; rec Finchcocks Kent. L'Oiseau-Lyre
      stereo D29D4 (4 lps 1977).
9.    Trevor Pinnock (hpsc) [3'10]; rec St Botolph's Church Swyncombe. CRD
      stereo CRD 1050 (lp), CRDC 4050 (mc 1978); digitally remastered CRD
      3350 [cd 1988].
10.   Tom Pixton (hpsc) 1'50; rec 7/1977. [Cambridge Mass.:] Titanic stereo
      Ti–20 (lp 1978).
11.   Elisabeth Garnier (msr) 2'23; rec Grand'Combe-Chateleu Church. Arion
      stereo ARN 36572 (lp 1980).

Sellinger's Round
1.    Glenn Gould (pf) 5'41. CBS stereo 72988 (lp 1973); MP 39552 (lp), MPT
      39552 (mc 1987).
2.    Lars Ulrik Mortensen (hpsc) 5'47; rec Banqueting Hall Gjorslev Castle
      1979. Canzone stereo CAN 101 [lp 1980].
3.    Christopher Hogwood (virg) 5'40; rec Finchcocks Kent. L'Oiseau-Lyre
      stereo D29D4 (4 lps 1977); DSLO 566 (lp 1980).
4.    Zsuzsa Pertis (hpsc) [6'22]. Hungaraton stereo HRC 079 (cd 1988).

*Sellinger's Round: [variations 1,3,2,6,8,9]
*1.   Margaret Hodsdon (virg) [4'45]; ed Hodsdon. His Master's Voice mono
      CLP 1633–4, stereo CSD 1487–8 (2 lps 1963).

*Sellinger's Round: [variations 1,4,6,9 [bars 161–175, 180–2]]
*2.   Erwin Bodky (hist hpsc) [2'54]. Parlophone mono R 1023 [ssp 1931].

The Carman's Whistle

1. Thurston Dart (hpsc) [4'44]; ed Donington. Decca mono X 540 [sp 1951]; LXT 2795–6 [2 lps 1953].
2. Paul Maynard (hpsc) [3'34]. [New York:] Decca mono DL 10040, stereo DL 711040 [lp 1962].
3. Susi Jeans (hist virg) [3'57]; rec 8/1961. Archiv mono APM 14301, stereo SAPM 198301 (lp 1964); 199001 [lp 1969].
4. Joseph Payne (hpsc) 3'46. Vox mono VBX 72, stereo SVBX 572 (3 lps 1966).
5. Sylvia Kind (hpsc) 4'54. Turnabout stereo TV 34200 (lp 1969).
6. Michael Thomas (clvg) [5'41]; rec Oryx Sound Studios 6/1967. Oryx mono 507 (lp 1968); Oryx stereo 1757 (lp 1971).
7. Christopher Hogwood (hpsc) 4'00; rec Finchcocks Kent. L'Oiseau-Lyre stereo D29D4 (4 lps 1977); DSLO 566 (lp 1980).
8. Trevor Pinnock (hpsc) [3'44]; rec St Botolph's Church Swyncombe. CRD stereo CRD 1050 (lp), CRDC 4050 (mc 1978); digitally remastered CRD 3350 [cd 1988].
9. Paul Nicholson (hpsc) 4'16; rec Forde Abbey 1/1988. Virgin stereo digital VC 7907221 (lp), VC 7907224 (mc), VC 7907222 (cd 1988).

The Maiden's Song

1. John Beckett (hpsc) [4'50]. Saga stereo 5347 (lp 1974).
2. Christopher Hogwood (hpsc) 5'35; rec Finchcocks Kent. L'Oiseau-Lyre stereo D29D4 (4 lps 1977).
3. Elisabeth Garnier (virg) 5'51; rec Grand'Combe-Chateleu Church. Arion stereo ARN 36571 (lp 1980).
4. Zsuzsa Pertis (hpsc) [4'43]. Hungaraton stereo HRC 079 (cd 1988).

The woods so wild

1. Alan Cuckston (hpsc) [4'11]. RCA stereo VICS 1693 (lp 1972).
2. Christopher Hogwood (virg) 3'20; rec Finchcocks Kent. L'Oiseau-Lyre stereo D29D4 (4 lps 1977).
3. Nicholas McGegan (virg) [3'34]. National Trust stereo NT 003 (lp 1977).
4. Tom Pixton (hpsc) 3'10; rec 7/1977. [Cambridge Mass.:] Titanic stereo Ti–20 (lp 1978).

Walsingham

1. Peter Williams (hpsc) [8'25]. Waverley mono LLP 1038 (lp 1965).
2. John Beckett (hpsc) [7'45]. Saga stereo 5347 (lp 1974).
3. Gustav Leonhardt (hist hpsc) [8'05]; rec Schloss Ahaus, Westphalia. BASF stereo BAC 3075 (lp 1975).
4. Christopher Hogwood (hpsc) 8'25; rec Finchcocks Kent. L'Oiseau-Lyre stereo D29D4 (4 lps 1977).
5. Tom Pixton (hpsc) 7'35; rec 7/1977. [Cambridge Mass.:] Titanic stereo Ti–20 (lp 1978).

6. Ton Koopman (hpsc) 8'48. Philips stereo 9502121 (lp), 7313121 (mc 1983).

Wilson's wild
1. Wanda Landowska (hpsc) [2'15]. His Master's Voice mono DA 1014 [ssp 1928].
2. Igor Kipnis (hpsc) [1'36]. Columbia stereo SCX 6159 (lp 1965).
3. Joseph Payne (hpsc) 2'13. Vox mono VBX 72, stereo SVBX 572 (3 lps 1966).
4. Elizabeth de la Porte (hpsc) 2'34. Saga stereo 5402 (lp 1975).
5. Christopher Hogwood (hist hpsc) [1'15]; [rec Fitzwilliam Museum Cambridge]. L'Oiseau-Lyre stereo D261D2 (2 lps 1982).
6. Zuzana Ruzickova (hpsc) 2'03. Orfeo stereo digital S 139861A (lp), M 139861A (mc), C 139861A (cd 1988).

*Pavans and Galliards*
Echo Pavan and Galliard in G, no. 5
1. Davitt Moroney (hist hpsc) 6'05; rec St Martin du Mejan Arles 5/1986. Harmonia Mundi France stereo digital HMC 1241–2 (2 lps), HMC 401241–2 (2 mcs), HMC 901241–2 (2 cds 1986).

Galliard in C, no. 4, Mistress Mary Brownlow
1. Peter Williams (hpsc) [2'39]. Waverley mono LLP 1038 (lp 1965).
2. Colin Tilney (hist hpsc) [3'11]. Pye stereo GSGC 14129 (lp), ZCGC 7053 (mc 1968).
3. Colin Tilney (hist virg) [3'15]; [rec German National Museum Nuremberg]. [Cologne:] EMI stereo lC 06330120 (lp 1974).
4. Davitt Moroney (hist hpsc) 2'58; rec St Martin du Mejan Arles 5/1986. Harmonia Mundi France stereo digital HMC 1241–2 (2 lps), HMC 401241–2 (2 mcs), HMC 901241–2 (2 cds 1986).

Galliard in D minor, no. 2
1. Fritz Neumeyer (hpsc) 1'54; rec Paulus Saal Freiburg 5/1954. Archiv mono AP 13026 [slp 1955].
2. Colin Tilney (hist virg) [1'47]; [rec German National Museum Nuremberg]. [Cologne:] EMI stereo lC 06330120 (lp 1974).
3. Davitt Moroney (hist hpsc) 1'36; rec St Martin du Mejan Arles 5/1986. Harmonia Mundi France stereo digital HMC 1241–2 (2 lps), HMC 401241–2 (2 mcs), HMC 901241–2 (2 cds 1986).

Passamezzo Pavan and Galliard
1. Christopher Hogwood (virg) 11'00; rec Finchcocks Kent. L'Oiseau-Lyre stereo D29D4 (4 lps 1977).
2. Colin Tilney (hist hpsc) 11'16; rec German National Museum Nuremberg 3/1977. Archiv stereo 2533379 (lp 1978); 2547069 (lp), 3347079 (mc 1982).

3.    Elisabeth Garnier (virg) 10'57; rec Grand'Combe-Chateleu Church. Arion
      stereo ARN 36571 (lp 1980).
4.    Davitt Moroney (hist hpsc) 11'28; rec St Martin du Mejan Arles 5/1986.
      Harmonia Mundi France stereo digital HMC 1241–2 (2 lps), HMC
      401241–2 (2 mcs), HMC 901241–1 (2 cds 1986).

\* Passamezzo Pavan and Galliard: Galliard
\*1.   Lionel Rogg (hist hpsc) [4'30]. RCA stereo LSB 4038 (lp 1971).

\* Passamezzo Pavan and Galliard: Galliard [sections 1–4, 6]
\*2.   Zuzana Ruzickova (hpsc) [5'41]; rec Supraphon Studios Prague. Supra-
      phon stereo SUAST 50787 (lp 1968).
\*3.   Zuzana Ruzickova (hpsc) 5'29. Orfeo stereo digital S 139861A (lp), M
      139861A (mc), C 139861A (cd 1988).

Pavan and Galliard in A minor, no. 1
1.    Fritz Neumeyer (hpsc) 4'22; rec Paulus Saal Freiburg 5/1954. Archiv mono
      AP 13026 [slp 1955].
2.    Colin Tilney (hist hpsc) [5'30]; [rec Colt Collection Bethersden]. Oryx
      stereo Oryx 1605 [lp 1970].
3.    Christopher Hogwood (hpsc) 6'00; rec Finchcocks Kent. L'Oiseau-Lyre
      stereo D29D4 (4 lps 1977).
4.    John Whitelaw (hpsc) 6'23; ed Brown. [New York:] Spectrum stereo SR
      139 (lp 1981).
5.    Davitt Moroney (hist hpsc) 6'32; rec St Martin du Mejan Arles 5/1986.
      Harmonia Mundi France stereo digital HMC 1241–2 (2 lps), HMC
      401241–2 (2 mcs), HMC 901241–2 (2 cds 1986).

\* Pavan and Galliard in A minor, no. 3: Galliard
\*1.   Isabelle Nef (hpsc) [2'13]. L'Oiseau-Lyre mono OL 76 [ssp 1939].

Pavan and Galliard in C, no. 1
1.    Christopher Hogwood (cha org) 4'05; rec Finchcocks Kent. L'Oiseau-Lyre
      stereo D29D4 (4 lps 1977).
2.    Davitt Moroney (hist hpsc) 4'14; rec St Martin du Mejan Arles 5/1986.
      Harmonia Mundi France stereo digital HMC 1241–2 (2 lps), HMC
      401241–2 (2 mcs), HMC 901241–2 (2 cds 1986).

Pavan and Galliard in C, no. 2, Kinborough Good
1.    Glenn Gould (pf) 5'16. CBS stereo 72988 (lp 1973); MP 39552 (lp), MPT
      39552 (mc 1987).
2.    Christopher Hogwood (hpsc) 6'00; rec Finchcocks Kent. L'Oiseau-Lyre
      stereo D29D4 (4 lps 1977).
3.    Davitt Moroney (hist hpsc) 6'06; rec St Martin du Mejan Arles 5/1986.

Harmonia Mundi France stereo digital HMC 1241–2 (2 lps), HMC 401241–2 (2 mcs), HMC 901241–2 (2 cds 1986).

Pavan and Galliard in C, no. 3
1.    Davitt Moroney (hist hpsc) 6'48; rec St Martin du Mejan Arles 5/1986. Harmonia Mundi France stereo digital HMC 1241–2 (2 lps), HMC 401241–2 (2 mcs), HMC 901241–2 (2 cds 1986).

Pavan and Galliard in C minor, no. 1
1.    Thurston Dart (hpsc) [6'02]. L'Oiseau-Lyre mono OL 50076 [lp 1955]; electronic stereo OLS 114–18 (5 lps 1971).
2.    Glenn Gould (pf) 7'11. CBS stereo 72988 (lp 1973); MP 39552 (lp), MPT 39552 (mc 1987).
3.    Christopher Hogwood (virg) 5'50; rec Finchcocks Kent. L'Oiseau-Lyre stereo D29D4 (4 lps 1977).
4.    Ton Koopman (hpsc) 6'35. Philips stereo 9502121 (lp), 7313121 (mc 1983).
5.    Davitt Moroney (hist hpsc) 6'27; rec St Martin du Mejan Arles 5/1986. Harmonia Mundi France stereo digital HMC 1241–2 (2 lps), HMC 401241–2 (2 mcs), HMC 901241–1 (2 cds 1986).

Pavan and Galliard in C minor, no. 2
1.    Colin Tilney (hist virg) [6'01]; [rec German National Museum Nuremberg]. [Cologne:] EMI stereo 1C 06330120 (lp 1974).
2.    Christopher Hogwood (hpsc) 6'25; rec Finchcocks Kent. L'Oiseau-Lyre stereo D29D4 (4 lps 1977).
3.    Davitt Moroney (hist hpsc) 6'26; rec St Martin du Mejan Arles 5/1986. Harmonia Mundi France stereo digital HMC 1241–2 (2 lps), HMC 401241–2 (2 mcs), HMC 901241–2 (2 cds 1986).

Pavan and Galliard in D minor, no. 1
1.    Gustav Leonhardt (hpsc) 6'32; rec Hause Skowroneck Bremen 2/1966. Telefunken mono AWT 9491, stereo SAWT 9491 (lp 1966).
2.    Tom Pixton (hpsc) 6'15; rec 7/1977. [Cambridge Mass.:] Titanic stereo Ti–20 (lp 1978).

* Pavan and Galliard in D minor, no. 1: Galliard
*1.   Violet Gordon Woodhouse (hpsc) [3'17]. His Master's Voice mono E 295 [ssp 1923].
*2.   Valda Aveling (hpsc) [1'30]. Oryx stereo EXP 52 [lp 1971].

Pavan and Galliard in F, no. 1, Bray
1.    Elizabeth Goble (virg) [5'44]. Decca mono AX 546–7 [2 sps 1951]; LXT 2795–6 [2 lps 1953].

* Pavan and Galliard in F, no. 1, Bray: Pavan
*1.   John Beckett (hpsc) [3'28]; ed Fuller Maitland. His Master's Voice stereo
      HQS 1147 (lp 1968).

Pavan and Galliard in F, no. 2, Ph. Tregian
1.    Colin Tilney (hpsc) [7'10]. Argo stereo ZRG 675 (lp 1973).
2.    Tom Pixton (hpsc) 6'10; rec 7/1977. [Cambridge Mass.:] Titanic stereo
      Ti–20 (lp 1978).
3.    Elisabeth Garnier (virg) 6'30; rec Grand'Combe-Chateleu Church. Arion
      stereo ARN 36571 (lp 1980).
4.    Ton Koopman (hpsc) 6'42. Philips stereo 9502121 (lp), 7313121 (mc
      1983).
5.    Davitt Moroney (hist hpsc) [6'27]; rec St Martin du Mejan Arles 5/1986.
      Harmonia Mundi France stereo digital HMC 1241–2 (2 lps), HMC
      401241–2 (2 mcs), HMC 901241–2 (2 cds 1986).
6.    Kenneth Gilbert (hpsc) 6'29; rec Schloss Leitheim 5/1987. Novalis stereo
      digital 1500181 (lp), 1500184 (mc), 1500182 (cd 1987).

Pavan and Galliard in G, no. 2
1.    Christopher Hogwood (hpsc) 3'55; rec Finchcocks Kent. L'Oiseau-Lyre
      stereo D29D4 (4 lps 1977).
2.    Davitt Moroney (hist hpsc) 4'31; rec St Martin du Mejan Arles 5/1986.
      Harmonia Mundi France stereo digital HMC 1241–2 (2 lps), HMC
      401241–2 (2 mcs), HMC 901241–2 (2 cds 1986).

* Pavan and Galliard in G, no. 2: Galliard
*1.   George Malcolm (hpsc) 1'25. Cantate mono 047704 [lp 1964]; Oryx
      stereo 3C301 [lp 1971]; Musicaphon BM30SL 1209 [lp 1981].
*2.   John Beckett (virg) 1'45. Pye stereo GSGC 14139 (lp 1972).

Pavan and Galliard in G, no. 3
1.    Paul Maynard (hpsc) [4'16]. [New York:] Decca mono DL 10040, stereo
      DL 711040 [lp 1962].
2.    Colin Tilney (hist hpsc) [5'10]; [rec German National Museum Nurem-
      berg]. [Cologne:] EMI stereo 1C 06330120 (lp 1974).
3.    Elisabeth Garnier (virg) 5'01; rec Grand'Combe-Chateleu Church. Arion
      stereo ARN 36571 (lp 1980).

Pavan and Galliard in G minor, no. 2, Sir William Petre
1.    Ralph Kirkpatrick (hpsc) [4'40]. His Master's Voice mono ALP 1518 [lp
      1957].
2.    Paul Maynard (hpsc) [5'53]. [New York:] Decca mono DL 10040, stereo
      DL 711040 [lp 1962].
3.    Colin Tilney (hist hpsc) [6'46]; Pye stereo GSGC 14129 (lp), ZCGC 7053
      (mc 1968).

4. Gustav Leonhardt (hist hpsc) [8'19]; rec Schloss Ahaus, Westphalia. BASF stereo BAC 3075 (lp 1975).

5. Christopher Hogwood (hpsc) 7'35; rec Finchcocks Kent. L'Oiseau-Lyre stereo D29D4 (4 lps 1977).

6. John Whitelaw (hpsc) 7'22; ed Brown. [New York:] Spectrum stereo SR 139 (lp 1981).

7. Davitt Moroney (hist hpsc) [6'46]; rec St Martin du Mejan Arles 5/1986. Harmonia Mundi France stereo digital HMC 1241–2 (2 lps), HMC 401241–2 (2 mcs), HMC 901241–2 (2 cds 1986).

Pavan and Galliard in G minor, no. 3
1. Joseph Payne (hpsc) 3'32. Vox mono VBX 72, stereo SVBX 572 (3 lps 1966).
2. Igor Kipnis (hpsc) 4'11; rec Unitarian Church Westport Conn. [Hollywood:] EMI stereo SB–3816 (2 lps 1974).

* Pavan and Galliard in G minor, no. 3: Pavan
*1. George Malcolm (hpsc) 1'47. Cantate mono 047704 [lp 1964]; Oryx stereo 3C301 [lp 1971]; Musicaphon BM30SL 1209 [lp 1981].

Pavan and two Galliards in A minor, no. 2, The Earl of Salisbury
1. Thurston Dart (hpsc) [5'50]. L'Oiseau-Lyre mono OL 50076 [lp 1955]; electronic stereo OLS 114–18 (5 lps 1971).
2. Colin Tilney (hist hpsc) [5'16]; Pye stereo GSGC 14129 (lp), ZCGC 7053 (mc 1968).
3. Robert Woolley (virg) 4'00; rec Eltham College London 11/1976. Saga 5447 (lp 1977).
4. Davitt Moroney (hist hpsc) 5'30; rec St Martin du Mejan Arles 5/1986. Harmonia Mundi France stereo digital HMC 1241–2 (2 lps), HMC 401241–2 (2 mcs), HMC 901241–2 (2 cds 1986).

* Pavan and two Galliards in A minor, no. 2, The Earl of Salisbury: Pavan and first Galliard
*1. Rudolph Dolmetsch (virg) [2'46]. Columbia mono 5712 [ssp 1930].
*2. Arnold Dolmetsch (clvc) [2'07]. [Haslemere:] Dolmetsch Recording mono DR 4 [ssp 1937].
*3. Elizabeth Goble (virg) [3'22]; ed Donington. Decca mono X 540 [sp 1951]; LXT 2795–6 [2 lps 1953].
*4. Joseph Saxby (virg) [3'10]. [Haslemere:] Chantry mono CRLP 3 [lp 1962].
*5. Paul Maynard (org) [3'00]; rec General Theological Seminary Chapel New York. [New York:] Decca mono DL 10040, stereo DL 711040 [lp 1962].
*6. Igor Kipnis (hpsc) [3'28]. Columbia stereo SCX 6159 (lp 1967).
*7. Christopher Kite (hist virg) 3'04; rec Bishopsgate Institute London 11/1981. Hyperion stereo A 66067 (lp 1983).

* Pavan and two Galliards in A minor, no. 2, The Earl of Salisbury: Pavan
*8.   Alice Ehlers (hpsc) [1'37]. Decca mono F 7726 [ssp 1941].
*9.   Susi Jeans (hist virg) [1'32]; rec 8/1961. Archiv mono APM 14301, stereo
      SAPM 198301 (lp 1964); stereo 199001 (lp 1969).
*10.  Simon Preston (hpsc) 1'25. Turnabout mono TV 4017, stereo TV 34017S
      (lp 1966).
*11.  Peter Cooper (hpsc) [1'37]. Pye stereo GSGC 14113 (lp 1969).
*12.  Igor Kipnis (hpsc) 1'48. CBS stereo 61132 [lp 1970].
*13.  Robert Aldwinckle (hpsc) [2'02]. Pickwick stereo digital CIMPC 873
      (mc), PCD 873 (cd 1987).

Pavan in A minor, no. 4
1.    Christopher Hogwood (cha org) 4'30; rec Finchcocks Kent. L'Oiseau-Lyre
      stereo D29D4 (4 lps 1977).
2.    Davitt Moroney (hist hpsc) 5'08; rec St Martin du Mejan Arles 5/1986.
      Harmonia Mundi France stereo digital HMC 1241–2 (2 lps), HMC
      401241–2 (2 mcs), HMC 901241–2 (2 cds 1986).

Pavan in G, no. 6, Canon 2 in 1
1.    Christopher Hogwood (cha org) 4'25; rec Finchcocks Kent. L'Oiseau-Lyre
      stereo D29D4 (4 lps 1977).
2.    Davitt Moroney (hist hpsc) 4'54; rec St Martin du Mejan Arles 5/1986.
      Harmonia Mundi France stereo digital HMC 1241–2 (2 lps), HMC
      401241–2 (2 mcs), HMC 901241–2 (2 cds 1986).

Quadran Pavan and Galliard
1.    Colin Tilney (hist hpsc) [13'45]; [rec German National Museum Nurem-
      berg]. [Cologne:] EMI stereo 1C 06330120 (lp 1974).
2.    Davitt Moroney (hist hpsc) 13'34; rec St Martin du Mejan Arles 5/1986.
      Harmonia Mundi France stereo digital HMC 1241–2 (2 lps), HMC
      401241–2 (2 mcs), HMC 901241–2 (2 cds 1986).

*Other dances, descriptive music and arrangements*
Alman in G
1.    Lionel Rogg (cha org) [1'06]. RCA stereo LSB 4038 (lp 1971).

Alman in G minor
1.    Fritz Neumeyer (hpsc) 1'32; rec Paulus Saal Freiburg 5/1954. Archiv mono
      AP 13026 [slp 1955].
2.    Joseph Payne (hpsc) 2'32. Vox mono VBX 72, stereo SVBX 572 (3 lps
      1966).
3.    Igor Kipnis (hpsc) 1'31; rec Unitarian Church Westport Conn. [Holly-
      wood:] EMI stereo SB–3816 (2 lps 1974).
4.    Christopher Hogwood (hist hpsc) [1'25]; [rec Fitzwilliam Museum
      Cambridge]. L'Oiseau-Lyre stereo D261D2 (2 lps 1982).

Coranto in C

1.   George Malcolm (hpsc) 0'55. Cantate mono 047704 [lp 1964]; Oryx stereo 3C301 [lp 1971]; Musicaphon BM30SL 1209 [lp 1981].
2.   Colin Tilney (hist virg) [1'33]; [rec German National Museum Nuremberg]. [Cologne:] EMI stereo 1C 06330120 (lp 1974).

Galliard (Harding, arr. Byrd)

1.   John Beckett (hpsc) [nt]. Saga stereo 5348 (lp 1974).
2.   Davitt Moroney (hist hpsc) [2'42]; rec St Martin du Mejan Arles 5/1986. Harmonia Mundi France stereo digital HMC 1241–2 (2 lps), HMC 401241–2 (2 mcs), HMC 901241–2 (2 cds 1986).

Jig in A minor

1.   Igor Kipnis (hpsc) [0'45]. Columbia stereo SCX 6159 (lp 1965).
2.   Roy Jesson (org) [1'10]; rec London. [New York:] Lyrichord mono LL 156, stereo LLST 7156 [lp 1966].
3.   Joseph Payne (hpsc) 1'08. Vox mono VBX 72, stereo SVBX 572 (3 lps 1966).
4.   Geraint Jones (hist virg) [1'10]; rec Fenton House London. His Master's Voice stereo HQS 1100 (lp 1967).
5.   Edward Power Biggs (hist org) 1'10; rec Staunton Harold Chapel 22/2/1971. CBS stereo 77237 [3 lps 1971]; 72980 [lp 1972].
6.   Christopher Hogwood (hist spt) [1'00]; [rec Victoria & Albert Museum London]. L'Oiseau-Lyre stereo D261D2 (2 lps 1982).

Lachrymae Pavan (Dowland, arr. Byrd)

1.   John Beckett (hpsc) [nt]. Saga stereo 5348 (lp 1974).
2.   Colin Tilney (hist virg) [5'09]; [rec German National Museum Nuremberg]. [Cologne:] EMI stereo 1C 06330120 (lp 1974).
3.   Colin Tilney (hpsc) 5'30. L'Oiseau-Lyre stereo DSLO 552 (lp 1979).
4.   Ton Koopman (hpsc) 6'27. Philips stereo 9502121 (lp), 7313121 (mc 1983).
5.   Davitt Moroney (hist hpsc) [5'40]; rec St Martin du Mejan Arles 5/1986. Harmonia Mundi France stereo digital HMC 1241–2 (2 lps), HMC 401241–2 (2 mcs), HMC 901241–2 (2 cds 1986).
6.   Zsuzsa Pertis (hpsc) [4'41]. Hungaraton stereo HRC 079 (cd 1988).

Lavolta in G, no. 1, Lady Morley

1.   Igor Kipnis (hpsc) 1'28; rec Unitarian Church Westport Conn. [Hollywood:] EMI stereo SB–3816 (2 lps 1974).
2.   Trevor Pinnock (hpsc) [1'13]; rec St Botolph's Church Swyncombe. CRD stereo CRD 1050 (lp), CRDC 4050 (mc 1978); digitally remastered CRD 3350 [cd 1988].
3.   Christopher Hogwood (hist hpsc) [1'27]; [rec Fitzwilliam Museum Cambridge]. L'Oiseau-Lyre stereo D261D2 (2 lps 1982).

Lavolta in G, no. 2

1.   Fritz Neumeyer (hpsc) 1′21; rec Paulus Saal Freiburg 5/1954. Archiv mono
     AP 13026 [slp 1955].
2.   Zuzana Ruzickova (hpsc) [1′29]. Supraphon mono SUEC 843 [ep 1959].
3.   Rafael Puyana (hpsc) [2′27]. Mercury mono MMA 11182, stereo AMS
     16132 (lp 1963).
4.   Michael Thomas (hpsc) [1′22]. Pan mono PAN 6202, stereo SPAN 6202
     (lp 1966).
5.   Joseph Payne (hpsc) 0′59. Vox mono VBX 72, stereo SVBX 572 (3 lps
     1966).
6.   Igor Kipnis (hpsc) 1′40. CBS stereo 61132 [lp 1970].
7.   Valda Aveling (hpsc) [2′23]. Oryx stereo EXP 52 [lp 1971].
8.   Lionel Rogg (hist hpsc) [1′18]. RCA stereo LSB 4038 (lp 1971).
9.   Christopher Hogwood (virg) 1′40; rec St John's Church Downshire Hill
     London 7/1977. Folio Society stereo FS 1001–2 (2 lps 1977); L'Oiseau-
     Lyre stereo D268D2 (2 lps 1983).
10.  Christopher Hogwood (hist hpsc) [1′14]; [rec Fitzwilliam Museum Cam-
     bridge]. L'Oiseau-Lyre stereo D261D2 (2 lps 1982).
11.  Zuzana Ruzickova (hpsc) 2′48. Orfeo stereo digital S 139861A (lp), M
     139861A (mc), C 139861A (cd 1988).

Monsieur's Alman in G, no. 1

1.   Joseph Payne (hpsc) 3′13. Vox mono VBX 72, stereo SVBX 572 (3 lps 1966).

Monsieur's Alman in G, no. 2

1.   Christopher Hogwood (hpsc) 6′30; rec Finchcocks Kent. L'Oiseau-Lyre
     stereo D29D4 (4 lps 1977).

Pavan and Galliard, Delight (Johnson, arr. Byrd)

1.   Elisabeth Garnier (virg) 6′15; rec Grand' Combe-Chateleu Church. Arion
     stereo ARN 36571 (lp 1980).
2.   Christopher Hogwood (hist spt) 6′35; [rec Victoria & Albert Museum
     London]. L'Oiseau-Lyre stereo D261D2 (2 lps 1982).

The Barley Break

1.   Christopher Hogwood (virg) 7′25; rec Finchcocks Kent. L'Oiseau-Lyre
     stereo D29D4 (4 lps 1977).

The Battle

1.   Susi Jeans (hist virg) [13′05]; rec 8/1961. Archiv mono APM 14301, stereo
     SAPM 198301 (lp 1964); stereo 199005 (lp 1967).
2.   Christopher Hogwood (virg) 10′45; rec Finchcocks Kent. L'Oiseau-Lyre
     stereo D29D4 (4 lps 1977); DSLO 566 (lp 1980).

* The Battle: The soldiers' summons; The march of footmen; The march of

horsemen; The trumpets; The Irish march; The bagpipe and the drone; The flute and the drum [bars 1–30, 56–75]; The march to the fight; The retreat
  *1.   Sylvia Kind (hpsc) [11'38]. Turnabout stereo TV 34200 (lp 1969).

* The Battle: The soldiers' summons; The march of footmen; The bagpipe and the drone; The flute and the drum
  *2.   Zuzana Ruzickova (hpsc) 5'28. Orfeo stereo digital S 139 861A (lp), M 139861A (mc), C 139 861A (cd 1988).

* The Battle: The bagpipe and the drone; The flute and the drum
  *3.   Paul Maynard (hpsc) [2'45]. [New York:] Decca mono DL 10040, stereo DL 711040 [lp 1962].

* The Battle: The flute and the drum [bars 1–30, 56–75]
  *4.   Zuzana Ruzickova (hpsc) [1'30]. Supraphon mono SUEC 843 [ep 1959].

The Galliard for the Victory
  1.   Sylvia Kind (hpsc) [1'58]. Turnabout stereo TV 34200 (lp 1969).
  2.   Christopher Hogwood (virg) 1'50; rec Finchcocks Kent. L'Oiseau-Lyre stereo D29D4 (4 lps 1977).
  3.   Zuzana Ruzickova (hpsc) 2'08. Orfeo stereo digital S 139861A (lp), M 139861A (mc), C139861A (cd 1988).

The Galliard Jig
  1.   Alan Cuckston (hpsc) [2'15]. RCA stereo VICS 1693 (lp 1972).
  2.   Christopher Hogwood (hpsc) 1'50; rec Finchcocks Kent. L'Oiseau-Lyre stereo D29D4 (4 lps 1977); DSLO 566 (lp 1980).

The March before the Battle, or The Earl of Oxford's March
  1.   Violet Gordon Woodhouse (hpsc) [3'13]. His Master's Voice mono E 294 [ssp 1923].
  2.   Christopher Hogwood (virg) 3'30; rec Finchcocks Kent. L'Oiseau-Lyre stereo D29D4 (4 lps 1977).

* The March before the Battle, or The Earl of Oxford's March: bars 1–26, 31–39, 49–56, 79–81, 85–113
  *1.   Sylvia Kind (hpsc) [2'34]. Turnabout stereo TV 34200 (lp 1969).

The Queen's Alman
  1.   Violet Gordon Woodhouse (hpsc) [2'16]. His Master's Voice mono E 294 [ssp 1923].
  2.   Thurston Dart [hpsc] [4'05]. L'Oiseau-Lyre mono OL 50076 [lp 1955]; electronic stereo OLS 114–18 (5 lps 1971).
  3.   Igor Kipnis (hpsc) [3'46]. Columbia stereo SCX 6159 (lp 1967).
  4.   John Beckett (virg) [2'40]. His Master's Voice stereo HQS 1151 (lp 1968).
  5.   Valda Aveling (hist spt) [4'53]; [rec Victoria & Albert Museum London]. Musica Rara stereo MUS 70 (lp 1968).

6.   Valda Aveling (hpsc) [2'32]. Oryx stereo EXP 52 (lp 1971).
7.   Trevor Pinnock (hist spt) [3'41]; rec Victoria & Albert Museum London. CRD stereo CRD 1007 (lp), CRDC 4007 (mc 1973).
8.   Christopher Hogwood (hist virg) 3'11; [rec Victoria & Albert Museum London]. L'Oiseau-Lyre stereo D261D2 (2 lps 1982).

Three French Corantos
1.   Igor Kipnis (hpsc) 2'44; rec Unitarian Church Westport Conn. [Hollywood:] EMI stereo SB–3816 (2 lps 1974).
2.   Elisabeth Garnier (msr) 2'39; rec Grand'Combe-Chateleu Church. Arion stereo ARN 36572 (lp 1980).

* Three French Corantos: The First French Coranto
*1.  Thurston Dart (hpsc) [1'39]. L'Oiseau-Lyre mono OL 50076 [lp 1955]; electronic stereo OLS 114–18 (5 lps 1971).
*2.  Christopher Wood (virg) [1'03]. [Haslemere:] Chantry mono CRLP 7 [lp 1966].

* Three French Corantos: The Second French Coranto
*1.  Paul Maynard (hpsc) [0'46]. [New York:] Decca mono DL 10040, stereo DL 711040 [lp 1962].

*Doubtful works*
Fantasia a 4 in D minor, no. 1
1.   Early Music Consort of London/David Munrow 1'56; ed Dart. His Master's Voice stereo SLS 988 (2 lps 1976).
2.   Liege Musica Aurea 2'44. [Brussels:] Alpha stereo DB 267 (lp 1978).

If my complaints (BK 103)
1.   Paul Maynard (hpsc) [2'36]. [New York:] Decca mono DL 10040, stereo DL 711040 [lp 1962].

Lullaby [Keyboard adaptation] (EK 53)
1.   Isabelle Nef (hpsc) [2'21]. L'Oiseau-Lyre mono OL 76 [ssp 1939].

Malt's come down
1.   Harold Lester (hist hpsc) 1'50; rec Colt Collection, Bethersden. Harmonia Mundi stereo HM 227 (lp 1980).

Medley (BK 111)
1.   John Whitelaw (hpsc) 5'13. ed Brown. [New York:] Spectrum stereo SR 139 (lp 1981).

Pavan and Galliard in A minor (BK 98)

1.    Paul Maynard (hpsc) [4'52]. Brunswick mono AXA 4515, stereo SXA 4515 (lp 1959).

Vide, Domine, quoniam tribulor
1.    King's Singers [3'22]; rec EMI studios Abbey Road London 1976. His Master's Voice stereo/quad CSD 3779 (lp), TC–CSD 3779 (mc 1977).

### Editorial note

A recording was made on 10 May 1990 of hitherto unrecorded music by, or attributed to, William Byrd. The music is played on the 1818 James Bruce organ of St Andrew's Scottish Episcopal Cathedral, Aberdeen, by Mark Duthie, from the editions by Alan Brown. It is available as a cassette number TD 0901 distributed by Top Note Music, 123 Crown Street, Aberdeen, Scotland. The pieces recorded are as follows: *The Ghost, Gypsies' Round*, three short Grounds, the paired Pavan in G, no. 8 and Galliard in G, no. 9, In Nomine (Parsons, arr. Byrd) and two anonymous pavans (EK 15 and 16) suggested by Alan Brown as possible compositions of Byrd though with reservations, amplified by Oliver Neighbour in his paper above.

# Index of Byrd's works cited

The order of entries is as in the Discography (see p. 202), except that doubtful and misattributed works are included in the main sequence. Where possible, references are given to *The Byrd Edition*. For the purposes of this index, the following editions have been added to the list on pp. xiv–xvi:

BE   *The Byrd Edition*

    5. *Gradualia I (1605): The Marian Masses*, ed. Philip Brett (London, 1989)

    6a. *Gradualia I (1605): All Saints and Corpus Christi*, ed. Philip Brett (London, 1991)

    11. *The English Anthems*, ed. Craig Monson (London, 1983)

BW  *The Collected Works of William Byrd*, ed. Edmund H. Fellowes

    12. *Psalmes, Sonets, & Songs (1588)* (London, 1948); rev. Philip Brett (London, 1965)

    13. *Songs of Sundrie Natures (1589)* (London, 1949); rev. Philip Brett (London, 1962)

## Mass settings

Mass for Three Voices (BE 4/1), 53, 136, 137n, 138, 205
Mass for Four Voices (BE 4/2), 13, 49, 53, 75, 137, 205–6
Mass for Five Voices (BE 4/3), 53, 74, 207
Assumption of the BVM (BE 5/23, 6, 22–5), 207–8
Corpus Christi (BE 6a/8–11), 22
Easter Day (TCM 7, pp. 262–80), 208
Nativity of the BVM (BE 5/6–11), 208
Nativity of our Lord Jesus Christ (TCM 7, pp. 210–29), 208

## Alphabetical list of Latin works

Ad Dominum cum tribularer (BE 8/7), 32n, 73, 208
Afflicti pro peccatis nostris (BE 3/17), 72–3
Alleluia, Ascendit Deus (TCM 7, p. 286), 208
Alleluia, Cognoverunt. Alleluia, Caro mea (TCM 7, p. 247), 208
Alleluia, Confitemini Domino (BE 8/1), 52, 61–2
Alleluia, Vespere autem (TCM 7, p. 196) 76
Apparebit in finem (BE 3/7), 73
Aspice, Domine, de sede sancta tua (BE 2/11), 57n, 73, 208
Aspice, Domine, quia facta est desolata civitas (BE 1/4), 39, 68, 208
Assumpta est Maria (BE 5/24), 209
Attollite portas (BE 1/5), 12, 57, 69, 209
Ave Maria, gratia plena (BE 5/14), 209

*English liturgical music*

*Other English Music*

# Index of names

Abraham, Gerald, 24n
Albrecht, Hans, 26n
Alwood, Richard, 159
Ammerbach, Elias Nicolaus, 180
Andrews, H. K., 56n
Andrews, Hilda, 161–2, 164–6, 177
Aplin, John, 85, 90n, 98
Ariosto, Ludovico, 112
Ashwell, Thomas, 159
Aston, Hugh, 31, 146–7, 159

Bach, J. S., 1, 73, 204
Baldwin, John, 77, 159–74, 177, 185
Battier, Marc, 51n
Beecher, D., 135n
Benham, Hugh, 29, 31, 83n
Bennett, John, 129n, 131n
Bent, Ian, 181n
Bergsagel, John, 159–61
Bernet Kempers, K. Ph., 26n
Bevin, Edward, 174n, 181n
Bishop, Martha, 135n
Bliss, Philip, 160n
Blow, John, 63
Bokingham, John, 30
Bonham, William, 38
Bowers, Roger, 79–82
Boyd, M. C., 160n
Brahms, Johannes, 82
Bray, Roger, 159n
Brett, Philip, 13n, 83n, 141n, 160
Brown, Alan, 132n, 147n, 162–3, 165n,
    174n, 183, 185, 193–5, 197, 264
Bruce, James, 264
Bukofzer, M. F., 135n
Bull, John, 142, 147, 157, 163, 165n
Bunbury, Priscilla, 163
Burnett, Duncan, 182f, 192
Burton, Avery, 159

Butterworth, Charles C., 28n, 32–3n, 36n

Caldwell, John, 143n, 176n
Campion, Edmund, 121
Campion, Thomas, 78
Carver, Robert, 80
Charnassé, Hélène, 51
Charteris, Richard, 69–70n, 73n, 75n
Clemens non Papa, 26, 37n, 75
Clough, Francis, 204
Clulow, Peter, 53n
Coates, W., 131n, 135n
Cockshoot, J. V., 28n
Cole, Elizabeth, 163n
Collins, H. B., 1
Colman, Charles, 129n
Colvig, Richard, 204
Cooper, Gerald, ixn
Coover, James, 204
Coprario, John, 78, 129n, 135–6, 141–2,
    155–7
Cosyn, Benjamin, 165, 167, 169, 186,
    192n
Crane, Frederick, 60, 61n
Croce, Giovanni, 83n
Cromwell, Anne, 186
Croucher, Trevor, 204
Cuming, G. J., 204

Dart, Thurston, 52n, 128, 162–5, 175n
Davis, Deta S., 51n
Davis, Walter R., 78n
Day, Timothy, 204
Dodd, G. J., 132–3n
Douglas, Robert, 37n
Dow, Robert, 160–1
Dowland, John, 113, 193, 260
Duffill, John, 64, 67, 82n
Dygon, John, 19n

273

## DATE DUE